Seagulls Don't Fly Into the Bush

The Wadsworth Modern Anthropology Library

Seagulls Don't Fly Into the Bush

Cultural Identity and
Development in Melanesia

Alice Pomponio
St. Lawrence University

Wadsworth Publishing Company
Belmont, California
A Division of Wadsworth, Inc.

Anthropology Editor: *Peggy Adams*
Editorial Assistant: *Tammy Goldfeld*
Production Editor: *Donna Linden*
Managing Designer: *Cindy Schultz*
Print Buyer: *Barbara Britton*
Art Editor: *Marta Kongsle*
Permissions Editor: *Jeanne Bosschart*
Designer: *Donna Davis*
Copy Editor: *Alan R. Titche*
Cartographer: *Mary Jo Zeidler*
Cover Illustration: *Adriann Dinihanian*
Compositor: *Bookends, Ashland, Oregon*
Printer: *Malloy Lithographing, Ann Arbor, Michigan*

1 2 3 4 5 6 7 8 9 10—96 95 94 93 92

Library of Congress Cataloging-in-Publication Data

Pomponio, Alice.
    Seagulls don't fly into the bush : cultural identity and
development in Melanesia / Alice Pomponio.
        p.   cm. — (The Wadsworth modern anthropology library)
    Includes bibliographical references and index.
    ISBN 0-534-16260-6
    1. Ethnology—Papua New Guinea—Siassi Islands. 2. Ethnicity—
Papua New Guinea—Siassi Islands. 3. Acculturation—Papua New
Guinea—Siassi Islands. 4. Siassi Islands (Papua New Guinea)—
Economic conditions. 5. Economic development—Social aspects—Case
studies.   I. Title.   II. Series.
GN671.N5P66 1992
305.8′009957′1—dc20   91-13311

*For my parents, Marian Addeo Pomponio
and the late Charles Angelo Pomponio,
who first instilled in me an appreciation
for cultural traditions and introduced
me to the wonders of human diversity.
Thank you for your understanding, your
encouragement, and your love.*

✿ Contents

CHAPTER TEN

Conclusions: Negotiating Development 186

🍃 List of Illustrations

🌿 List of Tables

🌿 Foreword to the Series

Modern cultural anthropology encompasses the full diversity of all humankind with a mix of methods, styles, ideas, and approaches. No longer is the subject matter of this field confined to exotic cultures, the "primitive," or small rural folk communities. Today, students are as likely to find an anthropologist at work in an urban school setting or a corporate boardroom as among a band of African hunters and gatherers. To a large degree, the currents in modern anthropology reflect changes in the world over the past century. Today there are no isolated archaic societies available for study. All the world's peoples have become enveloped in widespread regional social, political, and economic systems. The daughters and sons of yesterday's yam gardeners and reindeer hunters are operating computers, organizing marketing cooperatives, serving as delegates to parliaments, and watching television news. The lesson of cultural anthropology, and this series, is that such peoples, when transformed, are no less interesting and no less culturally different because of such dramatic changes.

Cultural anthropology's scope has grown to encompass more than simply the changes in the primitive or peasant world, its original subject matter. The methods and ideas developed for the study of small-scale societies are now creatively applied to the most complex of social and cultural systems, giving us a new and stronger understanding of the full diversity of human living. Increasingly, cultural anthropologists also work toward solving practical problems of the cultures they study, in addition to pursuing more traditional basic research endeavors.

Yet cultural anthropology's enlarged agenda has not meant abandonment of its own heritage. The ethnographic case study remains the bedrock of the cultural anthropologist's methods for gathering knowledge of the peoples of the world, although today's case study may focus on a British urban neighborhood or a new American cult as often as on efforts of a formerly isolated Pacific island people to cope with bureaucracy. Similarly, systematic comparison of the experiences and adaptations of different societies is an old approach that is increasingly applied to new issues.

The books in the Wadsworth Modern Anthropology Library reflect cultural anthropology's greater breadth of interests. They include introductory texts and supporting anthologies of readings, as well as advanced texts dealing with more specialized fields and methods of cultural anthropology.

However, the hub of the series consists of topical studies that concentrate on either a single community or a number of communities. Each of these topical studies is strongly issue-focused. As anthropology has always done, these topical studies raise far-reaching questions about the problems people confront and the variety of human experience. They do so through close face-to-face study of people in many places and settings. In these studies, the core idiom of cultural anthropology lies exposed. Cultural anthropologists still, as always, go forth among the cultures of the world and return to inform. Only where they go and what they report has changed.

James A. Clifton
Series Editor

✿ Foreword to the Book

Western visitors to Mandok Island in the Siassi group of Papua New Guinea have generally been favorably impressed and even charmed by what they see: the setting is sufficiently picturesque; the people are forthright yet affable; their physical attractiveness seems to connote a vigorous resourcefulness; and they seem refreshingly self-assured. And until recently, their two-masted sailing canoes, which seemed somehow outsized in their immediate surroundings, testified to the boldness and skill of the people who made and sailed them.

What lay behind such impressions—the islanders' way of life together with their modern history—are the subjects of this book. The author came to Mandok with a specific issue in mind—a practical problem having to do with the performance of local schoolchildren—but in the expectation that a full term of ethnographic field research would be required. In the end, Dr. Pomponio's research has extended over a decade, and not only has she solved the puzzle of why such capable children did so well at one point and so poorly later on, she has also explored the reasons for the successes and failures of adults in the modern context of village-level economic development. Success and failure are among the book's constant themes.

Traditionally, the Mandok Islanders, along with the other Siassi Islanders, were adventurous traders whose voyages distributed a variety of local and specialized products over a wide area. They were not merchants presiding over a central marketplace. Their small island was simply a home base from which they regularly set out to visit their foreign trading partners residing in the other communities of the region. They built seagoing canoes and made other goods for trade as well, but much of what they traded was produced by others. The extent to which they acted as middlemen in trade was unusual. Also unusual among Melanesians, most of whom were farmers, was that the Mandok, lacking arable land, imported vegetable food to meet both daily needs and festive requirements.

Traders rather than farmers, mobile rather than sedentary, the Mandok were nevertheless as much committed as other Melanesian villagers to a scheme of competitive politics in which calculated dispositions of wealth were the public indicators of achievement and social distinction. Disposable surpluses of wealth, gained through exchanges with partners abroad, were only the trader's proximate objective. The balance sheet of overseas trade was preliminary to contests of "strength" in the sociopolitical arena at home. The balance sheet that really counted entailed the comparison of careers of local festival sponsors: to not perform, or to perform inadequately—for example, the public rituals on behalf of firstborn children—was to lower one's status; to perform well in festive distributions was status-raising.

The successful man was not by any means a lone wolf, even though the Siassi societies are marked by a degree of individualism. Trading depended upon maintaining a far-flung network of partners in exchange, and this was a continuing process that Pomponio appropriately refers to as "investing in people." Partners were friends, protectors, kinsmen even, and most trade took the form of reciprocal gift giving.

The Mandok traders, then, along with other Siassi people, were at the center of the regional network. Theirs was the superior position with respect to knowledge of the people and products of the region, and also in the sense that they, as the principal voyagers, took the initiative. Perhaps it is not surprising that they thought of themselves as a superior breed of people, as "lords of the sea."

But now enter the European colonialists and rather suddenly their situation was inverted. Relatively speaking, the Siassi area is lacking in resources. This fact is "explained" in the cosmological account—the Legend of Namor (recounted in Chapter 2)—which explains as well why the Siassi people were destined, from the time of creation, to be traders. But the colonial economy, with its own centers in towns such as Rabaul and Madang, took little notice of Siassi, and the main lines of transport and communication bypassed their islands. Only in time did the Mandok realize that they had been demoted; no longer the center of the world, they were now peripheral players.

Living in a backwater, however, had its advantages. Encounters with Europeans were intermittent, disconcerting at first, and often confusing because European demands and interests differed, but overall the impact was less, or at least was absorbed more gradually, than in many neighboring communities. At the same time, the Islanders were able to obtain some of the new tools, goods, and knowledge offered by Europeans. As the Mandok continued their trading visits, they were in a position to observe the effects of relations with Europeans in a number of communities. Thus armed with comparative knowledge, they may have been more able to conduct their own relations with Europeans on terms favorable to themselves.

Following World War II, however, came a radically new departure in the relations of European colonialists and indigenous communities; in Papua New Guinea some administrators called it the "New Deal." The basic idea, entirely unprecedented in human history, was that the colonial powers, at their own expense (i.e., at the expense of the metropolitan taxpayers) were to "develop" the colonized peoples, prepare them for political independence, and help them develop their local economies along modern lines. Even the relatively resourceless Siassi Islands were to partake of this new dispensation.

Dr. Pomponio's book is both a record and an interpretation of what happened in the Mandok Island community during the era of development, which effectively began in the 1960s, when local readiness and the promise of outside assistance seemed to be favorably conjoined. The various strands of the story are woven together in a chronologically ordered account in Chapters 7–9. Informing the narrative is an ongoing community dialogue, in which the author herself has participated, about the meaning of development and the appropriate ways to achieve it. Mandok clearly is a village that has "chosen progress." But equally clear from Pomponio's account is their failure to achieve it. There has been no failure to innovate, to plan and organize new cash-earning activities, or to modify traditional cultural practices so as to release modernizing efforts. What, then, explains the failure?

Here lies the most intriguing and, perhaps, the most significant part of the story. At least in the Western view, the Mandok's main chance for achieving regular money incomes, which is how development is often measured, is commercial agriculture. Yet unlike most Melanesians, including most of their neighbors, they are not farmers by predilection, experience, or resource endowment. To devote themselves to cash cropping (combined with subsistence farming), now that land has been made available to them, would be to take the most radical course of all. It would mean abandoning their island way of life, and without that, they fear, they would cease to be the kind of people whose destiny is charted in the Namor creation legend.

The induced mode of development favored by democratic governments requires local, voluntary action. The Mandok have not failed to act, and from the 1960s through the 1980s they appear to have taken up every feasible option that is also consistent with their self-image as mobile sea people and traders. The effort to maintain that sense of cultural identity, however, does not explain the failure of particular projects or developmental schemes, such as those based on education, fishing, shipping, and so on. For this, as Pomponio shows in detail, one must examine limitations of resources and knowledge, and other factors as well. But it does explain both the kind of cash-earning activities they have chosen, as well as the one—cash cropping—to which they have refused to commit themselves. Each of their initiatives was simultaneously a positive action and a defensive maneuver in the face of rather persistent external pressure to forsake their island for an agricultural existence. Each project, whether short-lived or enduring for years, meant postponing the fateful decision about "relocation" and all that that portended. Though naturally disappointed by their repeated failures, the Mandok have the consolation that they have been true to themselves and to what has come to matter most to them in their cultural heritage.

Some readers may contest the idea that the Mandok's sense of cultural identity is an example of what anthropologists have variously termed "key symbols," "basic patterns," or "entrenched clauses" in order to indicate their inviolable or nonnegotiable character. Has the mobile-sea-trader image been an efficacious limiting cause in the other Siassi Island villages, or has their "conservatism" been less intense and differently grounded? And how much longer is the Mandok sense of cultural identity likely to constrain their choices when, for example, population growth forces a widening discrepancy between actual livelihoods and cultural ideals? I cannot offer answers to these questions. Nonetheless, I am convinced by my own ethnographic experience in the region and on Mandok Island itself, but mainly by Pomponio's lively and lucid analysis of Siassi culture and history, that Mandok cultural identity is fundamental to understanding their modern history. Surely they are not the only people, in the Third World or elsewhere, who have "made history" according to an historicomythic conception of their particular qualities and capacities as "persons."

Thomas G. Harding
University of California,
Santa Barbara

 # Preface

Studies of development are usually conceived in economic terms. Their focus tends to be on documenting either the conversion of subsistence activities into growth industries or the impact of the larger world system on a local one. In Papua New Guinea, for example, a study conducted by the World Bank concluded that "[t]he key constraints [on development] are inadequate support services for small-holders,[1] a lack of land security on estates, and a shortage of skilled and technical manpower that pervades the economy, interfering with efforts to overcome other constraints" (World Bank 1982:i). In such studies, "culture" becomes a secondary or residual category (Worsley 1984). The social and political interplay of economic relationships is downplayed in favor of more quantifiable forms of data and comes to be described in expressions like "other constraints," as in the World Bank report cited above.

What is often lost in discussions of development in Melanesia, as in other parts of the Third World, is that however abundant or limited local environmental resources might be, cultural factors often limit expansion or commercial exploitation of those resources that do exist. Rather than concentrate on particular forms of exchange or market dependencies, this book explores these cultural aspects of development: how local peoples view, symbolize, and express development problems, available options, and appropriate solutions.

In many ways Mandok development history, especially the community's experiences with several market shifts in local commodities, illustrates a larger dependency relationship for all of Papua New Guinea (PNG; see Amarshi, Good, and Mortimer 1979; Good 1986). As useful as a dependency-model perspective may be in a macro-level analysis, however, it is less useful in interpreting local responses or in understanding what the Mandok *think* is happening. Nor will it explain why they have resisted certain forms of development and actively embraced others. It is in these matters that Mandok behavior has been least understood by outside agencies and as a result labeled "paradoxical." Viewed in their cultural context, however, the values expressed in the Mandok people's decisions about development were consistent—more consistent, I will demonstrate, than those shown by outside agencies over time. The individual Mandok I spoke with were quite explicit about why they decided against certain development schemes. "Sure we might make more money if we cash-cropped," they would say, "but that is not who we are."

> We are sea people, not bush people. The Umboi Islanders—they are bush people, they know bush things. We are sea people—we know sea things. We *are* sea things.

This book offers an ethnographic perspective to the process of economic development that outlines perceived cultural identity as a major influence on the Mandok's conceptions of and reactions to dependency conditions. I will show how maritime middleman trade constituted for the Mandok a "cultural system" (after Geertz 1966) and a "key symbol" (after Ortner 1973) that patterned, summarized, and elaborated Mandok concepts of humanity in their culturally constituted "behavioral environment" (after Hallowell 1955). This cultural identity also influenced Mandok people's perceptions of "development" and their evaluations of specific development proposals in terms of perceived appropriateness to this identity.

I will analyze a series of seeming paradoxes. First, the Mandok had a long-standing tradition of entrepreneurial success in localized trading systems, and they experienced high achievement in the early years of a developing modern system. These successes were followed, however, by a sudden drop in performance in both contexts. Second, although Mandok children scored very high on tests measuring cognitive development, their actual achievement, as measured in national achievement tests, reached its all-time low in 1979. Third, though the Mandok have been in the forefront of "development" in Siassi, most of the business and development projects they initiated over the years ended in financial disaster. These seemingly disparate and unrelated events and sequences are really of one piece. They project a kaleidoscope of interfacing cultural and personal identities tumbling between the mirrors of national priorities and self-definition in a burgeoning nation.

BOOK OVERVIEW

This book is informally divided into four parts. The Introduction and Chapter 1 provide the reader with a general orientation to the Vitiaz Strait area and to the Mandok at the time of my fieldwork. This general description gives way to an account of several aspects of Mandok culture.

The Mandok creation legend that describes for them how their world was created, how it operated, and, implicitly, why it should stay that way, is the topic of Chapter 2. This legend lies at the heart of Mandok cultural identity, so it offers a vital introduction to Mandok culture.

Chapters 3 through 6 illustrate how the Mandok translated into everyday life the lessons gleaned from their creation legend. Illustrating my earlier statement that the Mandok saw themselves as "sea people" as opposed to "bush people," Chapter 3 considers the importance of the sea for subsistence and for Mandok culture, and how the sea's value extended beyond mere "economics." It demonstrates how the Mandok's definitions of humanity revolved around the sea and maritime middleman trade. Chapters 4, 5, and 6 examine the Mandok's social and leadership systems in terms of the Mandok's cultural identity as middleman traders. Chapter 4 describes the importance of firstborns as "persons" par excellence and as the linchpins of the social system. Chapter 5 examines social relationships as investments in trade. Chapter 6 discusses Mandok definitions and patterns of achievement and leadership.

Building on the basic foundation of Mandok culture and value systems, Chapters 7 through 9 describe how some of these changed in response to European contact. First were specific changes brought about by pacification, missionization, and market economics (Chapter 7). Next, Chapter 8 discusses outsiders' efforts to "develop" Siassi after World War II and the Mandok's responses, which included projects of their own. Chapter 9 describes selected examples of the Mandok's business ventures from the mid-1970s and the 1980s. The plans, natures, and eventual fates of these ventures illustrate both Mandok ideas about themselves and their understanding of what constitutes appropriate investments in the context of their identity. The book concludes with a discussion of how these projects became behavioral negotiations of "development" (Chapter 10).

I will tell the Mandok's story in the past tense, rather than use the traditionally accepted "ethnographic present" of my fieldwork period. This seems the more appropriate route to take for several reasons. First, over a period of more than 11 years there were two distinct fieldwork periods and interim times during which I have maintained contact with my Mandok friends and family. To choose any one year and call it the "ethnographic present" would be arbitrary and misleading. Second, I, along with others, feel that anthropologists' descriptions of the cultures they study are largely historical accounts. What I have done in this book is to convey my understanding of my informants' interpretations of their reality, to paraphrase Geertz (1973). That reality is not timeless.

Indeed, the point I wish to emphasize in my use of the past tense is precisely the *time boundedness* of anthropological accounts, a boundedness that has a historical rationale, not only in anthropology, but on Mandok. My portrait of Mandok development history offers but a glimpse of their plight, caught at one particular moment—a candid shot, if you will, of a continuing process. The Mandok Island I studied during 1986 and 1987 was different in very specific and definable ways from the one I first studied between 1979 and 1981. Underlying the changes were similarities that seemed "timeless," to be sure. Nor were these changes lost on the Mandok: they were quite articulate about them from the first moment I once again set foot on the island.

This brings me to the final point I wish to make. Some aspects of change in Siassi have been so drastic and so quick that by the time this book was printed, it was already out of date. Is that to say it is useless? I think not. For in the changes, I would argue, are embedded "samenesses" that show a pattern. This pattern is based on and illustrates more fundamental aspects of Mandok culture that last through time, despite apparent superficial changes in momentary details. Moreover, that culture plays a major role in development, not only on Mandok, but throughout the "developing world." The role of culture, which has been drastically underreported or ignored altogether in development studies, is what this book is all about.

In a filmed interview in which Margaret Mead was asked why she had written *Coming of Age in Samoa* for the general public rather than for her academic colleagues, she said that even though her book might be enlightening to specialists, it would most likely be used by people who needed it most, and these people, by and large, were not anthropologists. "So," she shrugged, "I wrote it in English." In a similar vein, I hope I have succeeded in writing an accurate, clear, and interesting ethnography that is at the same time enlightening to specialists and accessible to nonspecialists. This book is also written for people working in "development," whatever the level: administrators in third-world nations, international volunteers, students, lay readers, and those in the Third World who are concerned about their own culture's negotiations with external pressures to "develop."

Alice Pomponio
Canton, New York

✿ Acknowledgments

This book is the result of over two years of fieldwork and 11 years of correspondence with my Mandok friends and colleagues. The first research period, from September 1979 to March 1981, was funded by the Papua New Guinea Department of Education, Research Branch; the Frederica de Laguna Fund, Bryn Mawr College; and the Morobe Province Research Center. The Wenner-Gren Foundation for Anthropological Research and a St. Lawrence University Faculty Research Grant supported the second field trip from October 1986 to May 1987. The bulk of the manuscript was written as part of an Andrew Mellon Post Doctoral Fellowship in the Anthropology Department at the University of Pittsburgh. I thank all of these institutions for their support.

The present effort represents a major expansion, revision, and updating of my doctoral dissertation (Pomponio 1983). I thank all of those people and institutions again, but will not repeat the individual acknowledgments found therein except insofar as they pertain also to this work, with one exception. Jane Goodale directed my doctoral work and remains a source of encouragement and inspiration. To her I owe a debt of gratitude for her love of ethnography, her resourcefulness in times of uncertainty, and her patience with impatient students.

So many people gave unstintingly of their time and effort during my research and writing that I could not possibly thank them all here. My greatest debt is to the Mandok, without whose tolerance, patience, and participation my research would not have been possible, much less as enjoyable as it was. *Tenkyu Kat! Ngeu tiina inep toman gam.* Lewis Kusso-Alless, now Senior Librarian at the Administrative College in Port Moresby, extended his friendship to me and graciously wrote a formal introduction for me to his family on Mandok. This allowed me to live in the village and to become as much a part of a Mandok family as it is possible for a stranger to be. Kusso has also been a critical reader and consultant for all of my writing on the Mandok. My heartfelt thanks go to my "adoptive family" on Mandok—in particular, my "parents," John Aibung and Juliana Atene, who took me in and showed infinite patience at my clumsy attempts to participate in Mandok life. Gabriel Aipake, Church Deacon, was a diligent and insightful mentor on many aspects of Mandok custom, language, and mythology. Aipake and Michael Mote patiently told me the Legend of Namor (see Chapter 2) and painstakingly clarified linguistic and philosophical points. I thank all of the teachers of the Por-Mandok Community School, past and present, for their participation in the education parts of the study, and all the independent business owners on Mandok for their input, especially when the information caused them discomfort or embarrassment. Agnes Keke and Joe Hafmans were gracious hosts, critical readers, and valuable informants on many aspects of Mandok development, education, and business history.

Projects such as this would not be possible without the additional aid, encouragement, and friendship of many people off Mandok Island. The Morobe Province Research Committee approved my research and allowed me to work unmolested at a time when anthropologists were not popular. Sue and Hartmut Holzknecht were my mainstays in the field and provided me with a "home away from home" in Lae during 1979–81 and in Canberra during 1986–87. Rae and John Swan picked up where the Holzknechts left off, supplying me with needed goods from town and occasional goodies to keep my spirits up. Eddie and Sharon David also hosted me and gave valuable assistance. In Finschhafen in October 1986, Dr. John Hershey diagnosed my persistent backache as a herniated disk. He and his wife Vicky took me into their home, nursed me back to (almost) functional health, and endured my presence in the middle of their living-room floor for almost a month. The late Bill Abore, my Mandok brother and former Executive Officer of FISIKA, was a consistent source of encouragement and information both on Mandok culture and on development issues in Siassi. He will be sorely missed in both places. Manfred Bastian, head of the Finschhafen-Kabwuum Construction Company (the construction arm of FISIKA), was also a most helpful source of information on development history in Siassi. In Lablab, Verena and Friedrich Jakob opened their home and their hearts to me, offering cold drinks, good food, and warm friendship whenever my travels took me to Lablab. Gabriel Samol, Morobe Provincial Planner in 1986–87, added much to my knowledge of future development plans in Siassi.

I am indebted to Father Anton Mulderink, C.M.M., for many things through the years: language drills, his intimate knowledge of the Mandok, his gracious hospitality, his friendship, and his cogent criticisms of my work. He managed to keep up with my numerous drafts and recent developments on Mandok Island, even though he was transferred to different areas three or four times during the write-up period. Father Frans Lenssen, C.M.M., continued Father Anton's "open door" policy during 1980–81 and kept me current with major events between 1981 and 1986.

Librarians and archivists are often unsung heroes in research projects. Rev. Rufus Pech of the Australian Lutheran Mission opened the Lutheran Archives at Ampo to me and gave generously of his time, translations, and thoughts on early Lutheran missionary philosophy. Kathy Creely sorted through and helped me to decipher newly acquired and un-catalogued materials at the Melanesian Archives at the University of California, San Diego. Karen Peacock gave valuable help from the Pacific Collection at the Hamilton Library at the University of Hawaii, and Peter Brueggeman of the Scripps Institute of Oceanography Library helped me track down elusive information on the life cycle of sea cucumbers.

Many people contributed to the write-up of the manuscript. The following people read selected draft chapters: Lewis Kusso-Alless, James Clifton, Thomas Coburn, Agnes Keke, Timothy O'Meara, Marian Pomponio, Andrew Strathern, and Sara Sturdevant. The Okari Research Group at the University of Pittsburgh was a valuable forum in which to get feedback from graduate students and professional Melanesianists at that institution. I first worked out a rough outline for this book as part of an Association for Social Anthropology in Oceania symposium on cultural identity and ethnicity in the Pacific (Pomponio 1990a). My thanks to all the participants of those sessions, especially to James B. Watson and Michael Lieber for their insistence on the ethnographic and theoretical details.

Special thanks and a purple heart must be given to those troupers who slogged through uneven and very rough drafts and who forced me to write clearly and succinctly. Richard Scaglion, University of Pittsburgh, must have read through the entire manuscript at least four times, and he still stayed cheerful and encouraging about it. His valuable insights into Melanesian ethnology were complemented by an extraordinary sensitivity to the subtleties of undergraduate students' and other readers' needs. Thomas Harding offered both enthusiastic encouragement for this project from the outset and tenacious criticisms focusing on Siassi, which kept my thinking and writing mindful of the larger comparative framework of the Vitiaz Strait socioeconomic system. I also thank him for his graciousness in writing the Foreword. Anton Ploeg offered insights from Umboi Island and non-Austronesian culture in Siassi. Dorothy Counts and David Counts added comparative data and their expertise from neighboring western New Britain groups. Nancy McDowell, Franklin and Marshall College, gave incisive comments, which helped me gear the manuscript for classroom use. Richard Perry, Chair of the Department of Anthropology at St. Lawrence, endured the confusion and hassle of replacing me for my two leaves of absence during the researching and writing of this book and contributed editorial polish to the final copy. My late father, Charles Pomponio, did not live long enough to see the book completed, but he left his indelible editorial signature both on the book and on my thinking about writing. He lovingly charted a path of logic through my tangled prose and stuck to his own convictions about writing: first, that if it was not written clearly, no one would understand it; and second—''science, schmience''—if it was boring, no one would bother to try. Despite the earnest and loving efforts of all these editors, responsibility for the final product is, of course, mine.

Peggy Adams, James Clifton, Leo Wiegman, Donna Linden, and Alan Titche provided encouragement and editorial assistance. Mary Jo Zeidler drew the maps and Figure 3.1, Carol Barclay reproduced the photographs, Mary Haught helped with secretarial details, and Torre Seiniger helped prepare the bibliography.

Seagulls don't fly into the bush.
When their wings are tired,
       they perch on driftwood.

Mandok proverb

Seagulls Don't Fly Into the Bush

🦋 Introduction

The Siassi area of Papua New Guinea (PNG) has long been known to various government, mission, and education officials as a "backwater" whose physical environment impedes development. An archipelago of volcanic and raised coral islands located in the Vitiaz and Dampier straits, Siassi separates the islands of New Guinea and New Britain (see Figure 1.1, p. 7). Punctuated with coral reefs, these waters are quite hazardous for about eight months of the year. Prevailing winds can approach hurricane velocity in a matter of minutes, and just as abruptly the direction of the wind can shift. When wind is combined with variable currents, dangerous rough seas are the result. The region is a sailor's nightmare. Traveling in certain seasons becomes difficult to impossible, and the short distances between islands seem longer than they really are. Only nine of the 20 islands in this archipelago are inhabited.

The Siassi Islanders gained prominence as middleman traders in Thomas Harding's *Voyagers of the Vitiaz Strait* (1967). They formed the central hub of the Vitiaz trade system. This was especially true of Mandok Island, one of two islands described by Harding as lying at the "center" of the interdependent trading network that connects the Rai Coast with northwestern New Britain (Figure 1.1). Siassi Island traders were known for their sailing skills, their carving heritage, canoe manufacturing, and their obvious entrepreneurial talents.

Later in the 1960s, Mandok Islanders achieved esteem in urban areas of PNG by producing an increasing number of highly capable, well-motivated graduates of secondary schools and advanced education programs. While employed in the major towns, these graduates distinguished themselves through high achievement and rapid upward mobility. They became modern success stories in the emerging Papua New Guinean nation. In the spirit of independence and national development, Mandok villagers began investing in several types of business ventures. With their profits they formed a communal fund from which parents could borrow money to pay school fees for their children and thereby continue the cycle of success.

Funded by the PNG Ministry of Education, I first went to Mandok in 1979 to study the cultural foundation of this pattern of success. My original aim was to compare and contrast learning environments and achievement standards between the school and the village in order to study how children adjusted their performance in Western-style educational settings. I chose Mandok Island because it met all the requirements of my research interests and the research priorities of the Ministry of Education.

In planning my work in PNG, I had sought a community that had a government school in or near it and a populaton of 200–500 people who spoke an Austronesian language. Between 700 and 1,000 different languages are spoken in PNG (estimates vary), and these are divided into two broad types. Most Austronesian languages are spoken in coastal areas from Malaysia through Polynesia and are characterized by a relatively simple grammatical structure and easy pronunciation for English speakers. Although their vocabularies can be quite complex, learning these languages to the point of being able to function socially is a straightforward process.

The other language type in PNG is really a negatively categorized group. The major similarity languages in this type share is their distinctiveness from Austronesian languages. For lack of a better term this language group is called Non-Austronesian, and it includes all the languages that are not Austronesian. Non-Austronesian languages of New Guinea are generally much older than Austronesian languages, dating back to the original inhabitants of this area some 40,000 years ago. In contrast, Austronesian languages are thought to date only to about 4,000–4,500 years ago. Non-Austronesian languages are notable for having complex grammatical structures and difficult pronunciations (at least, for native English speakers). They cannot be mastered by outsiders as second languages in a short time.

Quick language facility was important because I wanted to be able to understand Mandok people's views about achievement, motivation, and success in a variety of contexts, from everyday village life to mythology and rituals. My initial plan was to compare and contrast these ideas with those being taught and expected in school. The Education Department wanted intensive follow-up ethnographic research to complement previous education research (see Lancy 1978, 1979a).

The decisive feature in my selection of Mandok as a research site was the children. They had scored in the top levels on cognitive tests (Lancy 1983), and graduates who were already employed in towns had an established reputation for being high achievers. Many had taken full advantage of their education by attaining well-paying, high-visibility positions in towns all over the country.

In contrast with such evidence of upward mobility in urban settings, the Mandok had retained a long-standing reputation for being an extraordinarily conservative, traditional society. From the perspective of the Education Department's research priorities, my task was to examine the cultural context of this success. Mandok seemed to be an ideal field site from which to view the tensions between "traditional" and "modern"

values in a dynamic, changing culture. Many traditional beliefs and practices were still strong, even though they had adapted to "modern"
achievement patterns via formalized schooling.[1]

When I arrived on Mandok Island in October 1979, the success stories
that originally lured me there had been replaced by accounts of frustration and apparent failure. No Mandok children had been sent to high
school between 1976 and 1979. Of the nine chosen for entry into
high school in 1980, only four were sent. In 1979, 20 children dropped
out of the elementary community school, and none returned to school.
In a survey of 62 provincial schools, the Provincial Superintendent
of Education rated Mandok's 6th-grade class of 1979 "poor," with an
average grade on the national exam of only 42.22 percent (Isoaimo 1980).
The school's Board of Managers was ineffective. The parents' reactions
toward the school seemed to range from laconic to apathetic. The
teachers suffered personal hardships just living on tiny, isolated Por
Island, and they were obviously frustrated in their futile attempts to
unite villagers to support the school and keep the children attending.
At the end of 1979, the triad of parents, Board of Managers, and teachers
were in gridlock. Each blamed the others for the "failure of the school."
The Catholic mission, formerly a guiding beacon for the community,
was also in a quandary. Recent political and administrative changes
suddenly made its role in education unclear. Mandok, along with the
rest of PNG, was in a period of transition. But transition to what?,
I wondered.

Education was not the only arena in which the Mandok were experiencing "failure." By this time, the village's business society had
defaulted on its bank loan when the motorized boat purchased with
the loan broke down. This became a focal point for a larger, more long-
standing political struggle in the village. In the end, the communal fund
went bankrupt, the bank repossessed the boat, and the village became
split down the middle.

What had happened to transform a reputation for success into such
a frustrating record of failure?

My first approach to answering this question was to describe and
analyze the rise and fall of Mandok's interest and participation in formalized Western schooling (Pomponio 1983). That analysis revealed,
however, that I had only scraped "the tip of the reef." The "real problem," I concluded in 1983, was not "education and development" but
"development" itself as it was variously defined in Siassi and by government, mission, and school administrators. For example, in compliance
with government plans for "rural development," several attempts were
made to induce the Mandok to relocate their community to Umboi Island
and grow cash crops. But the Mandok refused to move and instead proposed alternative development projects of their own. At every turn, it
seemed they were making decisions that defied sound economic
sense. As a result, administrators judged the Mandok's behavior to be

paradoxical and labeled them *bikhet,* a word in Tok Pisin (denoted TP; also called Melanesian Pidgin) for "big head," meaning "stubborn," "recalcitrant," "contradictory," or otherwise "contrary."

Mandok development history offers an extended case study in which cultural identity overrode crass economics. My approach to and definitions of Mandok cultural identity are based on Foster's reformulations of Barth's (1969) theory that ethnic identity is the result of a community's shared categories, which form the basis of their interactions with each other and with outsiders. In Foster's work on Mon traders in Thailand (1974, 1977), he departs from the widely held view of trade as a peace-maintaining mechanism (see Harding 1970 for a discussion of this in Siassi) and maintains instead that trade generates tension between traders and their customers. He further contends that the Mon are successful traders largely because they consistently maintain a certain cultural distance from the people with whom they trade. He asserts, moreover, that it is good business to do so.

The Mandok case differs from the Mon in several important respects. First, Mandok trade operated primarily as a barter system and was not rooted in commerce. Second, the Mandok notion of trade as an occupation was specifically confined within a maritime subsistence economy. The Mandok thus had a three-pronged view of themselves. First, they were sea people, as opposed to bush people. Second, they were episodically mobile, rather than sedentary. Third, they were primarily subsistence middlemen and fisherfolk who distributed other peoples' produce, not horticultural producers.

Nevertheless, Foster's general point—that traders consciously cultivate and maintain a separate ethnic identity and that it is good business to do so—is quite applicable and appropriate to the Mandok case. These factors provide running themes throughout this book. With them I will elucidate two things: first, the nature and content of Mandok cultural identity; and second, how this self-definition has influenced their participation in "development."

Typically, outside agents in Siassi defined the islanders as fishermen who traded their goods along the routes outlined by Harding (1967). Outsiders' suggestions for "development" historically stressed agricultural solutions to local demographic and environmental problems. For the Mandok, however, these "solutions" caused additional unwanted problems for them. As I will demonstrate, moreover, individual Mandok generally understood "development" to mean "personal access to cash." By receiving remittances from educated and employed children, for example, Mandok middleman parents believed they were participating in "development." These kinds of perceptions make sense in terms of their notions of trade and exchange, once trade is understood to be part of a more complex cultural system. That system forms the basis of Mandok cultural identity.

PHONOLOGICAL NOTE

There is no standardized orthography of the Mutu language. The orthography presented here is meant to aid the reader in approximating the pronunciation of Mutu terms.

VOWELS

/a/ (long and short): indicates allophones [a], [ə], and [æ], as in "ah," "uh," and "at"

/e/ (long and short): includes allophones [e] and [ɛ], as in "bait" and "bet"

/i/ (long and short): includes allophones [i] and [ɪ], as in "me" and "bit"

/o/ (long and short): includes allophones [o] and [ɔ], as in "go" and "bought"

/u/ (long and short): includes allophones [u] and [ʊ], as in "tune" and "put"

Diphthongs and triphthongs maintain an essential quality of all component vowels and are pronounced with equal stress on each vowel. Double vowels are pronounced with equal stress on each vowel. Double vowels are written as such (e.g., *tiina,* "big," as opposed to *tina,* "mother").

CONSONANTS

Most consonants can be pronounced as in English, with the following exceptions:

/ŋ/ voiced velar nasal, as in si<u>ng</u>ing

/r/ unvoiced alveolar tap /ř/ and voiced alveolar trill /ř/

/v/ voiced bilabial fricative /β/; different from /b/

/ɣ/ voiced velar fricative

Note that /m/ and /n/ constitute separate syllables when they appear before voiced consonants: /m/ before /b/ and /n/ before /d/ and /g/. For example, *ngar* is pronounced "n-GAR."

CURRENCY EXCHANGE RATES

From 1979–81 the approximate average rate of exchange was PNG K1 = U.S. $1.50. In 1986–87 the average rate was PNG K1 = U.S. $1.10.

CHAPTER ONE

✿ Voyage to the Vitiaz Strait

Things don't just appear from nowhere. God put the raw materials on earth, but humans must develop them and use them. For example, God gave us paper, so we can write things down and remember them later. We can read a book and learn all kinds of new things from it.

John Aibung, March 1980

My initiation into Mandok culture began with a splash—literally. On October 30, 1979, after enduring 21 stormy hours in the Vitiaz Strait, I could not wait to put my first experience with seasickness behind me. I was on the *M.V. Sungu,* a small motor vessel servicing the Siassi District of Morobe Province, Papua New Guinea (PNG; see Figure 1.1). From my position at the rail of the *Sungu,* the tiny 4-hectare coral islet of Mandok seemed to bob like a green-tipped cork in a brownish-gray sea. The realization that it was I who was bobbing while the island remained stationary made my stomach turn. I tried to ignore my queasiness.

When the boat finally docked, I was hesitant to follow my guide Dangeta's advice to climb out of it and into a canoe. Why not the perfectly sturdy-looking dock just off the bow of the ship? "No, no—that's the men's area," she protested, horrified. *"Misis"* (Tok Pisin, hereafter TP, for "Mrs.," or European woman), "you follow me." She tried again to convince me to climb over the rail. My other guide, a young man in his late twenties named Namongo, then informed me that it was quite all right to use the dock. In no mood to debate the issue, I stumbled off my rocking prison and followed him onto it.

The dock looked sturdier than it was. My rubber legs and thong-clad feet longed for solid ground. But the dock was built of slender tree limbs, barely smoothed of their bark, twigs, and buds, parallel to each other and nailed to thicker stanchions in the water. It bowed noticeably under its burden. With 20 or more men on it to greet the boat, the flexing poles alternately rose and fell when anyone moved.

I tried to supervise the unloading of my supplies from the ship's hold to the rickety dock and struggled to communicate in broken Tok Pisin I had acquired along the way in dribs and drabs. I smiled weakly and ventured an occasional glance at the crowded shoreline. Namoŋo informed

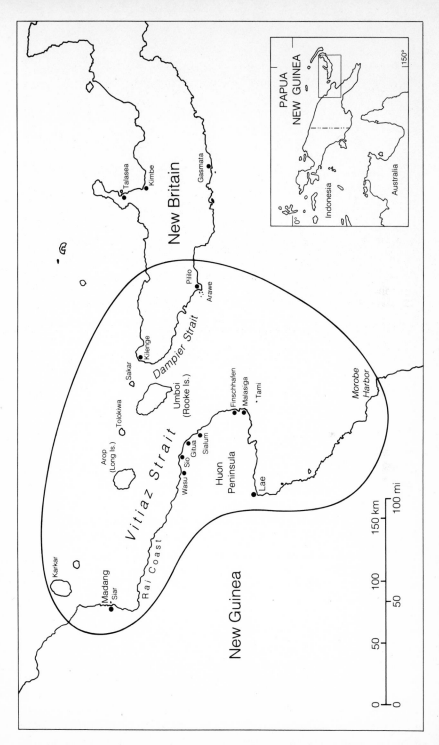

FIGURE 1.1 *Vitiaz trade system.*

F I G U R E 1.2 *Aerial view of Mandok Island, 1979.*

me that I was to stay at the mission on neighboring Por Island and that Father Anton (the missionary priest) had instructed the men to take me there. This was surprising because I had carefully mentioned to all officials and Mandok people I met that I wanted to live in the village. I turned to follow my cargo to the awaiting canoe and glanced again at the beach. It seemed to me that the entire village had turned out for the arrival of the boat, and all eyes were aimed at the *misis* on the dock. At that moment the lingering effects of seasickness, rocking legs, and anxious heart conspired against me to make every face I saw seem less than friendly. This was quite contrary to what I was told to expect from the various acquaintances (both Mandok and expatriate) I had met along the way to Siassi. Was this what people meant when they mentioned that the Siassi peoples had a unique welcoming ceremony? Couldn't be. Bolstering my courage, I tried to smile at anyone whose glance met mine. Nothing.

The walkway from the dock was a 20-meter-long lane of piled sea rubble: coral formations, stones, broken chunks of old concrete, and odd hunks of driftwood. It posed new balance problems. No stone was securely placed, so each step I took caused the ground underneath to rock, slip, or sink precariously. I tried to walk gracefully to the canoe that would take me to Por, my concentration focused on maintaining my balance for the seeming eternity—actually about five steps— separating me from my transportation. It would never do for me to slip on one of these rocks and . . . I landed with a great splash! I was sitting chest-deep in seawater, the full skirt of my dress billowed up in my face like an air pillow. That did it—I broke up with laughter at what I am sure was a hilarious sight. Once I laughed, the embarrassed hush of the onlookers was broken by scattered titters of laughter. When one of the two men appointed to paddle me to Por slipped and fell at my side, the entire village dropped its reserve and roared with unrestrained laughter. My comrade in salt water took my arm and helped me up. We shook hands and giggled some more.

Although this was my first "splash," it was not my last gaffe in front of the village (worse yet, in front of the men's area). Even my exit from Mandok Island a year and a half later caused commotion and climaxed with a dramatic swimming race against the *Sungu*. I say "swimming race" because my canoe got swamped in the rough sea, and I was forced to abandon ship. I let my nine-year-old companion do the bailing and paddling while I did a 50-meter freestyle sprint to shore, lest the boat come and leave without my luggage on board. By this time I had learned to take the mission boat to the airstrip at Lablab (Umboi Island) and fly out of Siassi to start my journey homeward. (In my own defense, I must note that during the first 18 months I spent in PNG I did learn to paddle my own canoe in the Mandok style, both literally and figuratively.)

Once on Por I got another surprise. Father Anton was nowhere in sight, nor was he expected back for two or three weeks. With no place to go, and no way to get there, I felt totally stranded. What would I do "by myself" on Por for three weeks? The tiny island hosted only the mission house and the community school buildings. The children paddled small single-outrigger canoes to school and returned the half mile across the channel to their Mandok homes every afternoon. No one lived on Por except the priest and two teachers. It was, culturally and geographically, an island. The cheerful singing of Mandok children, emanating from the school building about 30 meters from my room, offered me no solace from my misery. I wondered how I could endure the next 18 months in such isolation.

The next day the brilliant sun was shining. My stomach had settled back into its proper anatomical location. The bleakness of the day before was gone. I laughed at myself and determined to do what I could on Por. I tried to get my bearings. I busied myself talking with the teachers about my project, the school, and the community. With the help of Mary Nareko, the mission cook, and her sister Dong, a third grader, I began learning Mutu, the local vernacular. I also got my first formal lesson in poling a canoe across a reef.

During the week I spent on Por the village elders were also busy on Mandok, deciding what to do with me. An announcement from the Ministry of Education had been released to the teachers and to the mission, describing me as a "research officer" for the Ministry of Education. It explained that I would be "making a study of the school." While in the capital city of Port Moresby I was fortunate to meet Lewis

Kusso-Alless, a Mandok, then a student and librarian at the University of Papua New Guinea.[1] He wrote a letter of introduction for me to his family and the other *bigmen* ("leaders," "elders"; see Chapter 6). It also explained my presence (in terms more comprehensible to the Mandok, I hoped). Because it would have been improper by Mandok standards to have a stranger (especially a woman) wandering around alone, Lewis's family was entrusted with my care. I was thus adopted into the family and was to share one-third of a house then being constructed. Later I learned that this was also part of the reason the Mandok were happy to paddle me to Por when I arrived. The house did not yet have a ladder by which I could climb into it. Because all the houses in Siassi are built on stilts that are about a meter and a half tall, the ladder was essential. The walls were not finished, either, and I used a shower curtain as a "door" for the first six months. But I was so eager to live on Mandok that I did not mind. In this region the next change of season meant heavy rains and a change in direction of the prevailing high-velocity winds. When I got drenched with deluges from the southeast monsoon, my new door was built in a few days. I also added shutters over the window holes in my walls.

On Sunday, one week after my arrival, I was picked up from Por and paddled across the channel to attend Sunday mass. It was celebrated by the church deacon during the priest's absence. On the way across the channel our canoe got caught in a sudden squall, and we all got soaked. I was given a *laplap* (TP, a two-meter by one-meter strip of cloth) to wear as a skirt, and a very blousy top called a *meri blaus* ("lady's blouse," or woman's blouse; *meri* is the TP term for "woman" or "female") to wear for church.

After church my new "sister-in-law" Malaka took me to see my house. I had no place else to go except back to Por, and my clothes were not yet dry. I negotiated the new ladder (no more than six two-by-fours at almost regular intervals) and readjusted my *laplap*. Malaka got a small bench, sat me on the veranda, and disappeared. Unable to communicate well, I waited and watched the village go by. When Malaka returned she handed me a long garfish that had been formed into a teardrop shape and roasted on the fire. With her other hand she offered me a kind of bread made from sweet manioc and grated coconut. Because by this time breakfast was a distant memory, I accepted the food gratefully and ate with relish. Malaka smiled at me and nodded her approval. Then she turned and made the following announcement, to no one in particular but to anyone who could hear it: "Hey—she's alright, this *misis*. I gave her one garfish and a piece of tapioca bread; she ate both, and thanked me for them! She is sitting on her veranda now, eating the food I gave her." I later learned that my Mandok family was willing to take me in but anxious about whether a *misis* would eat their food. They were also worried about their ability to take care of me. Their concern did not last long, however. With Malaka's announcement and with the help of Sakael, my new "brother," Sopol, a classificatory "brother," and

Dolau, my "son," I was moved into my new home on Mandok. I celebrated the move by hosting a "tea party" for my family. We all relished the coffee and cookies, both rare treats at that time.

My modus vivendi on Mandok was simple. I ate whatever was offered and reciprocated periodically by supplying meals of rice with canned meat or fish. I also became the family's source for a seemingly endless flow of coffee, tea, hot chocolate, sugar, milk, cookies, crackers, peanut butter, and popcorn. This appeared to be a satisfactory arrangement all around. I generally depended on my "mother," Juliana Atene, or Malaka, and on other female kinswomen to decide how much of which foods we would eat when it was my turn to be host. But it was either my mother or my sister Josephine Kamunggi who did the actual cooking.

Living in the village had both advantages and disadvantages. There were personal hardships such as lack of water, a toilet, and privacy. These were compensated for by intensive participation in village life and increased personal rapport with the Mandok. Living in the village I was able to learn Mutu quickly; it was total immersion. I received the patient explanation and drilling of many tutors, young and old. The Mandok and all the Siassi speak a very clear and fluent Tok Pisin, but I did not. With the determined cooperation of my new family and friends, I was able to learn both languages simultaneously.

Sometimes, school-aged children were my best tutors. Accustomed to verb paradigms and the repetition of school lessons, they were tireless in their efforts to teach me their language. Agnes Abiua, my "daughter" and a fourth grader at the time, sat with me for hours, saying, for example, not much more than *"iit* means 'all of us together, you too'; *yei* means 'all of us, but not you.' Push, pull, in, out, up, down, chop, slice, rip, tear," and so on. As I progressed we looked at magazines and picture books. We recited the names of different fish and animals in a teasing game. "You have a face like a frog," got a swift reply of "You have a face like a hammerhead shark," and so on. Though they learned English in school, most of the Mandok were hesitant to speak it, especially to a stranger whom they knew to be a native speaker. This reserve dissolved, however, when I took out a guitar and offered them the opportunity to sing. Mandok children were excellent and exuberant singers who won awards locally for their talents. We spent many balmy evenings on my veranda, singing folk songs in a joyous attempt at cross-cultural communication.

At the end of seven months I was fluent enough to understand what was said at town meetings and in the narrations of myths and stories. Explanations were given in Mutu rather than in Tok Pisin. All my interviewing thereafter was in Mutu. At first the Mandok were less than ebullient informants on any but the most trivial subjects. Once they felt I had command of their language, however, I became a source of pride to them. Any visitor to the village was immediately informed, either directly or indirectly, of "how well Ali knows our language." I found (as others had before me) that the entire process of language learning was a useful way of establishing long-lasting friendships and general rapport. Knowing the language also helped me to understand the various nuances of meaning and the many metaphors that expressed values. This contributed greatly to my initial interests in achievement and success, but more importantly, perhaps, to my greater understanding of Mandok mythology and culture.

Most of the elders of the village remembered Thomas Harding and Michael Freedman, two earlier anthropologists who studied in Siassi. My "father," John Aibung, and many other family members were key informants for both. Therefore, they were all convinced they knew exactly the information I sought, and they reassured me of this from the first fireside chat we shared. What they did not understand was why the American *bigmen*—in particular, Harding's professor *Masol* (Marshall Sahlins)—had sent another anthropologist (a woman, no less) to do it again.[2] *Masol* even came to Mandok with Harding (in 1964). Was it not all written in their books? One prominent elder suggested that perhaps they were "confused" because both of my predecessors went *nabaut nabaut* (TP, "all around," with the implication of aimlessness) in their research. "This is no good," my father declared. "If one wants to gain Mandok knowledge, one should find one particular man of knowledge and learn many things from him. Too many voices make one dizzy."

I immediately set out to explain that, no, the American *bigmen* were not confused by either Harding's or Freedman's accounts, and no, *Masol* was not my teacher; it was the PNG Ministry of Education who had asked me to come. I tried to spark their memories of the other researchers who had come a year or so before to test the school children. I appealed to the positive image of Mandok workers in towns. I told them my job was to learn Mandok knowledge, language, and customs so the *bigmen* in Port Moresby could understand more clearly how other schools could be as successful in educating their children. "Ah," a voice came up from the far side of the fire, "now you see the power of books. The *bigmen* in Moresby and in the United States have read those books, and now they know how great we Mandok are. Now Ali will write another book, and very soon the whole world will know about us Mandok."

From the perspective of my informants and friends on Mandok, my account will perhaps be a disappointment. I, too, departed from Mandok custom, for I spoke with as many and as diverse an aggregate of informants as possible. Male, female, elder, youth, important people, "just plain folk," teachers, students, and missionaries—as varied perspectives as possible on as many topics as possible.

By living and participating in the village I was my own most effective research tool, for doing so enabled me to watch children at play, adults at work, or the village as a whole perform sacred rituals. In addition to observing, interviewing, and chatting with anyone who was available—by just being there—I participated in Mandok activities to whatever extent possible. I accompanied women on fishing expeditions. We dug holes and planted yams in the garden. I traveled on trading trips and even scraped my own trochus-shell armlets. Most evenings I sat around the fires and told stories. Throughout, of course, I practiced paddling my own canoe. In the Vitiaz Strait, this last task is not as easy as it sounds.

SIASSI DISTRICT

Most ethnographies set in tropical climates describe the seasons as either "wet" or "dry"; "dry" periods are usually broken by "wet" monsoon rains. In the small islands of Siassi, however, it is misleading to speak of "wet" and "dry" as distinct seasons, even though they are so described on Umboi and in other parts of PNG. The distinguishing climatic feature of the Vitiaz Strait is the seasonality and relative intensity of the winds. The more important distinction in describing weather patterns is therefore "windy/calm." The windy seasons bring with them rain; the calm bring dry. The "northwest season" is short, officially lasting from January to March, and is considered to be the milder, "drier" of the seasons for the smaller islands. The "southeast season," May to November, is the longer, "rainy" season. Periods of relative calm are usually limited to the months between seasons: March through April, and November through December. During these transitional times the winds are variable and unpredictable. Winds might change direction without losing intensity many times during any given day. When I departed for Siassi in 1979, acquaintances in Lae had remarked on how lucky I was to be traveling at the "start of the calm season." At the time I could only be grateful it was not the "height of the windy season."

Although the mean annual rainfall for the area as a whole is about 5,100 mm (about 200 in.) per year (Patrol Report Finschhafen 1, 1950), precipitation varies greatly between the smaller low islands and the high volcanic islands and from year to year. Umboi generally gets much more rain than the small islands, most of which are situated less than 3 kilometers from Umboi's southern shore. The difference in rainfall is due to the large mountain in the center of Umboi that causes higher precipitation on the windward side of the island. When the prevailing wind changes, so does the rainfall (Patrol Report Finschhafen 1, 1952:6).

The sizes of the nine populated islands in Siassi District range from the large "mainland" of Umboi, whose area is about the size of metropolitan Boston, to tiny Mutumala and Aromot, whose total land mass combined would barely accommodate a football stadium. The islands that concern us here are the high volcanic island of Umboi (Rooke) and the small coral islets that encircle its southern tip: the "inner" islands of Aromot, Mutumala, Mandok, and Aronaimutu and the "outer islands" of Malai and Tuam (Figures 1.3 and 1.4).

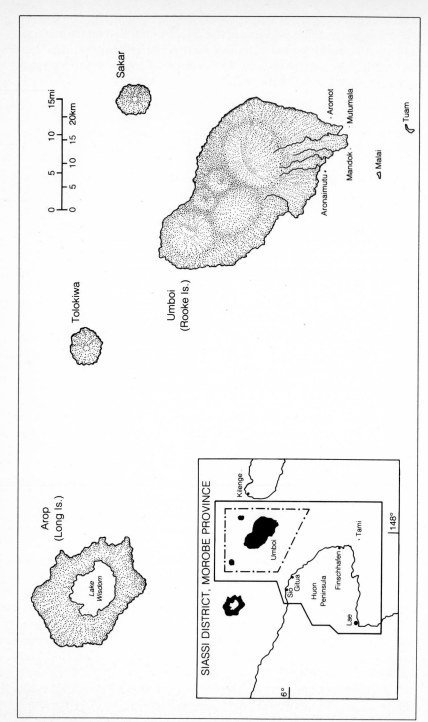

FIGURE 1.3 *Siassi social sphere.*

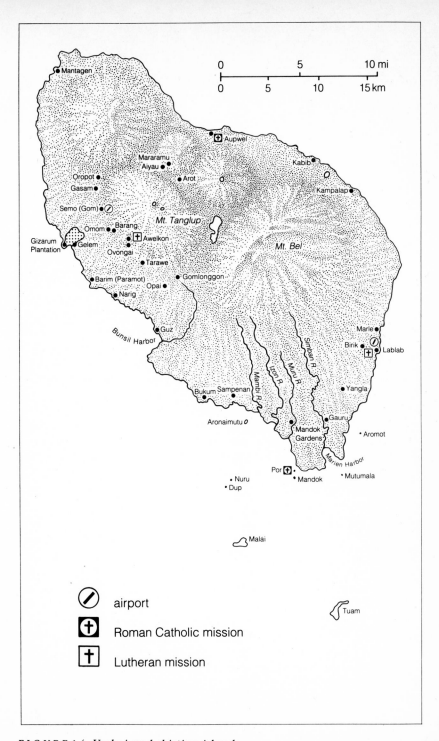

FIGURE 1.4 *Umboi and skirting islands.*

T A B L E 1.1 *Small-island populations, 1926–87.*

ISLAND	1926	1963	1980	1987
Aromot	156	398	549	604
Mandok	120	343	435	508
Malai	300	448	365	464
Tuam	250	496	275	286
TOTAL	826	1685	1624	1862

SOURCES: The figures for Aromot Island include Mutumala Island for the 1980 figures. For the first entry for Aromot, the source is Neuhauss (1911, I:135). All other figures for 1926 are from Chinnery (n.d.). Those for 1963 are from Harding (1967:14*n.*), and those from 1980 are from the Morobe Province Preliminary Field Counts (1980:409). Aronaimutu Island does not appear in the earliest sources; its population was formed much later from immigrants from Barim (west Umboi Island) and Mandok Island (see text). All figures from 1987 are mine.

The islanders make up approximately one-fourth the total population of Siassi District. As the numbers in Table 1.1 indicate, the total population of these small islands has increased by more than 250 percent since 1926. This striking population growth most likely stems from the curtailment of population-limiting techniques such as abortion and infanticide. Increased hygiene and health care are certainly contributing factors as well.[3]

Throughout this book references will be made to the population growth of these islands and to the overcrowding on the inner islands, especially on Aromot and Mandok. Recognition of overpopulation was a primary catalyst for the establishment in this area of different development programs (discussed in Chapter 8).

"SEA PEOPLE" AND "BUSH PEOPLE" IN SIASSI

The Siassi region is usually considered to be a political and social unit. Within that basic unit, however, as already noted, are great geographic differences that are matched by cultural and linguistic differences. The combination has always impeded outside governance and rural development. For example, there has been much confusion in the literature over the inclusiveness of the name "Siassi." Politically the entire region inset in Figure 1.3 is called "Siassi." Locally, however, the small coral islets that ring the southern tip of Umboi Island are considered "the Siassi Islands proper." Here we will use the terms as follows: "Siassi" refers to the entire area; "small islands" refers to the small coral islets of Aromot, Mutumala, Mandok, and Aronaimutu, plus the two somewhat larger islands of Malai and Tuam; and "islanders" refers to their inhabitants.

The three major volcanic islands Umboi (Rooke), Sakar, and Tolokiwa are considered locally to be mainlands; I therefore refer to each by name.

Additional distinctions must recognize geographic, political, and cultural boundaries. Although Tami Island, off the coast of Finschhafen, and Arop (Long) Island to the west in Madang Province (see Figure 1.1) do not belong to "Siassi District," they did figure into "Siassi culture." Some Siassi Islanders traced their origins back to these islands through trade, adoption, and marriage ties (see Chapter 5). Many customs, legends, masked figures, and feasts also found their way to the small islands from these "Siassi outliers." They will thus be included in this discussion when pertinent.

Siassi peoples recognized ethnic differences among themselves based on the following four criteria: (1) a distinction between "sea people" and "bush people," (2) a distinction between gardeners and fisherfolk, (3) language, and (4) locale and time of ancestral origin. Within the relatively small geographic area of Siassi District there were two different subsistence economies, four different languages spoken, and a complex "fishnet" of interweaving and crosscutting social networks based on kinship and trading relations.

The local distinction between "sea people" and "bush people" seemed to summarize the differences between the islanders and the inhabitants of Umboi. The Siassi island traders historically traveled to distant shores and returned with a wealth of material goods and stories. Because of this, they enjoyed a more cosmopolitan status than the Umboi "bush people." The islanders were a relatively homogeneous population in terms of language, economy, rituals, and cultural identity, especially compared to the different populations on Umboi. Linguistic distinctions highlighted these basic cultural differences and contributed to local perceptions that the two groups constituted different worlds.

Local people did not usually refer to Umboi Island as a whole, but rather by reference to one or another particular named area. One can divide Umboi linguistically with a diagonal line drawn from northeast to southwest, separating the Kowai language group of the northwest mountain district from the Kaimanga language group of the southeast lowlands (Figure 1.5).[4] Speakers of Paramot, the third language group, lived in Barim (formerly called Paramot) and Mantagen and on Aronaimutu (a bilingual island), Tolokiwa Island, and Arop Island. The Siassi Islanders "proper" spoke three different but mutually intelligible dialects of a language they called "our language," named Mutu after the local term for island.[5]

The various language groups were important to the islanders for many reasons, not the least of which was mutual intelligibility (or the lack of it). The Kowai language of northwest Umboi is non-Austronesian, whereas the Kaimanga language of southeast Umboi, as well as Paramot and Mutu, are Austronesian. These languages have all been classified as

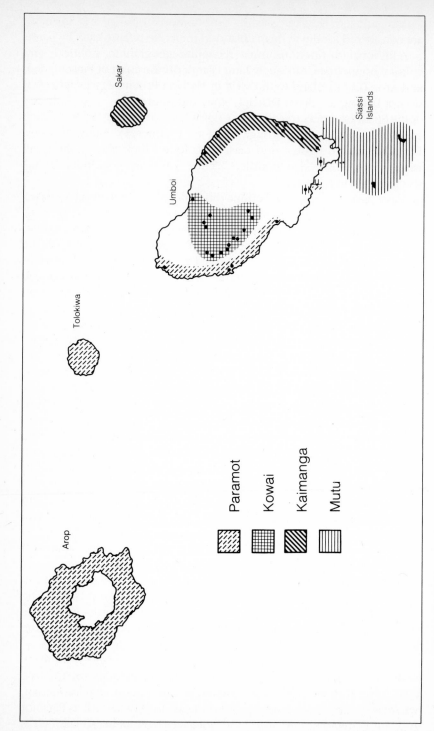

FIGURE 1.5 *Siassi language groups.*

members of the Siasi [*sic*] Family of languages (Hooley 1971).[6] A basic cultural similarity was thus recognized among groups speaking the three Austronesian languages and, though not mutually intelligible, speakers of one language had little difficulty learning another of the same family. These similarities seemed to mitigate some of the differences between the "sea" and "bush" designations. In contrast, peaceful contacts and trade with Kowai-speaking communities were very recent—only since pacification in the early part of the 20th century—and were not stabilized until after World War II (Ploeg 1989). Linguistic and cultural differences seemed in this case to highlight the sea/bush distinctions among the islanders. In general, most islanders were more knowledgeable about, and hence more comfortable with, Kaimanga-speaking populations than with those on the Kowai side of Umboi.

The subsistence economies of the different populations corresponded to geographic and linguistic groupings. Inhabitants of Umboi and its satellite islands to the west, Tolokiwa and Arop, depended primarily on swidden horticulture and arboriculture. In contrast to these sedentary horticulturalists, the Siassi Islanders historically were maritime middleman traders. Voyaging in huge two-masted sailing canoes, they connected mainland New Guinea with western New Britain by distributing finished material goods, rituals, magical spells, and raw materials. In exchange for these largely nonedible objects and edible shellfish and smoked fish, the Siassi traded for both ceremonial and food items. Pigs were always at the top of the list of desirable trade goods. Pork was an essential ingredient to any large feast and the major item of wealth throughout Siassi (as in other parts of Melanesia). Other valuables sought included two kinds of clay pots (instrumental in bridewealth and other kinds of ceremonial exchanges), obsidian, dogs, dogs' teeth, pigs' tusks, necklaces of fruit bat teeth, tapa cloth, taro, sweet potatoes, yams, net bags, and a wide variety of raw materials.[7]

Also valuable were the indigenous crafts of the small islands, including canoe building (especially two-masters), fishnet weaving, carving, weaving of pandanus sleeping mats and sago-frond skirts, and the making of incised trochus-shell armlets. A more complete list is presented in Table 1.2.

In addition to long-distance overseas trade, the islanders traded "locally" with communities on Umboi, Arop, Tolokiwa, and Sakar islands, as well as among themselves. From these various sources the traders obtained serial and cyclical sources of vegetable staples (because growing seasons and crops varied). They also got the raw materials used in canoe manufacture, the carving and craft industries, and house building. In this barter system, the cultural value of comparable toil balanced out to the satisfaction of the traders. The people of Umboi did not, for the most part, manufacture trade goods, with the exception of woven vine armlets (*ngas*, discussed in Chapter 2). The Kowai-speaking mountain people dug red ochre out of the soil; the Kaimanga-speaking

TABLE 1.2 *Village exports in the Siassi sphere.*

	SMALL ISLANDS				UMBOI ISLAND COMMUNITIES		SATELLITE ISLANDS		
	MANDOK	AROMOT	MALAI	TUAM	KOWAI-SPEAKING	KAIMANGA-SPEAKING	AROP	TOLOKIWA	SAKAR
canoes	●	●							
fishnets	●	●	●						
trochus-shell armlets	●	●	●						
kwila bowls	●	●							
grass skirts	●	●							
betel-nut baskets	●	●	●						
coconuts	●	●	●[a]	●		●			
fish	●	●	●						
shellfish	●	●	●						
lime	●		●						
betel nut	●	●			●	●	●	●	
tortoiseshell armlets		●							
net bags				●[b]					
red ochre					●				
taro					●				
logs						●			

Singapore

taro

pigs

dogs

sweet potato

sweet manioc

oranges[c]

vines[d]

sago

banana

pineapple

pawpaw

watermelon

tobacco

dogs' teeth

flying-fox-
tooth necklaces

drums

tortoiseshell

pitpit

[a]*Kingfish (sup)*
[b]*Recent introduction (1987)*
[c]*Barim (Paramot speakers)*
[d]*Mantagen (Paramot speakers)*

lowlanders obtained the raw materials traded with the islanders from the bush. Their labor went into their gardens. On the other hand, the Mandok (and other islanders) spent comparatively more time working on their crafts than they did on subsistence activities. If the catch was good, for example, one day of fishing could convert into one or two weeks' worth of vegetable food. The nutritional balance of trade is obvious: the Umboi gardeners relied on the islanders for protein supplements, and the islanders relied on the Umboi gardeners for their vegetable staples and for variety in their fruit and vegetable diet.

Despite frequent intermarriage, trade, and generally congenial relations, there existed even among the small islands of Siassi an underlying current of competition and parochialism. If a Malai woman, *A*, married a Mandok man, she was often called "Malai *A*" or "that Malai woman," particularly in times of disagreement. Each small island population had a vested interest in maintaining its identity vis-à-vis the others. This seems to be a common feature of trading societies (see, for example, Foster 1974). Even within single island populations, as we will see with respect to Mandok, there was an informal hierarchy of lineages based on place and time of origin of the ancestral immigrant group to which any person belonged. The subject of status differences among groups was brought up in times of disagreement and stress. For the most part the rivalry was tempered, however, by intricate networks of trade and kin relations and by the perception that all depended on one another for survival and prosperity.

Trade was supplemented by reef fishing. After pacification, Australian government officers introduced limited horticulture and arboriculture to the islanders as a supplementary means of subsistence (see Chapter 7). Malai and Tuam were large enough to support limited gardening, but the other islands were much too small and lacked a source of fresh water.

FISHERMEN WHO TRADE VERSUS MIDDLEMEN WHO FISH

Most Melanesian societies trade. Trade systems in Melanesia usually fall into two categories: subsistence trade and prestige trade (Harding 1970). The Vitiaz system is distinctive because it involves both types of trade. Within this system the Siassi Islanders stood out for three reasons. First is their reliance on trade for subsistence: they had to trade to eat. Second, the importance of trade provided the foundation of Siassi status and prestige systems (see Chapters 4–6). Third, the Siassi region was distinctive in its reliance specifically on *middleman* trade—that is, the connecting of two or more endpoints through a complex network of food and craft specialization, exports, imports, and reexports for profit.

In a comparison of ten different trading societies, Harding rated Mandok society among the highest in its reliance on reexported goods:

> In spite of the importance of Mandok's local craft specialties . . . almost the entire content of the overseas [i.e., beyond Siassi] trade, as well as much of the local trade, consisted of re-exports. (Harding 1989:28)

The Siassi Islanders enjoyed a more cosmopolitan status than their Umboi trade partners. They traveled the straits, met different peoples, spoke different languages, and came back with a wealth of stories. As a result of this worldliness they maintained an edge on local social and political interactions. This seems to be a common feature of trading societies in general (Foster 1974) and of maritime traders in particular. Sahlins (1972:282), for example, noted that maritime-trading specialists "are typically the richest people of their area" and that "this prosperity is the dividend of trade." The Mandok expressed this prosperity as their just reward for "breaking the straight." "People pay us for our sweat," the Mandok would say.

For these and other reasons, I consider the Mandok not as fishermen who traded but as maritime middlemen who fished. This shift in emphasis makes a tremendous difference to our understanding of Mandok behavior and of specific choices during their development history.

EXILES, REFUGEES, AND MAVERICK DRIFTERS

Where did the Siassi Islanders come from? How did they get to their respective islands? How long have they been there? If the environment of the Vitiaz Strait is so harsh, why did they stay? These questions are more easily asked than answered. Siassi migration patterns provide a key to contemporary social relationships, which in turn explain some of the problems faced by various outside agencies in their attempts to unite the Siassi region under one set of administrative guidelines and development programs.

We know very little about the origins of these intrepid traders. Reconstructing prehistoric migration and settlement patterns in Siassi is a complex and frustrating endeavor. The archaeological record is scant because the shoreline has changed so drastically over the years: Much of the evidence is buried under the sea. Because Siassi is in the Pacific "Ring of Fire," volcanic and tectonic activity in this area wreak additional havoc with material remains. Moreover, much of the prehistoric tool kit was composed of nondurable materials. What remains, then, are scattered heaps of marine debris (clamshells, fish bones), occasional deposits of animal bones, and obviously imported obsidian flakes and pottery sherds. The extensive and complex trading systems all over the northeast New Guinea region further complicate the picture by creating a constant shuffling of people, objects, and customs. Archaeological research in Siassi is just beginning, and so far the results are tentative (see Lilley 1986:448–479; 1988). There is evidence for human activity on Tuam dating as far back as 2,500–2,800 years ago, but the first evidence of intensive habitation does not appear until around 1,600 years before the present (B.P.; Lilley 1986:450). On Mandok there is evidence of human activity as early as around 1,200 B.P. (1986:457). According to Lilley, the earliest evidence for trade relations ancestral to the Siassi trade system as it has been recorded ethnographically dates at 300–350 years B.P. (Lilley 1986:103–104; 1988), but such activities could be more ancient.[8]

For example, although there is no archaeological evidence for intensive habitation on Tuam from around 300–350 B.P., "some 150 people lived there at [the time of European] contact" (Lilley 1986:473). Lilley noted that this discrepancy in evidence "suggests that people may have lived in the islands continuously from ca. 2,500–2,800 B.P., or at least ca. 1,600 B.P., but left no remains which [sic] survive today" (1986:473). Until more archaeological research is conducted, we can only guess about the antiquity of settlement and trade in this area.

The different Siassi peoples had their own accounts of how this area was settled, who settled it, when, and why. This information was contained in oral histories for each island, in genealogies of important families, and in the creation legend of Namor (see Chapter 2). Each source of information imparts a characteristic twist to events and interpretations; much of this information agrees with Lilley's broad outline for settlement. One thing is certain: these islands were settled by people who originally were just passing through, presumably on trading expeditions. Various historical episodes encouraged individuals or family lines to remain on various islands. Many of the oral narratives suggest that the first settlers were "mavericks," rebels, or some other kind of refugees from "bush" societies. The complex and far-flung trade system recorded by Harding (1967) did not occur randomly but instead was the result of a series of cataclysmic and disruptive episodes that scattered bits of several populations across the archipelago. Space limitations here preclude a comprehensive account of each island's settlement history. Although the settlement history of Mandok is more recent that those of Malai, Aromot, or Tuam, it can be considered typical and will serve to illustrate the pattern.

The island that is now called Mandok was once an uninhabited resting place for traders on their long journeys both within the Siassi region and from the Rai Coast to western New Britain. The first settlers on Mandok came from Aromot. These founders traced their roots back to key, named forebears from Kilenge. Both Mandok and Aromot elders described a fight between "brothers" that took place in the *pulat* (the men's area) on Aromot. The *pulat* in each village was a sacred area in which all the secret and sacred paraphernalia for the ritual life of the community was stored and in which male initiations were performed. Discussions of all important political, social, and economic decisions affecting the village were conducted there. Because of its identification as a place of decision making, respect, and law and order, the *pulat* was also a sanctuary in which fugitives could find refuge. No fighting or carousing was permitted within its boundaries.

According to the story, while the men were assembling for a meeting one day, two brothers were joking with each other. One of them was having an affair with a married woman, and the other was teasing him about it. The woman's husband, who was trying to call the meeting to order, became suspicious when he heard the teaser calling "*Ove,*" the ritualized call for attention used when a man wanted to address the assembly. The man had already suspected the affair, and seeing the two brothers laughing convinced him that they were laughing at him. He then challenged the brothers to a fight. Because aggressive behavior was forbidden within the boundaries of the *pulat*, the incident was gravely disruptive. One of the brothers left Aromot, taking his group with him to Mandok (it is unclear whether he was expelled or went voluntarily). Thus the members of *Mandoog* moiety moved and settled Mandok. (A moiety is one of two approximately equal parts, in this case one-half of a society. Each moiety often includes smaller divisions into clans, lineages, and so on.) At the time of the split, Aromot Island contained the *Aromot* (presumably the island's founder group) and *Mandoog* moieties. At first the immigrants named their new island *Ove*, perhaps to commemorate the circumstances of its settlement. Later they renamed it *Mandoog* (Mandok) after themselves (see Chapter 5 for a discussion of Mandok moieties).

The leader of the *Mandoog* had been using the little island for some time as a sort of private fishing ground. When the fight broke out it was no real hardship to leave, for he and his group had someplace to go (Mulderink 1989). The fight itself, then, might be a secondary explanation for a political split that was developing anyway. At any rate, this is the Mandok version of how they came to live on their island.

The particulars of this and other smaller migration episodes bear striking similarities to features of the migration legend of Namor (see Chapter 2). This migration, however, accounts for only those Mandok who traced their ancestry through Aromot to Kilenge. This story was important because it told of the migration that established "ownership" of Mandok. These points will be pursued in more depth in subsequent chapters.

During the precontact era the islanders formed the hub of the Vitiaz trade system. They did not share the same craft specializations or networks of trade relations. The Aromot and Mandok were canoe builders, for instance; in contrast, even though Malai and Tuam islanders were overseas traders, they did not build canoes. Instead they purchased their sailing canoes from Mandok and Aromot and specialized in plaiting pandanus sleeping mats for export. As fisherfolk, Aromot, Mandok, and

Malai islanders also produced and exported large fishing nets and trochus-shell armlets used for adornment in dancing feasts. Tuam has no fringing reef but does have the largest landmass of all the small islands. The Tuam therefore were less active fisherfolk and considered themselves more "Siassi gardeners" than "sea people." But they did participate in both local and overseas trade. As they traveled the trade routes the Siassi traders exchanged all sorts of things throughout the region. An example from my own Mandok family's history will demonstrate.

The inhabitants of Tami, an island off the coast of the Huon Peninsula, were wood-carvers. They carved oblong bowls of *kwila* (TP for *Intsia bijuga*, a very valuable hardwood, sometimes called ironwood both because of its hardness and its reddish hue). These bowls were an important item used in bridewealth payments, land purchases, and ritual exchanges throughout the Vitiaz trade system. The Mandok historically traded their canoes at Tami for these carved bowls and for pigs. Just before the turn of the 20th century, a Mandok trader named Sopol adopted a baby girl from his Tami trade partner and named her Aikiba. This consummated the trade relationship, making it a "true" kinship relationship (see Chapter 5).

When Aikiba came to Mandok she brought many things with her, though she was but an infant. Through her Tami father and other relatives on Tami, she had rights to Tami names, carving and house designs, spells, rituals, and trading partnerships. The rights to these resources passed through her to her children (in particular to her firstborn son: my Mandok father, Aibung) and through them to her grandchildren. By the time Aibung was coming of age (in the late 1920s), missionaries were already active in Siassi (see Chapter 7). Tami evangelists on Aromot taught the Aromot, and through them the Mandok, to carve the oblong bowls (Mulderink 1989). Mandok and Tami islanders spoke as if they exchanged crafts, so that the Tami learned how to construct and lash two-masted canoes, and the Mandok gained the rights and knowledge to carve the wooden bowls. Once the Mandok began to carve the Siassi bowls, they traded them throughout the Vitiaz and Dampier straits to western New Britain, thereby establishing their own heritage as fine carvers. Aibung was sent to Tami to learn carving from his mother's brothers. He was thus among the first Mandok men to learn how to carve the oblong bowls so characteristic of the Vitiaz trade network.[9]

Although they chronicle particular episodes of Mandok history, these examples typify the nature of the trade system as a whole. In addition to goods characteristic of the system, rights to designs, skills, and even particular human beings were exchanged through trade relations. These themes will be developed in subsequent chapters. Oral histories and creation legends also traveled the trade routes, providing additional documentation of and justification for these and other aspects of Mandok personal and cultural identity. The next chapter explains how.

CHAPTER TWO

The World That Namor Made: Creation, Cosmos, and Culture

Today we have the explanation of the Bible. Before, our ancestors had these legends of this man who came from the Rai Coast and did these things, just as God did them. It is the same. This is the Bible of our ancestors.

Gabriel Aipake, Mandok Church Deacon, 1980

In this chapter we examine the Legend of Namor. This legend lies at the core of Mandok cosmogony, cosmology, and religion. It therefore lies equally at the heart of Mandok views of personal and cultural identity. Here we use Geertz's definition of religion as a "cultural system." According to Geertz, a religion is:

(1) a system of symbols which acts to (2) establish powerful, pervasive, and long-lasting moods and motivations in men [*sic*] by (3) formulating conceptions of a general order of existence and (4) clothing these conceptions with such an aura of factuality that (5) the moods and motivations seem uniquely realistic. (Geertz 1966:4)

One cannot separate "religion" from "culture" because each implies the other. Just as culture is a complex system of symbols, so too is religion. A "religion" may thus be studied as a symbolic subsystem of a culture of which it forms a part, though it might not be so distinguished by its followers. There is also a normative aspect to religion, for it provides its adherents with both models of, and models for, behavior (Geertz 1966:7). It provides *models of* behavior (both desirable and undesirable) considered "natural" in the world to buttress the received morality conveyed in *models for* behavior as that religion or culture defines ideal human action. In this chapter we will see how the Legend of Namor provided these things for the Mandok.

As the quotation that began this chapter indicates, the Mandok viewed the Legend of Namor as an integral part of their culture. It had "religious" or sacred value, as Aipake explained to me by use of an analogy with the Bible. Like the Bible in the Judeo-Christian world, this story constituted only part of a larger tradition of oral literature found in Mandok "culture."

Mandok oral tradition contained two categories of stories, each re-counted slightly differently. The term *vuvuaŋ*, "story," was used generally for tales in both styles. It could be extended in the verb form *-vuvub*, "to [tell a] story." The root could also be changed to a noun, indicating a body of knowledge transmitted orally. The process of *vuvuaŋ* contained two kinds of tales. *Vuvuaŋ sorok*, "just a story," could be re-counted by anyone; they were told to children and anthropologists, primarily for entertainment. The other kind of tale, called *kamos*—a sacred history or legend—included the allegories that explained impor-tant aspects of community knowledge and heritage held as vital to Man-dok culture. They were recounted for their didactic value. It was in *kamos*, and in their telling, that Mandok notions of ideal culture were preserved, taught, and continued. The story of Namor is classified as *kamos*.

I follow Mandok usage in translating *kamos* as sacred history or "legend" instead of "myth" for two reasons. To many specialists such an epic would be considered a creation myth: It is a sacred story presented as having actually occurred in a previous age, it explains cosmological and supernatural traditions, and its purpose is explanatory. The *Standard Dictionary of Folklore*, however, notes that

> a myth remains properly a myth only as long as the divinity of its actor or actors is recognized; when the trickster becomes human rather than divine, when the hero is a man rather than a god, myth becomes legend, if explanatory or limited to some specific loca-tion. . . . (1972:778)

A legend, in contrast, is

> a narrative supposedly based on fact, with an intermixture of tradi-tional materials, told about a person, place, or incident. . . . The legend is told as true; the myth's veracity is based on the belief of its hearers in the gods who are its characters. (1972:612)

When interpreting oral histories of the sort anthropologists study, often only a fine theoretical line separates history, legend, and mythology. The story of Namor contains elements of myth, legend, and codified history. The Mandok told it as part of their history and considered it true. We will examine their sense of history in some detail at the end of the chapter.

The second reason I prefer "legend" over "myth" is that when non-specialist native English speakers hear the word "myth" applied to non-Western oral traditions, they tend to think of "just-so stories" and falsehoods. The term "legend," on the other hand, implies a germ of truth. In legends, embellishments and codifications of some real events are woven into a mythical fabric of fantastic accomplishments. Such an interpretation is more appropriate to this case.

There was no special category of "storyteller" or one particular "keeper" of *kamos*. The ability to remember and "to know" these stories was, however, attributed to certain *bigmen* (see Chapter 6). Women for the most part did not tell them and considered themselves not "to know" the details. Women could and did tell *vuvuaŋ sorok*, however. Older women were especially likely to tell them while comforting or baby-sitting their grandchildren.

There are many versions of the legend of two brothers recorded all across northeast New Guinea through eastern New Britain (see Figure 1.1, p. 7).[1] Though minor details may vary, the different versions are strikingly consistent. The story has several features that concern us here. First, the text describes Mandok creation history. The Mandok were missionized during the late 1930s, and their own traditions remained prominent in their worldview and philosophy. Second, the legend illustrates how the Mandok synthesized their own cosmogony and cosmology with ideas introduced by European missionaries. The tellers' comments on points of juncture between the knowledge of Siassi forebears and Christian teachings give pertinent clues about how the Mandok understood their world and syncretically embraced those aspects of Christianity that they understood to be "the same." In discussing its philosophy and in trying to place a time frame on the events in the story, the Mandok I spoke with referred to this legend as "Eden"; that is, as Gabriel Aipake explained to me, it occurred during

> the time before the Catholics came and preached the Word of God to us. Before they came, Siassi was like the Garden of Eden, and the Siassi people were like Adam and Eve. They did not know any better. Once the missionaries came, then they taught us, and now we know. This is like "New Testament" Mandok; the time before—the time of Namor—was like the "Old Testament."

The third important feature of the Namor legend is that each episode maps out significant places, peoples, and material goods in the Siassi environment, as well as the culturally sanctioned relationships among them (see Figures 1.3 and 1.4, pp. 14, 15). The odyssey in the legend usually ends in the region in which a particular version is told. For example, the Arop version ends on Arop Island, and the Kilenge version ends in Kilenge, with Namor leaving for Siassi. The Siassi version includes a final episode that explains how the two-masted sailing canoes came to be built on Aromot.

The hero's travels take him from the Rai Coast, through Siassi to Kilenge (western New Britain), and back to Siassi. By noting significant material goods and their indigenous locations, the story outlines the interrelationships among the various Siassi communities. It also maps out schematically overseas and local trade. By recounting the exploits of their culture's hero, the Mandok also conveyed their ideas about relationships between people: male and female, elder and younger, and man to man. These relationships cued the patterns of social life as Siassi Islanders expected to find them in their contemporary world.

A particularly important feature of this legend is its depiction of implicit notions of leadership and success in Siassi culture. The Mandok stressed learning by example, by watching and experiencing their environment. The hero's travels illustrate both several primary personality characteristics of *bigmen* and the culturally acceptable or assumed routes to success. These personality characteristics provided the behavioral and psychological prototype for the renowned Siassi traders. It is in the world of Namor that these themes are most vividly portrayed.

Finally, the Legend of Namor encapsulates Mandok views of history and change, discussed at the end of the chapter.

The legend actually has several protagonists, depending on the geographic location of the episode. The Mandok referred to the entire epic as "The Legend of Namor," taking the hero's name from the Kilenge part of the story (see Episode V). In the Madang area and on the Rai Coast, it is known as the story of Manup and Kilibob (spellings vary). The Mandok version presented here includes the several name and character changes as part of the narrative. To alleviate confusion, such changes are apparent in episode titles; Mandok names are used for the characters.

The epic narrative falls naturally into five episodes. Each episode charts fairly discrete geographic areas (see Figure 2.1). Items of special importance will be discussed after the text of each episode. Significant departures from details recounted to me will be noted in footnotes only insofar as they shed additional light on each episode or offer contrasting information. In the course of condensing lengthy transcripts I have taken a certain editor's license; for the sake of brevity I have condensed Siassi rhetorical and recounting style into an "anglicized" form.

EPISODE I: KILIBOB LEAVES MADANG

▼ Once upon a time . . . there were three brothers living in Madang. One day the oldest, Mandip, went fishing with his younger *runai* [patrilineal group] brothers and left the youngest, Kilibob, at home. Kilibob went bird hunting with his bow and arrow. He shot an arrow high into the sky. It missed its target and fell into the center of the village. Mandip's wife, who had been sweeping the area around her house, saw the arrow fall and retrieved it. She recognized the beautiful design carved into the arrow's shaft and she hid it.

In his search for the lost arrow Kilibob came upon his sister-in-law. When he asked her about it she admitted hiding the arrow, but rather than give it to him she seduced him into tattooing the arrow's

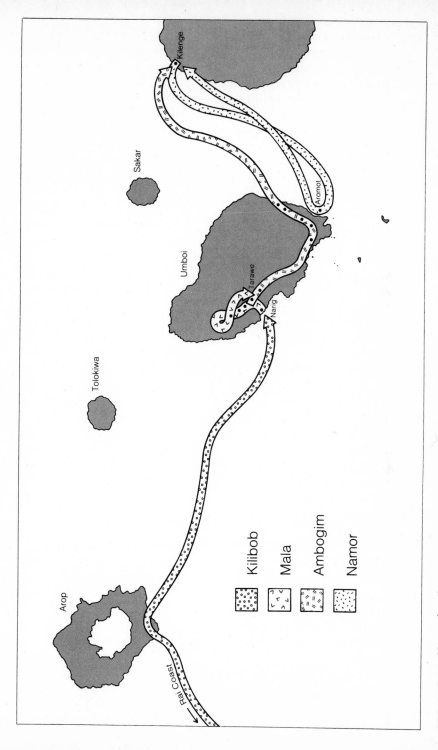

FIGURE 2.1 *Namor's odyssey.*

▼ design on her groin.[2] He agreed, and the two sat down together [i.e., they committed adultery]. Afterward, he tattooed her groin with the arrow's design, just as she asked. When he finished, he took a *benben* leaf and wiped away the blood. After he applied soot to the wound, he threw the leaves into the river.

The leaves were swept out to sea, and soon many birds came and circled over them. Mandip saw the circling birds and thought they might be over a great school of fish. He ordered his brothers to paddle toward them. When they reached the spot, he saw the bloody leaves and sensed instantly that something was amiss. So as not to arouse suspicion, he feigned illness so that the expedition would return to the village.

The tide was high, so they floated the canoe offshore a bit and called out to those standing on the shore to help beach it. Mandip's wife, assigned to the outrigger, was in waist-deep water. She protested that the waves were cresting too high, but her husband scolded her, so she waded to the outrigger. As she did so, a wave came and pulled away her grass skirt, revealing the tattoo. Mandip saw this and thought, "Aha! Now I've got her number!"[3]

After the canoe was ashore and the women collected their respective shares of the day's catch, he confronted his wife about the new tattoo. She tried to deny it, but he had already seen it. She let him look, fearing that if she disobeyed him, he might beat her. He examined it and instantly recognized his own family's design. With this, he got very angry and started fighting with Kilibob. They fought viciously for days. Finally, Kilibob suggested to his mother that they leave.

The next day they gathered their belongings and loaded the canoe with some sand, some dark soil, some wood from the beach, many indigenous plants, and other supplies. They launched at nightfall, paddling toward New Britain. Now, New Britain is a long way off. When they reached Arop, Kilibob estimated that they were about halfway there, so he decided to stop. He anchored the canoe offshore and began his work.

He dropped some stones and beach sand. The beach started extending out to sea until it met the canoe. Then he took more stones, sand, and cane and constructed a hearth. Next, he spread the dark soil and planted the many plants and trees he had brought. The two of them settled there; they worked hard creating many things.

One day he told his mother he was lonely. With this, he got an idea. He started carving a chunk of wood into a drum. As he carved, his mother asked him why he was doing all of this work, since they were alone on the island. He just shrugged and kept on carving. Next, he constructed a headdress for the feast dance called *Sia*. He made several. His mother kept asking him why he was making all of these things for nothing, since there were only the two of them. But he

▼ answered confidently that he wanted to get everything ready. Each time his mother questioned him he shrugged her off and kept carving.

When all of the dancing accoutrements were completed to his satisfaction, he started shaping the sand into paired figures: one male, one female; a male, a female; and so on, until there were many couples. He created these things just as today we understand God's work. As soon as he finished molding the sand, he took some lime, just like the lime we use for chewing betel nut [areca palm nut],[4] and blew it into the sand models' noses. They started to breathe, and finally they came to life, just as God blew his own breath into humans. Our story says it a bit differently: He blew lime into their noses, and they came to life. Soon they were all alive. He returned to his mother and instructed her to make a stone oven for the taro, sweet potato, and manioc, declaring that the next day there would be a great feast. His mother protested that there was no one besides themselves to eat all the food. He shrugged her off again and told her that people were coming from a nearby village. So they prepared for the feast.

When the food was ready he went into his men's house [*rumai*] and started beating the drum. Instantly a man and a woman appeared. He kept on beating it. More and more people came until the place was crowded. He instructed his mother to take them to their houses. As people arrived from different directions, he allocated to them houses in the direction from which they came. If they came from the west, for example, their house lay to the west of the village, and so on. He had already made many things in anticipation of their arrival. He built them houses and created the dancing feast called *Sia*. [The dance called *Sia* is famous throughout PNG as a characteristically Siassi dance. It was originally imported from Arop.] He created the headdresses, the drums, grass skirts for clothing, and so on. After they danced the complete Sia and ate all the food, the visitors settled there. Eventually he married one of the women.

Now, women are like this: They are always angry and jealous. So of course one day Kilibob's wife got angry with him. He decided that he would leave and find another home. This was his personality. He saw Umboi Island and decided to go there. As he was leaving Arop, he noticed a group of women who were bathing near the trunk of a fallen tree. The tree's trunk lay on the beach, and the top lay out to sea. The women had spread their grass skirts on the log to dry. One woman in particular caught his fancy. He took her grass skirt and hung it on one of the outer branches. When the women finished bathing, each put on her grass skirt for the return to the village. But Gainor could not find her skirt. Finally she spotted it hanging on the outer branch. She waded out into the deep water and climbed up onto the trunk to retrieve it. As she climbed up, Kilibob hopped

▼ onto it, and the log shot out into the sea, heading for Umboi Island and Siassi.

Episode I: Comments

Readers will notice that this legend does not describe the creation of the universe; the universe was a given in Siassi cosmology. Mandok informants said that the old men believed "the world just came up by itself." Once there, however, humans developed culture. Kilibob did not create humans as a species; on the Rai Coast were humans who lived in a village, sailed canoes, and so on. What he did was populate Arop Island and develop a distinctive culture associated with that particular place. These threads run through the entire epic. The premise that Kilibob did not create the human race may also indicate the relative recency of Austronesian settlement in the Vitiaz and Dampier straits. What requires explanation is not "how humans got created," but "how they got *here*."[5]

The original impetus for Kilibob's travels was sparked by an argument between two brothers over a woman. Brothers were supposed to be allies and help each other; they should not fight. However, ownership rights to trees, land, wealth, and other resources sometimes caused competition between supposed allies. According to Siassi mores and notions of male-female relations, women were often the cause of trouble; adultery was a sure way to break up a family. The protagonist "proves" this repeatedly at each new place he visits as the episodes unfold. But "woman trouble" could also be used as a convenient excuse to save face in the midst of other conflicts.[6] To solve the problem, one competitor left. Because Kilibob was the younger brother and the cause of the trouble, it was he who had to leave (see Chapter 4 for an expanded discussion of elder/younger sibling relationships).

Kilibob's betrayal of his brother was signaled by the bloody leaves. Circling birds usually indicate the position of a school of fish. Instead, when the older brother arrives at the spot and sees the bloody leaves, he interprets them as a bad omen. When he discovers his wife's tattoo, he knows the whole story. Carving and tattoo designs were often unique to and controlled by particular family lines and/or *runai*. Siassi people kept track of each other's movements by recognizing these designs on any item: a moored canoe, a stray arrow's shaft, a drum, a canoe paddle, and so on (see also Mulderink 1980). When Mandip saw his family's design tattooed on his wife's groin, he knew it had to be Kilibob who made it because Kilibob was the only one in the village at the time who had the right to use that motif.

Once he lands on Arop we begin to see the more creative aspects of Kilibob's personality. He is a creative man of knowledge—an artisan. Using his magical powers he created the Siassi environment and named different species of dance, flora, and fauna. (By using these specific names, the teller asserted his rights of usage/ownership to the episode, as well as to the species, objects, and events listed in it.) Just by observing Kilibob's interactions with his mother and his creations of people, places, and things we learn that *bigmen* are creative, knowledgeable, convincing, and manipulative. These are common personality traits of *bigmen* in other parts of Melanesia, and they have a very important function: They attract people to the *bigman* (cf. Watson 1970). Kilibob enticed people to stay with him and build a village by hosting a lavish feast. He built a village by supplying plenty of food, decorations, and housing for his guests. His actions established a social network of visiting, sharing, exchange, mutual familiarity, and knowledge of geography necessary for safe travel. He even got himself a wife, establishing local customs of intermarriage in the process.

We also learn, too, that *bigmen* can be moody and fickle. With a vague announcement about "typical" female behavior (as expected in Siassi), Kilibob decides to leave. He embarks on a new venture, but not alone: he takes Gainor with him. She becomes his new wife, and the wife of Mala, in the next episode.[7]

EPISODE II: MALA'S TRAVELS ON UMBOI

▼ Kilibob and Gainor settled at Narig, on the creek with the same name. [Narig is an uncharted spot between Barim and Tarawe, west Umboi; refer to Figures 1.4 (p. 15) and 2.1 for village names and odyssey paths, respectively.] At this point Kilibob's name changes to Mala [Malo in the Aupwel version]. They lived at Narig for a long time. Mala went net fishing or spearfishing and brought his catch home to Gainor. She traded his fish for vegetables with the Umboi Islanders. The couple also made a small garden and planted taro.

One day, as usual, Mala went to cast his fishnet, and his wife went to the garden. She brought his food back and boiled it. Absent-mindedly she put Mala's food into the pig's food basket and vice versa. When she hung up the food, she hung Mala's food in the pig's place and the pig's food in Mala's place. Gainor was outside sweeping the area around their house when Mala came home, so she just told him to go and eat. He went into the house and began eating the pig's food, thinking it was his. When Gainor entered the house she shrieked that he had the wrong food and explained her absentminded mistake. He tried to make light of it but was obviously upset about it. He changed the subject by showing her taro corms he had just brought home. He suggested that she go to the garden and plant them.

The next morning, after she left for the garden, he packed his belongings, shaved, painted himself, put on the beads that she had made for him, and started walking to Tarawe. When he arrived in Tarawe people he met asked him where he was going. He answered that he was going to Ovongai.

▼ As he approached Ovongai, he looked over and noticed the elders sitting in the men's house. They were all old and gray. He slipped behind a house to disguise himself. He took *reg,* the white flower from the tall grass, and dusted its powder into his hair. Then he took cordylline sap and smeared it on his forehead. He bunched some leaves up and tied them around his ankles. His disguise complete, he cut a leaf and started shooing away flies and mosquitoes with it. Grabbing a stick, he hobbled toward the village like an old man.

When the elders saw this decrepit stranger hobbling feebly toward them, they beckoned for him to come and join them in their meal. One of them asked his destination. In a quavering voice, he responded that he wanted to go to Barang. After he ate their food and chewed betel nut with them, he continued on his way until he reached Barang. He entered Barang in the same disguise he used at Ovongai. He felt that the village elders, who might fear an approaching stranger and kill him, would not fear an old man. Instead they would take pity on him and invite him to the men's house and offer him food and shelter, which they did. Again he set out. Near the end of the road to Gom, he sat down to rest. He chewed a betel nut and wove himself some black vine armlets called *ngas.* Continuing, he finally arrived at Gom.

At each village he usually came upon the women first, since women's chores usually led them to the outskirts. As he entered the village he proceeded to the men's house, where he sat and ate with the village elders. At each place they asked him to stay on. But each time he declined, choosing instead to keep going.

On and on he walked, until he arrived at Gasam. There he saw two beautiful women filling their gourds with water. They were so beautiful that he decided he wanted to marry them. He climbed a nearby tree and started chewing betel nut. When his wad was good and red, he spit it down between them. They looked around, and finally one of them spied him up in the tree. These two women were sisters. They both wanted this man. He climbed down from the tree and announced to them that he wanted to settle down there. The two sisters returned to the village and told all their friends about him. The next day all the women went back to get water. They stayed to talk with this handsome man, to make love with him, and generally to have fun. This went on for days, until the men of the village started wondering why their wives went every day to fetch water and never got any work done. Finally one man hatched a plan. He told his young son to throw a tantrum the next time his mother went to draw water, and to keep it up until she took him along.

The little boy obeyed his father and really created a scene. The other women reassured the irritated mother by pointing out that he was only a child: "What does he know?" They also argued that he was old enough to walk by himself. So they all went.

▼   The women carried on with this man at the riverbank all day. The little boy watched. At sunset they returned to the village. As soon as they reached home, the little boy ran straight to his father and described what he had seen. The father reported what was going on to the other men in the men's house. They were all outraged and wanted to kill the intruder. The father suggested that all the men take their weapons, their pig nets and wallaby nets, to catch him.

During the night, while the women slept, the men went out and surrounded the whole riverbank area. Their nets were set, and all of their weapons were ready. They hid and waited. At dawn the women came down from their houses. When they arrived at the riverbank, the man emerged.

But when they saw him the men hesitated. Should they catch him or kill him? The little boy was right: He really was a handsome man who could "steal your heart" (*isad atem*). The older men wanted to invite him into the village; the younger men wanted to kill him because he had violated their wives.

They started shouting and chasing the intruder toward the nets. He turned and ran. He jumped into the water, and, changing himself into an eel, dived under the mud. The men scrambled about, groping for him with their hands and feet under the murky water. In the confusion, the man who had sent his son out to spy on the women found and caught the eel (Mala), who was slithering away. The man grabbed Mala and slipped him into his pandanus mat. Then he cried out in feigned agony, pretending to have a cramp in his groin. He excused himself and returned to the village. Once safely inside the men's house, he opened the mat, let Mala out, and laid him down. Later, when the others returned, the man confessed his deception. He suggested that, rather than kill Mala, they should accept him into the village as an elder. They gave Mala food, and they all lived together. Since the first two women who flirted with him were unmarried, he married them both, and they all lived in Gasam.

Episode II: Comments

This episode reveals more about the personality and cunning of Siassi *bigmen* and provides models *of* expected behavior. Mala is a trickster, a womanizer, and a vagabond. His physical beauty is complemented by a social and political shrewdness that attracts both women and men to him. (Siassi charm and sexual prowess were legendary in surrounding areas.) He is a charismatic maverick. These themes, among others, appear again and again in the legend. It is important to note how the hero first *creates* the trouble, usually by adultery, and then transforms an adverse situation into a winning one by using his wits and magic. That conflicts arise was an assumption of everyday life on Mandok. Mala's instigation of his own problems was thus interpreted by the Mandok as a sign of his humanness. His clever manipulations and escapes, however, coupled with his physical beauty and metamorphic abilities, made him "superhuman" and separate.

Ultimately, Mala is *admired* for his cunning and invited to stay on as an elder of the village. Thus, although much of his behavior would not normally be condoned, the fact that he gets away with his antics is considered admirable and is yet another demonstration of his personal power. He is renowned and successful because he is clever. Instead of asserting his manhood through acts of physical prowess, Mala is a talented artisan who creates the many wealth objects, dance forms, fish, and even human populations found in Siassi. He is a man of knowledge, a man of controlled action, and a very wily opponent. Instead of openly confronting his opponents (real or potential), he outsmarts them and essentially swindles them out of the objects of his desire. He achieves his goals by manipulating the social or physical environment through disguise, magic, or by changing his physical form.

These legendary events mirror episodes in Siassi genealogical and migration histories. The Siassi Islanders were, after all, pragmatists: Why kill such a powerful person if they could get him to work for them?

EPISODE III: AMBOGIM

▼ Meanwhile, Gainor was searching for Mala. She was pregnant, and her delivery time was near. Each time she arrived at a village its inhabitants told her that she had just missed him. Still searching, she wound up in Tarawe.

One day she had a yen for some fish. She talked some other women into going with her. Now if they were island women, they would have said, "Let's go diving for sea clams." But these were bush people, so the Umboi women decided to follow the riverbank and find themselves some shrimp. They prepared their shrimp nets and left for the river.

Along the way, Gainor went into labor. She walked off into the bush and gave birth to a boy. She left the baby at the base of a ficus tree.[8] A snake, Ambogim, who lived in this tree, took the baby to raise as his own. When Gainor returned to the other women, they asked her where her baby was. She just shrugged and told them she threw it away. "It's not as if he had a father—his father took off a long time ago." They returned to the village.

A long time passed, and while Gainor remained in Tarawe, the child Ambogim grew up in the bush. You see, the snake gave the child his own name. One day, some of the women returned to the very same place, again looking for shrimp. They came upon a huge branch of a ficus tree from which some vines were hanging. As the wind blew, the leaves rustled against the vines, and the women thought it was

▼ about to rain. But when they looked up, they saw that it was just the leaves, so they kept shrimping along the riverbank. Suddenly one of them cried that she saw a handsome man up in the tree. The women started chattering hopefully about enticing this man to go with them.

The snake Ambogim heard them. He came out and announced that this was the baby they had discarded. He explained how he took the child in and gave him his own name, Ambogim. He refused to let the child go without compensation of one *ti* basket [a large, tightly woven round basket with sloping sides] and some money shells. The snake wanted to decorate his forehead with the money shells and then curl up to sleep inside the basket. The women gave him these things and took the young man back to Tarawe. There Ambogim settled down and married two women.

One day a message came that there was to be a great feast at Opai and that Ambogim was among those who would receive a pig. Several other Tarawe men were also receiving pigs. They invited Ambogim to accompany them to Gom to trade for some vine armlets.[9] The entire village gathered their wealth objects together—betel nut, tobacco, and other exchange objects—and walked to Gom.

Ambogim did not know that Mala, the father he had never seen, lived in Gom. By this time Mala was an old man. He had left Gasam and now lived in his men's house (*rumai*) in Gom. From there he could see that one by one all of the different people were met by their trade partners—all, that is, except for Ambogim, who did not have a trade partner in Gom. Neither man recognized the other. The old man just saw a young loner and asked him for some betel nut and betel pepper. Ambogim gave him these things. At once Mala recognized this betel nut and pepper because they were very special. He himself had planted them many years ago. [These two species grow wild near Barim.] They are both red. The betel nut is called "Mala's sweat" [also called "Mala's wad"] and the pepper, named after his wife, is called "Gainor's blood." This recognition told Mala that this loner was his son. He chewed. As he chewed he began to sweat. It was a sultry day, and "the betel nut speared him" [*bolai ingali,* e.g., intoxicated him]. Mala wiped the sweat off his brow and flicked it onto Ambogim. As they chatted, he kept wiping his brow and flicking the sweat onto his son. To size him up, Mala kept Ambogim talking. He asked Ambogim why he had come. Ambogim told him of the upcoming feast and explained his need for vine armlets. He took out the wealth object he had brought to trade and showed it to his father.

The Tarawe expedition was gathering in the plaza; it was time to go. As Ambogim rose to leave, the old man took out a tiny parcel and handed it to him. Ambogim slipped the parcel into his pandanus pouch. But when he tried to give the old man his wealth object in return, the old man refused. Instead he predicted, "One day you will

▼ see a breadfruit leaf spiral in the air and glide to the ground. This will be my sign to you that I am dying, and you must come."

With this farewell, Ambogim started walking home with his friends. When they reached the riverbank closest to the village, they stopped to rest. They started comparing and admiring each other's purchases. When it was Ambogim's turn, however, he was reticent because his package was so small. They pressed him to open it anyway. When he started unwrapping it, he realized that this was a really long and exquisite set of vines. The onlookers marveled at their beauty. They had all been fooled by the tiny package, for inside it lay beautiful, long vines. Once they returned to the village, Ambogim realized that they were long enough for three sets of four each: a set for each of his two wives and a special set for himself. Not only did they have armlets; they each had a special set of leglets, too.

At last the appointed day arrived. All the Tarawe participants prepared their dancing paraphernalia for the feast. Early that morning Ambogim sent his wives out to collect some of his special betel nut and pepper to take along. As they set out, however, a breadfruit leaf spiraled above their heads, sailed down, and stuck in the ground at their feet. Recognizing the sign, he instructed his wives to put away their feasting regalia and prepare to leave for the funeral.

When they arrived at Gom, the old man had already been placed inside the grave. All were awaiting Ambogim's arrival. When the three appeared, Ambogim was invited to pay his last respects. Clutching his pandanus mat, he removed his cassowary-bone knife and jumped down into the grave. He cut his father's skin at the forehead, then zipped off the skin and folded it up into his pandanus mat. He gave the order to bury his father as he climbed out of the grave. They left for home right after the burial.

Along the path he sent one wife off to find him a coconut to drink. When she returned he drank the whole thing and ate all the meat by himself. When they reached the crossroads, he excused himself to go into the bush to urinate, blaming his need on the coconut. But instead, he ran into the bush and took out his father's skin. He fitted it over his own skin and ran ahead of his wives. He came out of the bush and sauntered toward them.

His wives started screaming. They thought his father's ghost had come to kill them.

Ambogim ran back into the bush, removed the skin, and doubled back to come out from behind them. Feigning real concern, he asked why they were screeching like colic babies. When they told him what had happened, he scolded them and accused them of lying.

They argued about it as they walked. The women had barely calmed down when he complained of stomach cramps and ran back into the bush. He donned his father's skin and again scared his wives. Once again he doubled back and pretended innocence and skepticism

▼ of their hysterical tale. He repeated this over and over until they reached the village.

Most people had already left for the feast by the time they arrived in Tarawe. A few who were waiting for Ambogim and his wives remained. The two wives collected their betel nut in different baskets and started packing their things. As they packed, Ambogim donned his father's skin again, lay down, and curled up around the fire like an old man.

When his wives came into the house and saw him, they wailed in frustration, for after all they had been through on the path, now Ambogim was sick. They were supposed to receive a pig at this feast; who was going to accept it now? He told them to go with their brothers and have them accept the pig on his behalf. After bickering about it (for they were really fed up with him), they stoked his fire and left.

Ambogim went out onto the veranda and started chewing betel nut. Next door was a woman who had recently given birth and so was still confined to her house. Since the rest of the village had gone to the feast, the two were alone. They chatted awhile. Eventually the woman failed to answer Ambogim's idle chatter; she had fallen asleep. He jumped up and grabbed his huge betel-nut basket. He donned his headdress, painted his eyes with red ochre, and took his shrubs, armlets, and grass skirt worn for the *Bukumu* feast. His costume complete, he took off for Opai. By the time he arrived the dancing was in full swing. He hid behind a house and sent a small boy to get the main dancer to surrender the dancing frame to him so he could dance [see Figure 2.2].

As Ambogim adjusted the frame, he sent the boy to tell the elders which song set to sing. As they started singing, he stumbled out into the center of the dancing, lurching and staggering clumsily as if he couldn't dance. Some of the men protested and tried to get Ambogim removed. An old man stopped them with the admonishment that everyone came to dance, good or bad, and everyone had the right to try. He speculated that the clumsy dancer was from a distant village.

The old man finished the set and then began a set of the main songs. As these commenced, Ambogim stopped faking and started dancing seriously. Once he started dancing well, everyone cheered in unison. He really "beat his dancing to death." He was so good that all the women danced closer and closer to him, and one by one, they slipped betel nut into his basket [a sign of flirtation and an invitation for a tryst].

He kept dancing, waiting for his own wives to slip him some betel nut. Finally, just as "the face of the place came" [i.e., dawn broke] and the birds began to chirp, his two wives slunk up to him and slipped betel nut into his basket. All night they had danced behind the handsome dancer, singing as they danced. "That's it," he thought to himself, "it's all over now."

FIGURE 2.2 Bukumu *dancer with frame, Kilenge.*

▼ Ambogim stopped dancing, replaced the frame, and took off because it was already getting light enough to see clearly. As he turned to run off, the women all protested. He escaped quickly so as not to be recognized. The elders sent some boys after him to find out who he was, but he had run too swiftly. This confirmed the elders' theory that he was from a distant village and had decided to get an early start on the path.

Back at the house, Ambogim put all his things away, hung up his full basket, and hurriedly wiped off his face paint. His father's skin donned once more, he curled himself around the fire and went to sleep. While it was still early morning the others returned, congregating in front of his house to discuss the night's events. The two wives unpacked their food gifts, and their brothers tied Ambogim's pig under his house. The women put down their baskets and went up into the house, calling Ambogim to wake up. He moaned that he was cold and that his fire had died. He kept moaning pathetically,

▼ pretending to be deathly ill. His wives spoke wistfully about the feast and about this handsome stranger who had stolen all the women's hearts. Ambogim feigned ignorance as his wives sang this mysterious dancer's praises to him. They described his seductive charm on all the women in lurid detail. Ambogim let his wives babble on, until he injected slyly, "I bet you two flirted with him, too."

They denied it, giggling. Then he mentioned casually that this stranger awakened him during the night and, complaining of a long journey ahead, had given Ambogim some of his betel nut. He pointed to his bulging basket that hung from a rafter. With this his wives got suspicious and accused him of lying. He insisted that they take down his basket and look. He made them take out each betel nut, one by one, until their own red betel nut dropped out. They dropped the basket, giggling. Ambogim scolded them with, "See? What did I tell you? I knew you two would slip him betel nut, and there's the evidence."

The two women glanced at each other, embarrassed, and tittered nervously. Then one of them spotted a tiny speck of red in the corner of Ambogim's eye. You see, when he cleaned his face he missed a spot, right in the inside corner of his eye. They both pounced on him, smacking and punching him playfully. It was his turn to be ashamed, because they had caught him in his own deception, and what he had done was shabby.

He confessed and told them he was testing their faithfulness. They had failed the test, so he got up and left.

Episode III: Comments

Ambogim (Namor from Kilenge) is really the central character of this epic. He starts life as a discarded waif, yet he emerges as the hero of the legend. Two clues suggest that he has already gained some renown and is an up-and-coming *bigman*. The first is that he has two wives. Before European contact, the Mandok practiced polygyny, though it was predominently the prerogative of *bigmen*. The second clue is that he is receiving a pig in a formal exchange in a village other than his own. Competitive feasting was a vital part of Siassi social, political, and economic life before missionization. Men displayed their strength through these feasting competitions, and they also resolved arguments and rivalries without violence (see Chapter 6).

Mala, Ambogim's biological father, recognizes his son by his possession of Mala's own special hybrid betel nut and pepper. Though initially Ambogim has no trade partner in Gom, he soon gains one in the old man. By having Mala's sweat flicked onto his skin, Ambogim also receives some of his father's "substance" (discussed in Chapter 4). Perhaps this is a clue to his subsequent behavior. He becomes "just like his father"—a rogue, a wanderer, and a creator of wealth, custom, and (as we see in the next episode) material culture. Mandok notions about heritable personality traits are further dramatized by Ambogim's taking of his father's skin (more substance) and donning it in disguise to deceive his wives and test their fidelity. The ability to change skin at will is a mark of his immortality (Mulderink 1989; see also Chapter 3). The disguise is also effective against real or potential adversaries.

Why Ambogim terrorizes his wives on the trail and later deceives them into adulterous behavior is unclear, except insofar as it is consistent with his roguish image throughout the narrative. This aspect of the legend may be a Siassi view of males and of male-female relations. We surmise from his behavior that he is a trickster who, one way or another, always succeeds in getting what he wants. Even when discovered (as, in this episode, by a telltale speck of ochre), his objectives are achieved and he moves on.

EPISODE IV: THE TREE OF WEALTH AND PLENTY

▼ Ambogim left Tarawe and headed for Gauru, on the Simban River. Along the way he noticed at Sampenan that on their way to market, the Mandok kept stepping on stonefish and squashing them. He fashioned poisoned spines for the stonefishes' backs so they wouldn't be squashed in the future. When he came upon the Izon River, the Gauru shared their breadfruit with him. Finally he arrived at Gauru village. He went straight to the men's house, where the elders were pounding taro pudding. As they distributed the food as payment to the workers, Ambogim called for some leaves and showed the Gauru people a special way to wrap this pudding. He lived with them for awhile, and then he moved on.

Just at the head of the path he met an attractive woman. This woman was menstruating, but this did not bother Ambogim. He made love to her and then took some *bou* leaves and wiped her vagina clean. Today this leaf is red, signifying this woman's menstrual blood.

Ambogim left her and walked on to Birik. When he arrived at the village plaza, he noticed that there were no men around. He saw the woman Atambalau [Atakabala in Allace (1976:11)], who was in post-partum seclusion in a nearby house. Approaching the house he asked her where all the men were. She told him that they had all left to chop down a *malaz* tree.

As Ambogim turned to leave, she suggested he sit down and catch his breath first. He climbed up and sat on the edge of her veranda. She offered him some betel nut, and he began to chew. As he chewed, he whispered a spell for rain. It began to drizzle. The rain fell harder, but he just kept on chewing his betel nut. He pulled out his lime stick to add lime to his wad, and the lime stick grew longer until it poked

▼ a hole in the roof. Atambalau noticed that the roof was leaking right over him, so she bid him come inside.

Once inside, he pulled out another betel nut and began to chew some more. Once again, as he pulled out his lime stick it poked a hole in the roof, and the roof leaked. Once more she invited him to move inside to avoid getting wet. He kept on doing this until they were inside her house and sitting on her bed. He seduced her. When they finished, he told her to take his semen and baptize her baby with it.

She did this, and the child grew up instantly and called Ambogim "Daddy." Ambogim spat [at the] rain [i.e., performed a spell for rain] so that it would stop, and he announced that he was leaving. But when he jumped down from the house, the woman packed her things and followed him. The child tagged along behind her.

As Ambogim neared the site where the elders were chopping down the *malaz* tree, he noticed that a big crowd had gathered, so he donned his father's skin and resumed his disguise as a decrepit old man. Next, he dusted his hair with the white flower powder. He grabbed a stick and hobbled up to the younger men who were chopping at the base of the tree. He offered to take a turn, but, seeing his old, hunched figure, they refused. He insisted, and he added the disclaimer that he did not want to eat their food [their payment to the workers] without working for it.

You see, this was no ordinary *malaz* tree. There was all sorts of wealth in its branches at the top: cockatoo, cassowary, bird of paradise, black ochre, clay pots, pigs, dogs, wooden bowls, black beads, and— oh, boy!—everything you could possibly imagine of any worth. They were chopping down this tree for these valuables.

The young men escorted Ambogim to the old men and resumed their work. Ambogim then "spit [at the] rain," and it began to pour. All of the men ran to a nearby lean-to to escape the downpour. Once they were gone from the site he spit again, and the rain stopped. As the men came out of the hut to resume their chopping, Atambalau and her son arrived on the scene, asking for her husband. But when the men pointed to where her [actual] husband stood, she protested that he was not the father of her baby and that she was looking for someone else who had come this way before them.

They reasoned that the only man to come this way was the old man by the base of the tree over there . . . Hey!—where did he go? The old man had disappeared. They all looked around, but it was Atambalau who spotted him up high in the tree. She hollered as she looked up, and all eyes followed hers.

The men looked up into the treetop, and there was Ambogim. He had shed his disguise and was all dressed up in his feasting finery. He was a spectacularly handsome man. Realizing that they had been fooled, the village men were very angry. They started hacking away at

▼ the tree trunk in an effort to fell it and kill him. They chopped and chopped. Finally the tree started swaying. Ambogim rocked it even more, and it really bowed. It swayed toward Tami Island and the Huon Peninsula. The open clay pot, cockatoo, and wooden bowls fell out. The tree swayed back and over toward the Rai Coast. Bows and arrows, black clay pots, wide-mouthed pots, cockatoo, cassowary, bird of paradise, and black ochre fell out. Then it swayed toward New Britain; short-tailed pigs, hairless pigs, spears, tapa cloth, and boar's tusks dropped, and obsidian fell into Garua [near Talasea]. It arced once more toward Kilenge, and then it snapped. It rained more cockatoo, cassowary, and black beads. This time, Ambogim fell too.

The tree snapped so that the trunk remained at Wanduad Point [near present-day Marle], and the top reached over to Kilenge. This trunk provided a bridge between Umboi and New Britain [over the Dampier Strait]. One species of cockatoo tried to fly back to Umboi, but its wings were not very strong, so it fell into the sea and perished. The species that went to the New Guinea coast has strong wings and can fly well, but it was too far from Siassi, so it stayed on the mainland.

When this wondrous tree fell, it dispersed all of the most valued goods. The Umboi mountain was left barren. You see, today in Siassi, we have no cockatoo, no cassowary, no bird of paradise. . . . Siassi doesn't have anything—it is empty.

Before, even the wooden bowls were carved only on Tami. But because of the two-masted canoe, the bowls eventually came to Siassi. And that is the next part of the story. . . .

Episode IV: Comments

In Episode IV we see a bit more about male-female relations. Ambogim confirms his roguish reputation by having sexual intercourse with a parturient woman—behavior that is normally forbidden. More important, we learn why the Siassi environment is "empty."

Some speculative informants drew an analogy between Ambogim's adulterous affair with Atambalau and Eve giving the apple to Adam in the Garden of Eden. This "original sin" caused the barrenness of wildlife and wealth objects in Siassi. Instead of a "Tree of Knowledge," in Siassi it is a "Tree of Wealth and Plenty." All of the wealth objects that the Siassi acquired on their trading voyages thus had their mythical origins in this tree. In anticipation of Episode V, the arcs of the swaying tree describe the trading points and the objects sought in each place. They might also describe migration waves of various Siassi forebears. This part of the story shows a close resemblance to the migration and genealogical histories of Aromot, Tuam, and Malai islands. We cannot prove this, but the speculation is given some credence by the linguistic similarities between Siassi languages and those in western New Britain (Ross 1986).

But the image of a tree in Melanesian cosmology implies more than a distribution of wealth or the codification of migration legends. The symbolism of trees often plays a role in religious attempts to reach for the supernatural or spiritual realms.[10] In the men's area of Mandok there was an old rain tree that was treated with reverence (see also Chapter 3). When Ambogim climbed the *malaz* tree he took possession of it. In so doing he claimed a certain authority over the realm of the spiritual, and he demonstrated this authority by shaking the tree and consequently distributing precious goods.

The teller of the legend, in this case a Mandok man, identified himself with Ambogim. He, like Ambogim, claimed a certain authority in the realm of the spiritual. He too received this authority through ancestral channels, analogous to the way Ambogim received the wisdom of Mala and Kilibob (i.e., models *for* behavior). The teller demonstrated his authority by recounting the tale. The Mandok said that "a 'man of knowledge' [see Chapter 6] knew the old sacred histories." By knowing the "word" he had spiritual contact with and access to its power. Telling the story correctly demonstrated his own internal knowledge and capacity for spirituality. Knowing *kamos* was part and parcel of a *bigman*'s personal power and a spiritual asset to the whole community.

EPISODE V: NAMOR'S ARK

▼ Once in Kilenge, Ambogim's name changed to Namor. Since this part of the story comes from there, we too call him Namor.

We do not know what Namor did in Kilenge.[11] He was "sorry" because all of the wealth objects were gone from Siassi. He lived up on Mount Naventame, between Tangis and Talabei mountains. He built a canoe named *Erevel Time* and brought it to Siassi so that the Siassi peoples could sail to various places and retrieve some of their lost wealth. He whispered a spell on a pig-bone knife, stabbed it into the ground, and cut a long groove to the sea. This became a river, and it washed *Erevel Time* down to the sea. Just as Noah's ark landed on Mount Ararat, Namor built his two-masted trading canoe on Mount Naventame. This was Namor's Ark.

He was angry with the Kilenge, so he took the canoe away from them.[12] He sailed it out to Aromot and sold it for two pigs, Ankionk and Savaŋai. He taught the Aromot how to sail to various points to recover some of their lost wealth. You see, we are really one village. We Mandok have our roots on Aromot, so this is why we Mandok also make canoes. Later, the Tami Islanders came to Aromot/Mandok and learned how to make canoes (see Figure 2.3). Likewise the Mandok went to Tami, sailing in their two-masted canoes, and learned to carve the wooden bowls that we use in brideprice and other important purchases. The two islands exchanged these two carving traditions.

FIGURE 2.3 *Two-masted sailing canoe, 1964.*

(Photo courtesy of Thomas Harding.)

▼   Namor's crew for the Siassi trip were from Kilenge. They became
angry with him for selling the canoe [i.e., the knowledge and rights
to production]. Plotting to kill him, they sent him down into the hull
of the great vessel to help guide the masts into their supporting
sockets. They wanted to replace the mast and return home to Kilenge.
But Namor anticipated their trickery. He took some red sap from the
isis tree to look like blood and some white sap from the *simbam*
tree, to look like smashed brains, and poured them both into a
cylinder of bamboo. When the mast came hurtling down, aimed to
crush his head and kill him, he slipped the bamboo container under
it at the last moment. The mast shattered the bamboo and splattered
the red and white saps all over the hull of the canoe. Convinced he
was killed, the Kilenge cheered triumphantly. They retrieved the pigs
and the canoe and sailed back to Kilenge.

▼   Of course Namor was not dead. He had cleverly faked his death. Turning himself into a mouse, he scurried the length of the canoe inside the hull. Then he dived off the stern into the sea and swam to Kilenge. [There was a square hole in the washboard of all two-masted canoes by which the board was lashed to the canoe's platform. It was called "Namor's door" and was believed to have been his escape route.] When his betrayers set sail, Namor cast a wind spell to blow them off course. He preceded them to landfall and was strolling along the beach as they came ashore. By the time they saw him it was too late to escape. Was he a ghost? Had they failed to kill him? When they finally saw him they were petrified with fear. They secured the canoe hastily and ran. The two pigs, Ankionk and Savaŋai, were left behind. They each rooted a furrow in the sand and stayed there. If you go to western New Britain, you can still see the depressions they made in the sand.

Namor took the canoe and sailed it back to Aromot. This is how the two-masted canoes came to Siassi. And that is the end of the story.

Episode V: Comments

In this episode we see some of the consequences of wrongfully usurping authority and of breaking the law. When the tree fell into New Britain, Namor was "sorry." This was the first instance in which he showed the slightest remorse for any of his escapades. He created the two-masted canoe and offered it as compensation to the Siassi. It was through his amorous exploits that they were deprived of their wealth objects and wealth potential (the tree itself and all of its wealth objects). He sold the canoe to them for two pigs. Namor thus supplied the *means* by which the Siassi could retrieve for themselves some of the lost wealth. He also supplied it at a bargain: The customary price for such a vessel was three pigs; one for each named section of the canoe.

Note that all of the land activities described in the legend are located on Umboi. The smaller islands do not enter the Siassi picture until the very end. They do appear in the sequel to this legend (presented in Chapter 3). The Siassi region as a whole is described as having lost its capacity to produce wealth as a result of Ambogim/Namor's roguishness. In telling this aspect of the story, the teller is acknowledging Namor's (human) weaknesses but does not lose his sense of the consequences of succumbing to them. Siassi peoples lost the right to possess the wealth objects. To get them back, Namor (and, by extension, the Siassi Islanders) had to work hard. The Aromot (hence the Mandok) *in particular* were given the knowledge to manufacture two-masted canoes. Although this gave them the means by which to recover the lost wealth, such recovery could be accomplished only through their own initiative and efforts as traders.

By describing historical events in this way, the tellers were also expressing and legitimizing a prior claim to the wealth. One cannot "lose" something one did not first "own." Thus we see a Siassi version of how the Siassi Islanders "began" their careers as maritime middlemen and staked their claim to *access* to the wealth objects characteristic of the Vitiaz trade system. From the Mandok (and Aromot) perspective, we see that they were the symbolic protagonists throughout the epic.

OF HEAVEN, EARTH, AND EDEN

When translating significant Mandok concepts communicated in the Legend of Namor, people have continually stressed the analogues of their "historical" tradition with those of Western "historical" tradition as documented in the Bible (as taught by the Roman Catholic missionaries). In the absence of a written record, Mandok elders documented historical episodes by means of physical features of their environment (cf. Kahn 1986, 1990). Depressions on the beach at Kilenge marked out (and provided concrete evidence of) the location where the two named pigs rooted in the sand. A fenced-off cordyline plant on Aromot marked the place where Namor closed the deal that brought the first two-masted canoe to the Aromot. More poignant, perhaps, is the story's explanation for the barrenness of Siassi with regard to indigenous environmental resources (as compared with other points in the trading circuit), which necessitated adaptation to a mobile maritime existence. In this case the proof of history lay in the marked *absence* of significant concrete objects.

The Namor epic and the Bible did not present an either/or proposition to the Mandok (cf. McDowell 1985). Their interpretations reflected a consistent syncretic alternation and a synthesis of both Western and Melanesian expository styles. Rather than underline the differences between methods of recording history, the points of juncture indicated historical *analogues*. By locating the legend in "Eden," Mandok philosophers documented European contact and synthesized introduced Christian explanations for the creation of the world. This is what Aipake was saying in the quotation that opens this chapter. Before missionization, the Mandok reasoned, their elders "did not know any better" than to think that the sea (indeed the world) just "came up by itself." They also owned the rights to a different story (see note 11). When they became Roman Catholic, they obtained the rights to biblical accounts of the creation of the world. The Mandok then considered themselves to "understand."

The Bible and the Legend of Namor (and other *kamos*) offered the Mandok complementary and mutually supportive interpretations of history. Each tradition filled in blanks left by the other. Part of the reason the Mandok understood history in this way resulted from a 20-year relationship with a popular missionary priest who stressed the similarities, rather than the differences, between Christianity and already extant Mandok beliefs (Mulderink 1988). The other part reflects, I think, the way the Mandok interpreted history to begin with. Thus although change was recognized to be the result of significant historical episodes (e.g., the coming of the missionaries), these episodes did not rewrite or replace the past but rather became woven into explanations of the present.[13]

A recent example will illustrate this reasoning. In 1982–1983 the Mandok built a new church. Each *runai* had its best artisans carve the supporting posts. The most powerful *runais*, *Mandog Sala* and *Tavov Puɤu* (see Chapters 4 and 5 for the reasons why they were powerful), also carved the tabernacle stand and the holy-water font. The current priest had gone on leave; when he returned, he was anxious to see the carvings for the new church. But when he opened the door he saw, standing in the center aisle, a huge wooden head. It stood over a meter high and was carved of the finest *kwila* wood (see Figure 2.4). Inset in the top was a stone basin for the holy water. The stone, which had been left on Mandok during the German colonial period (see Chapter 7), had writing incised on it that at one time some Mandok believed to be magical. The men eventually discarded it. Women used the stone to scrape off the outer layer of trochus armlets. All that scraping caused a grooved depression in the surface of the (previously flat) oblong stone that was sufficient to contain water. In the meantime, however, the stone had been reappropriated by the men and stored in the men's area. The priest had never before seen the head. It was most definitely not in the original plans for the holy-water font.

The priest went to see Gabriel Aipake, a church deacon, for an explanation. Aipake explained that the head was that of Giliŋ, guardian spirit of *Tavov Puɤu runai* (and hence, by extension, of Mandok; see Chapter 5). His presence in the church confirmed that "this is a place of truth, a place of law." That law was absolute. The priest responded with a biblical counterexample. Aipake parried with the statement that Giliŋ belonged to "Old Testament Mandok." The biblical example was also true but, Aipake noted, belonged to the "New Testament." The priest eventually reasoned that many devout European Catholics still believed that ghosts, ghouls, and goblins haunted the spires of their cathedrals; such beliefs were relics of more archaic ones. Why shouldn't other cultures have equivalent psychological leftovers? The head stayed.

The explanation offered by Aipake illustrates the same kind of thought processes the Mandok used to interpret "history." *Kamos* justified and explained the world "as it is now," how it got to be that way, and why it should stay the way it is. Just because Christians today follow the New Testament does not mean they reject and have completely abandoned the Old Testament (as occasional fundamentalist Protestant debates over

FIGURE 2.4 *Holy-water font, Mandok Church, 1987.*

the teaching of evolution in U.S. schools remind us). To some, the proof
of history lies in the fact that the Old Testament underpins New Testament theology. Likewise, the Mandok reasoned, whether one called a
creator "Namor" or "God" did not change the basic story line. Names
changed with geographic and historical progessions in both accounts.
Moreover, each account records that the son replaced the father as hero
(e.g., Mala/Ambogim and God/Jesus). Mandok church elders recognized
many such parallels and were quite interested in noting and discussing
them. Nevertheless, there were certain "truths" that were timeless. Siassi
Islanders carved canoes and caught fish for food; Umboi people grew
yams and taro. Men were tricksters and rogues; women were jealous
by nature. The islanders were sea people who sailed the trade circuit

for wealth; the Umboi were bush people who stayed put. The trappings might be new, but the plot remained "the same."

The epic tale of Namor explained the universe to Siassi peoples in a way that was comprehensible to them. Whatever strategic or pragmatic implications there might have been in drawing analogies to the Christian Bible (some of which are discussed in subsequent chapters), the Namor story painted a verbal portrait of physical and social realities that they understood to be at the very least analogous, if not identical, to those in their own lives. The next three chapters illlustrate how the Mandok transformed "legendary history" into contemporary everyday life.

CHAPTER THREE

🐚 Things of the Sea: Maritime Foundations of Cultural Identity

Our ancestors taught us to kill a pig in honor of a child's first sea crossing. But many are not clear about why they throw water on the children when they return—why the sea water. It is the same for [Christian] Baptism. We must explain this clearly to the *bigmen,* and then show the children and explain to them too: "This is the sea—it has many things inside it. It is where we get food." Later, when the children eat fish, they learn that life comes from the sea. God made this come about. He put the many good things in the sea for us to have. It is the same with Baptism: The Holy Spirit is in the water; it is the true source of life.

Gabriel Aipake, christening sermon, September 1980

The Mandok liked to describe themselves as *mbeb to te,* "thing(s) of/from the sea." The centrality of the sea for them found expression in many different contexts. It provided a major source of food and the highway for trade. The value of the sea extended beyond subsistence and crass economics, however; it had deep psychological, emotional, and spiritual value as well. The sea and its resources provided the Mandok with cognitive and emotional templates that oriented individuals in their culturally constituted "behavioral environment" (Hallowell 1955).

Hallowell's concept of a "behavioral environment" recognizes that human adaptation is not just a matter of conquering the physical environment but of understanding a behavioral field that is *culturally* constructed. In a culturally constituted behavioral environment,

culturally reified objects . . . may have functions . . . directly related to needs, motivations and goals of the self. Symbolically represented, such objects are integral parts of the psychological field of the individual and must be considered as relevant variables because they can be shown to affect actual behavior. (Hallowell 1955:87)

The Mandok behavioral environment oriented individuals over-whelmingly to the sea and to maritime activities. It extended beyond these physical surroundings and included other-than-human "persons" important to Mandok culture. The most important of these were also related in some way to the sea, and they personified Mandok notions about humanity and life in general. This chapter explores how the sea and its resources provided the Mandok with the foundations for the economic, psychic, and spiritual life of their community.

SPACE, TIME, AND THE SEA

Every culture orients the individual in space and time (Hallowell 1955). Space, seasons, and directional coordinates in Siassi were organized around the winds and sea formations. The northwest and southeast winds provided baseline directional coordinates in much the same way that Westerners use cardinal points on a compass. The origins of the winds provided the major orienting directions for fisherfolk and sailors alike. The two major wind seasons had names: *Yavar* was the name and the season of the northwest wind (November–March), and *Rag* was the name and the season of the southeast wind (May–October). The expression "Go to *Rag*'s origin" gave a directional coordinate of southeast. Lesser winds were also named, and they also provided these kinds of spatial coordinates. Each of the reefs, mangroves, sand cays, channels, prominent boulders, and so on were named, distinct places.

Among the small islanders, the sea was bounded territory; the boundaries delimited each community's fishing areas. Figure 3.1 shows the recognized boundaries that separated the small Siassi islands. The boundaries overlapped somewhat. At the time of my fieldwork these were informal divisions; they did not restrict fishing activities. At one time, "Mandok waters" were also subdivided into usufruct rights among the *runai*. But, as one man insisted,

> anyone can go anywhere, nowadays. We are all Christians, and we know that God put the fish in the sea for all men, so we shouldn't fight [about it].

In Chapter 1 we considered the seasons in Siassi in terms of the northwest and southeast winds. The Mandok (and other Siassi groups) had a more detailed system for reckoning seasonality. Time in a cyclical (Leach 1961) or "ecological" sense (Evans-Pritchard 1940) was traditionally reckoned by the changes in the sea and winds and by the motions of the stars. According to older informants, there were also months or "moons" divided roughly into two groups of six for each wind. Two months marked the in-between times (see Figure 3.2), which were notable for calm, windless seas and hot, dry weather. At one time all of

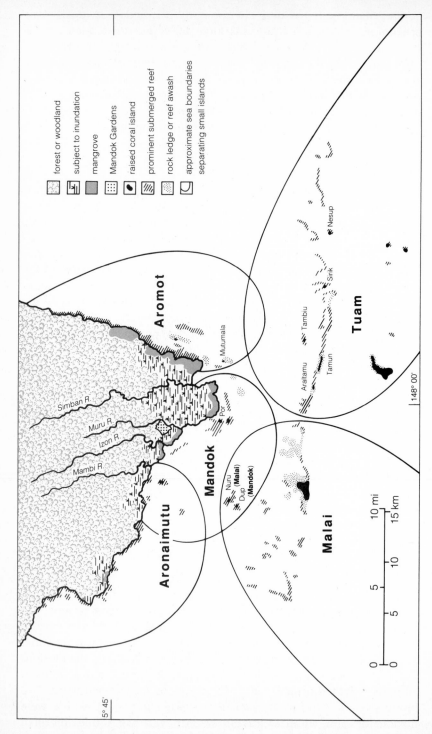

FIGURE 3.1 *Sea boundaries separating the small Siassi islands.*

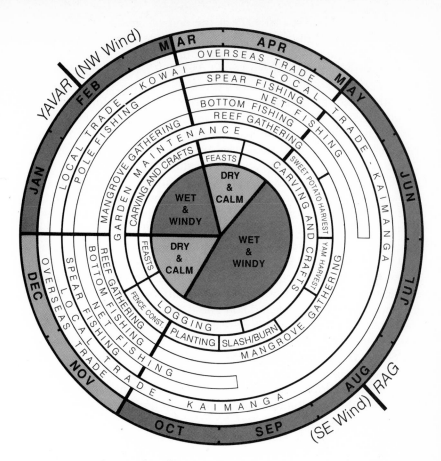

F I G U R E 3.2 *Seasonal cycles.*

the months were identified by name and relevant activity; only some
of these names were in use while I was on Mandok, and they referred
to more general seasons rather than to individual months. We will not,
therefore, consider them in detail here. As my Mandok father explained,

> when the government and the mission came, we dropped the calen-
> dar our ancestors gave us and started following the European Pope's
> calendar [i.e., the Gregorian calendar], so everyone got mixed up, and
> they forgot.

Each month of each season was associated with significant weather
features, tidal movements, floral and faunal availability, and specific subsistence and/or ceremonial activities. Although expressed here in the
"European Pope's" system, the time periods described next were determined more by the weather than by the calendar.

I arrived on Mandok in 1979 at the end of October. October and November were formerly the time to sail to the New Guinea coast to trade. By the time of my fieldwork these months were devoted to planting. Once the gardens were planted, Mandok traders hopped a commercial boat or a motorized dugout canoe for their trade trips. December was one of the "good times" months: it brought beautiful weather and plenty of fish. Relatives living in towns came home to celebrate Christmas and "first-accomplishment feasts" for their firstborn children (see Chapter 4). Once gardens were planted, everyone took advantage of the calm seas to go hook-and-line fishing.

When the *Yavar* winds were up (January and February), women and adolescent children fished in the rocky shallows near the mangroves. A Mandok saying described this period as the time for "big winds and small fish." In this season, some people fished with bamboo poles, whereas others wound fishing tackle around an empty bottle or a whittled chunk of wood. Wind permitting, women gathered trochus and other shellfish off reef edges and in the mangroves. They also harvested smaller sea clams to deposit into individually owned clam beds in the channel between Mandok and Por. These clam beds provided food during the times when the winds were too strong to go fishing or to gather food off the reefs. Men and older youths went in large work groups to get timber from Umboi Island for carving, house building, and canoe manufacture. Immediately after the Easter feasts there was often no food in the village. Crops planted in November would not yet be ready for harvest, so the Mandok relied on their Gauru trade partners and other Umboi markets for food.

During mid- to late March through April the seas were once again calm. This was the "Easter season." During May and June, low tide occurred during the daylight, which provided ample opportunity for gathering shellfish on the reefs, even if the winds were up. July and August marked the "bad time." The heavy rains and strong winds of *Rag* made travel especially difficult and dangerous. July marked the rise of the Pleiades and with them the yam harvest. This initiated the time to "sit down and eat what you planted" the previous November.

CLASSIFICATION OF SEA RESOURCES

Linguists have long appreciated the relationship between important objects and activities in a culture and the linguistic elaboration of these things in that culture's language. Many students studying introductory anthropology, for example, have been regaled in their lectures with the many and varied terms Inuit use for "snow" (estimates of the actual number of terms vary). For the Mandok, maritime resources and activities received the highest degree of linguistic elaboration.

In two surveys I conducted in 1980 and 1987, Mandok men named over 110 separate species of fish (*ig*), and women named about 80 categories of mollusc (*gol*). Their taxonomic system, which was similar to that recognized by Western marine biologists, was based predominently on physical features. There were, however, a few notable departures that illustrate that the Mandok perceived marine resources somewhat differently than would a Westerner.

For example, the category *ig*, which I gloss here as "fish," really meant "moving creatures of the sea." I learned this while reviewing *Grant's Guide to Fishes* (Grant 1973) with my Mandok father and several other family members of various ages (14–65) and both sexes. They all felt that Grant "forgot" to mention some of the most important *ig*. He omitted turtles, dugong (sea mammals related to the manatee), dolphins, and, less important but noted nevertheless, whales. Whales and dolphins were classified as the same "family" of "fish." This is not too different from Western marine biological classification, which classifies the dolphin as a species of "toothed whales." To the Mandok, the whale is the "mother fish" of the dolphin. They are both, however, "fish." Sharks with white skin and no other prominent distinguishing features were just *korau*, "shark." Two-toned sharks (dark on top, white on bottom) were "the mother of them all."

Fishermen described a lot more than physical features of separate species. Within each category they also indicated: *where* found (deep sea, reef edge, reef, coral or rock bases, mangroves, rivers, etc.), *when* available (wind season, tide, time of day), and *how* caught (large or medium fishnets, hook and line, spear). They knew which fish were poisonous or, in some cases, during which season or which parts of them were most poisonous (e.g., liver or head).

In contrast to the general category *ig*, the Mandok also distinguished the generic category of *gol* (also *ngol*), "mollusc." As with fish, they were distinguished according to physical features such as shape, size, color, and location. Several species had special functions, such as food, craft material, traditional currency, or decoration. Some were poisonous and were therefore to be handled very carefully or avoided altogether. Several mollusc species had ceremonial or decorative significance: white cowries were used as canoe decorations, and bailer shells as house roof ornaments, for example. Certain types of coral and smaller shells were important personal decorations for feasting regalia and were marked specifically with *runai*- or family-owned designs.

Any discussion of marine life in Siassi requires some mention of maritime birds. Many different species of sea birds had various significances to daily or spiritual life. The Mandok invoked seagulls as a metaphor for a generic mobile sea creature; hence their prominence in the proverb that inspired the title of this book. Circling birds figured in the Legend of Namor (see Chapter 2) as omens and in other *kamos* as helpers or heroes.

The most important bird, perhaps, was the sea eagle. Hunters par excellence, sea eagles were admired for their power, their speed, and their deadly accuracy. Certain land formations (e.g., mangroves, deserted coral islands) provided homes for eagle eyries. Certain named eagles became protagonists of different *kamos*; others had totemic value for Mandok *runai*. If a man speared a fish successfully, for example, he might call out the name of his sea-eagle totem in jubilation (as a celebration and to give thanks for his fishing success). The sea eagle provided one of the characteristic carving motifs for the Siassi carvers. It was most often depicted struggling with a crocodile over a fish. This motif seemed to summarize for the Siassi peoples the struggle and balance among the forces of the universe on the land, in the sea, and in the sky. During my fieldwork visits, younger Mandok used the names of their totemic sea eagles for their intramural sports teams.

In addition to this complex classification of marine life, the Mandok described the sea itself in minute detail. They noted changes in its temperature, the shape and size of its swells, whirlpools, and currents. This knowledge was crucial to successful overseas sailing in the precarious environment of the Vitiaz and Dampier straits. Even subtle changes could be significant: to misread the wind, water temperature, or swells might result in shipwreck and drowning in the volatile sea.

THE DAILY CATCH

The Mandok devised a general division of sea labor based on sex. Men fished off the reefs with large nets in which they caught several varieties of large schooling fish and dugong. Women collected shellfish on the reefs and in the mangroves. Women also dived for several species of sea clam (*Tridachna* spp.) in the deeper channels off the larger reefs. They "farmed" immature sea clams close to Mandok to provide emergency resources for the lean times. Chinnery (n.d.:36) described the use of hand nets for collecting on the reefs. These were mentioned frequently in legends, but I saw none in use during my stays on Mandok. Mandok women mentioned these nets more in reference to catching shrimp in rivers on Umboi, but they said that this was a long time ago; they apparently discontinued the practice. Women also fished with hook and line.

For less-involved collecting trips on the reefs, women either went alone, with one or more of their children, or in groups of closer consanguineal and affinal kinswomen. Teenagers and younger children also went in groups to collect shellfish or to bottom fish with hook and line. More recently they engaged in spear fishing by sling-shotting a meter-long iron rod propelled through the water by a large rubber band most likely fashioned from an old inner tube. Though mostly a male activity, I have seen older teenage girls spear fish, too.

In the precontact era, fishing expeditions were usually organized according to *runai* or extended family membership. A person could also go alone or with only one other person. A husband and wife might go together, leaving their children with a grandparent or other kinsperson. By the time of my fieldwork, several new techniques and types of fishing equipment had been introduced. These innovations allowed the Mandok more flexibility in their choices of fishing companion and of the kind of fishing to do. Crosscutting kinship ties, adoption, and (increasingly) school-based play groups also extended social attachments beyond kin groups.

Net fishing for the Mandok was not only a major male subsistence activity; it was a process imbued with symbolism of the sacred past. The Mandok's Legend of *Las, Nan̄ur,* and *Sup* provided the "proper" means by which these sacred schooling fish should be caught. Originally part of the Legend of Namor (see, for example, Allace 1976), it could also be told as a separate episode. It was "owned" by the Malai, but, just as other islanders had the use of the Aromot's versions of the Legend of Namor (see Chapter 2), so did they have the rights to this episode. Time and space limitations preclude a full presentation of this legend here; a short synopsis will have to suffice (for a fuller, annotated version, see Pomponio 1991).

In Allace's version (1976:4–5), the Legend of *Las, Nan̄ur,* and *Sup* comes after Kilibob created the *Sia* dancing feast. This legend would fall between Episodes I and II in Chapter 2 (cf. Pomponio 1991). After providing spouses for everyone else, he made a woman for himself and married her. This was Gainor, who was originally from Tarawe (not from Arop, as in the version recorded in Chapter 2). At any rate, she bore Kilibob two sons *before* she conceived Ambogim (see Episode IV). At this time, Kilibob also created the three sacred fish: *nan̄ur* (trevally), *las* (leatherskin or queenfish), and *sup* (kingfish). He put these fish in a lake on top of a hill on Arop (Long) Island, with only a small trap door from which to extract the fish, and showed his mother how to catch them (Allace 1976:4).

Recall that in Episode IV of the Namor legend, the hero's wife Gainor, after realizing that her husband had deserted her, went off to find him. She ended up in Tarawe on Umboi Island. Her other two sons stayed with their paternal grandmother on Arop. The grandmother is the protagonist of the Legend of *Las, Nan̄ur,* and *Sup.* Through her actions the Malai (and hence, the other Siassi Islanders) learned how these three sacred fish migrated to Siassi from Arop. The fish fled when the boys tried to spear them, and traveled along the south coast of Umboi in search of people who spoke a different language from that of their tormentors. Eventually, they reached Malai Island. The old woman visited a Malai man in a dream and, in exchange for a safe haven, instructed him in the proper techniques for catching these fish. From that time onward, the Siassi Islanders have fished for them with nets, as the old woman instructed.

This story's most obvious message concerns the instructions for catching these species of fish. Some species were caught inside the nets and then speared. One lesson is that kingfish, which school close together and jump, must never be caught this way, although trevally and queenfish could be speared. But because the three fish were often found together, it was best not to risk spearing any of them.

At the time of my fieldwork the Malai, Mandok, and Aromot fished with nets using the methods prescribed in this legend. They also used this legend to explain why they did not fish with traps: they "did not know how." There are two meanings to this phrase. First, the Mandok had neither a legend that explained fishing with traps nor a spell to ensure that the fish would go into the traps, once constructed. Without the legend and the spell, the traps would have "no power to attract fish." Second, without these forms of "knowledge" they had *no right* to use fish traps.

In addition to explaining what must be done in order to catch fish, tradition also dictated certain things *not* to do in order to ensure a good catch. During the construction of the great nets (*palpal*) there must be absolute harmony between a man and his fellows. He could not fight with his wife. He had to be generous to all who sought help, and he could not deny anyone anything asked of him. He was obliged to provide food distributions at each stage of the net's construction and to provide a final large distribution for the entire village upon its completion. A fight or any ill will between the owner of the net and another person endangered the power of the net to catch fish.

A man could not have sex before going on a fishing expedition, and a menstruating wife disqualified him from fishing as well. It was poor etiquette and bad luck to ask "Where are you going?" to a man carrying a net or paddling a canoe with a net on board. The Mandok did not even acknowledge that person's presence—call out his name or otherwise attract attention—for fear of bad luck. If a man took a great net and was going to fish, his wife used to mark off his path from their house to the beach. It was taboo to cross this path until the net was thrown into the water, for such a breach of taboo could ruin the expedition. Wives also left their husbands' sleeping mats unfolded until their return; to fold them would "cover up the fish" and jinx the expedition.

Large fishnets (*palpal*) were usually owned by the *runai*. While I was on Mandok, the few remaining *palpal* in the village were stored in the men's area, which avoided the taboo about crossing the path. Smaller nets, *maluum*, were in greater abundance. However, most Mandok used store-bought nylon nets. One could see traditional rolled-bark fiber nets hanging under a couple of houses; but if men went fishing, they were more likely to use store-bought nets than the bark ones because the former were sturdier and easier to repair. By 1987 the only traditional nets I saw were on Malai.

When the weather was bad, women's fishing and gathering activities focused on the mangroves, which were sheltered and easily reached. Later we will consider two particularly important types of bivalves called *tiwai* (*Polymesoda cyrenoididae*), which are like cherrystone clams, and *motak* (?*Polymesoda palustris*), which are like steamer clams but rounder (Cragg 1982). The women also collected several types of snail, shrimp, and mud crabs. As one woman observed on my first mangrove expedition, "a mangrove is like an ice box—it keeps fresh food for us. It is like the ice box of our ancestors."

Diving for sea clams (*Tridacna* spp.) was perhaps the most important women's activity from the perspective of cultural symbolism. It deserves special note here because it was considered the epitome of "women's activities." Several essential tools were used for hunting sea clams: a long sturdy rope, a black oblong river stone, a large knife, a crowbar, and goggles. The labor on the expedition was divided into two groups. One group of goggled girls and women swam on the surface, scanning the coral reef beds for open sea clams among the various sea flora and fauna. Four or five remained on board to paddle the canoe and to haul in the catch. Once a clam was located, the spotter kept her face in the water and her eyes fixed on the clam while she trod water in place. Another woman brought the stone, which was affixed by rope and vines to a stronger rope. The other end of this rope was held securely by three or four women on the canoe. The woman with the stone dived to where the clam lay, as far down as 20 to 30 meters (60 to 90 feet) in some cases. She dropped the stone into the clam's gaping mouth, which caused it to close instantly. By yanking on the rope she signaled to the women waiting above to haul it in. Because these clams grew up to 227 kg (500 pounds) or more, it took several women to haul the clam up to the surface (see Figure 3.3).

Once on board, the clam was prized open with the crowbar. The meat was cut out in one piece and left in the canoe hull. The shell was tossed overboard or taken back to the village for use as a pig trough. If a clam was too large to pull up into the canoe without tipping the canoe over, it was tied on either side of its shell, and the rope was secured to the canoe platform. The women quickly paddled to the nearest reef, where, in shallow water, they extracted the meat.

Just as men observed certain taboos before going net fishing, women observed taboos before they went clam diving or mangrove culling. For instance, when a woman was menstruating, pregnant, or had had sex the night before a sea clamming expedition, she could search for sea clams, paddle the canoe, and help clean out the meat of the clams. It was taboo, however, for her to hold the rope to which the stone was attached and dropped into the open clam. To fail to observe the taboo was considered an invitation to bad luck. It could cause the rope to slip and the clam to fall. For this reason, unmarried girls usually held the

FIGURE 3.3 *Bringing a giant sea clam on board.*

rope. Assuming that the first clam was pulled up successfully, the woman who first dropped the stone in kept on "holding the rope," because the Mandok believed that to change rope holders (i.e., stone droppers) was bad luck. On one trip that was being conducted as a firstborn, first-accomplishment celebration (see Chapter 4), the rope slipped several times, causing the women to lose six giant clams. The older women on the trip grumbled that the younger women were not comporting themselves properly—that is, that they were engaging in (illicit) pre-marital sex and that they were to blame for such a bad catch.

To ensure a big catch of sea clams, one of the women picked up "something from Mandok" to take along with them on the canoe. One time the women I was with took a starfish, but I was assured that it could be anything. About halfway to the final destination, each woman in the canoe, from front to back, took the starfish in her left hand (whether it makes any difference which hand is used is unclear). Each one spit on it, knocked it on the side of the canoe, and passed it on to the next woman. The last woman threw the starfish overboard. (This custom seems to be analogous with that of the old woman in the Legend of *Las, Naŋur,* and *Sup,* who threw a stone into the water to attract the fish. In this case, the women were "attracting" sea clams.)

Similar taboos applied when the women went to the mangroves to cull *tiwai* or *motak* clams. Prior sex was forbidden, but menstruation did not enter into taboos for mangrove activities. Good-luck charms for expeditions to the mangroves differed from those of fishing expeditions. Instead of involving "something from Mandok," these were extracted in situ. Each member of the expedition took a leaf from a mangrove tree, spit on it, hit it on her leg and then against the side of the canoe, and then tossed it overboard. This practice was said to ensure two things. The two types of bivalves were harvested by probing with the feet in the silty marshes of mangrove swamps; hence the focus on the legs. By spitting on the mangrove leaf and smacking her leg, the woman hoped to be surefooted and prevent serious injury. (The danger was slipping and possibly impaling herself on the sharp mangrove roots.) Second, *motak* is a soft-shelled clam; thus concentration on her legs ensured that she would step gently and not crush the shell, for to do so would ruin the delicate-flavored meat of the clam.

Women were also quiet on fishing expeditions. Silence was mandatory when larger groups dived for sea clams, culled *motak* or *tiwai* from the mangroves, or bottom-fished with hook and line. Children learned at an early age not to ask questions and to observe fishing taboos. Once my "daughter" and language tutor Agnes Abiua was pulling her pole and canoe paddle out of the rafters of her house. She balanced a small basket on her head as she pulled. Some women who were making trochus armlets nearby asked, "Abiua, where are you going?" She did not answer them; she never even looked their way. She just silently pulled out the desired objects, turned, and walked away. When one of the women realized that Abiua was going fishing, she shushed everyone else, saying, *"Tikia—pa moi"*—"Hush, [you'll spoil] her luck!"

THE "HIGHWAY" TO TRADE

The Mandok exchanged fish for vegetables and fruit at several points on Umboi (Figure 1.4, p. 15) as well as in longer-distance overseas trade (Figure 1.1, p. 7). A regular "market" operated at Barang, on the Kowai side of Umboi, before and after World War II and continued through the 1960s. By 1986, wind and weather permitting, Mandok were fairly "regular" merchants at Lablab on Saturday mornings. Other trading sites were visited sporadically.

The Mandok traditionally traded for all of their vegetable staples, and even though they did garden during my stay, they still relied on Umboi trade for the majority of their vegetable foods. When the weather was good (especially in December and around Easter), the schooling fish (gar, tuna, leatherskin, kingfish, and trevally) started running. The sea was calm then, and the Mandok seemed to do little else but fish day and night. Spearfishing and net fishing were accomplished at night with

the aid of dried coconut-frond torches. The luckier and wealthier fishermen had kerosene pressure lamps. At these times the entire village
became a great barbeque, everyone smoking the catch for future trade
on Umboi. If the weather was good, a man could net enough fish in
one day to trade for one or two weeks' worth of vegetables (sweet potato,
taro, *pitpit*, manioc) and for special treats of banana, *pawpaw* (papaya),
watermelon, pineapple, and litchi nuts.

METAPHORS FOR HUMANNESS

The Mandok linguistically distinguished humans from other beings in a
variety of ways. Though there is a clear separation of "animals" from
"humans," Mutu has no cover term for "animal," although it does for
"fish." The Mandok defined humans (as distinct from animals) based
on two characteristics. The first was that humans had the capacity for
ngar, "knowledge" or "wisdom," which was considered partly to be
a function of hearing; humans could hear and listen and hence learn.
Animals were *borou*, "deaf," "mute," "stupid," "retarded," or otherwise
lacking in *ngar*. The second distinguishing feature of humans was that
they had an *anunu*. *Anunu* has many meanings in English, including
"self," "likeness," "reflection," or "life substance." During my field stay
many Mandok likened *anunu* to the Christian concept of "soul." Because
of its variety of meanings, I prefer to use the Mandok term *anunu*; the
term's precise meaning in any particular instance can be gleaned from
the context in which it is used.

The Mandok believed, as did many other Melanesian societies, that an
inherent aspect of an individual's (and a culture's) identity was assimi-
lated from that individual's residence and subsistence economy. It was as
if people absorbed all of the life-giving forces from their land and from
the food grown in that place. That "substance" was then transformed,
through the food and liquids ingested and the air breathed, into human
life. For most Melanesian horticulturalists, this "substance" comes from
the ground (see, for example, Watson 1990). For the Mandok, it came
from the sea.

As in other Melanesian societies, the Mandok identified with particular
environmental features that were most significant in their subsistence
economy. For instance, most Melanesian horticulturalists expressed concepts of the "self" and humanness in terms of botanical metaphors. Thus,
in those areas where yams are the primary staple and the crop of highest
prestige, elaborate metaphors using the yam express the concepts of the
human body and of growth (Tuzin 1972; Fortune 1932). Where taro is the
primary staple crop, human beings are described in terms of taro parts,
growth, and reproduction (Panoff 1968; Kahn 1986). Other societies emphasize pandanus (Herdt 1981). Some societies use features of animals

such as pigs (Goodale 1985) or cassowaries (Gell 1975; Schieffelin 1976) in their metaphors for humanity.

One distinctive feature of Mandok exegetical conceptual style in describing the general form of the human body was the use of both land-based and oceanographic metaphors for the self. For example, the firstborn child (discussed in Chapter 4) was called the *aidaba*, or "head of the tree" (*ai*, "tree"; *daba*, "head"). When describing where in the body the *anunu* ("self," "soul," etc.) resides, one informant explained that *"anunu inep ila patu lolo,"* "the *anunu* resides inside of the container" (i.e., the skin of the body). However, instead of continuing these metaphors to describe the body as a tree with bark (skin), sap (blood), and so on (cf. Panoff 1968), my informant described the human body as "just like a tin can that has canned fish inside." He went on to clarify:

> Just like we say the women go diving for *gol* [generic term for "molluscs"], it is like this: when there is meat inside, it is a *gol* ["clam"], and the *gol* lives inside of the *gol patu* ["clam container," "clamshell"]. But after you take the meat out, then the *gol patu* is a *diwar*, an "empty shell" you see lying about on the beach. Alright, it is the same with humans. The *anunu* resides inside the skin [of the human body]. Once the *anunu* goes out of the body you die, and a person is then a "corpse."

Among the Mandok infant sickness and colic could be interpreted as a loss of *anunu*, and must be remedied quickly, lest the baby die. If an infant became ill or "cried incessantly for nothing," the Mandok said that *ipul anunu*, that "he/she lost his/her *anunu*." In 1980 two specialists in the village had the ability to "call the *anunu* back" to the child. Both called out to the baby by name (i.e., to the child's *anunu*) and referred to significant features of the Siassi environment in order to "call the baby back into its skin." Likely features might include reef grasses, large holes into which the baby's *anunu* might have fallen, or large fish, which might have swallowed it. The species of fish invoked in the spells range in weight from about 12 to 227 kg (25 to 500 pounds) and in lengths up to 2 meters (7 feet)—large enough to swallow an infant.

SPIRIT BEINGS OF THE SEA

Though the sea was the source of life, it was also a source of danger. We have already seen this reality expressed in the spells for loss of *anunu*. Part of this danger came from *mariam*, "spirits," "ghosts," "spirits of the dead." Different kinds of spirits inhabited the Mandok behavioral environment. These other-than-human "persons" interacted with the Mandok in different contexts (cf. Hallowell 1955). *Nakamutmut*, masked figures (see Chapter 4), were one kind of *mariam*; certain other *mariam* were ancestral guardian spirits, limited to specific *runai*. For example, the head of Giliŋ carved into the holy-water font (see Chapter 2) was an example of this kind of *mariam*. Other *mariam* belonged to everyone. Many were depicted on the carved wooden bowls used in bride-price exchanges, land purchases, and, more recently, for sale to tourists. Some *mariam* inhabited the deep sea; others lurked about on the reefs.

Some *mariam*, called *puɤun*, took animal forms, with anthropomorphic features, and they were dangerous. *Puɤun* usually appeared as snakes, lizards, or crocodiles, sometimes with two heads. They inhabited certain points in mangroves, reefs, and river mouths. Elders seemed to know these *puɤun*'s habits and how to avoid or appease them. *Puɤun* that inhabited the bush areas were less well known and therefore doubly feared. A distinctive characteristic of *puɤun* was that they had no *anunu*: once you killed them they died. One story tells of the sea *puɤun* Baluan Tidi, a two-headed snake that lurked among the reefs near Mandok. He was not especially "bad" unless you took too many sea clams or oysters from him; then he made storms come up, fish jump away from the nets, hurricane-velocity winds blow, and generally wreaked havoc until you appeased him by throwing back whatever you took. "But," as one older man informed me, "when the Europeans came to Siassi they brought dynamite[1] and blew Baluan Tidi up, so he died."

Since missionization the Mandok had become more reluctant to talk about these spirits. But the belief in them was still strong during my stay. When a person died, for example, the *anunu* left the body and the body became a corpse. Upon leaving the live body the *anunu* became a *mariam*. The priest encouraged people not to fear the deceased's *mariam*. He emphasized that if the person was a good person in life, then to fear him or her in death would be an insult to that person's memory. A special mass was celebrated on All Souls' Day to revere the spirits of deceased Mandok, especially the recently deceased. However, as soon as night fell, people still got nervous. And when a child fell unaccountably ill, the blame usually fell on either a *mariam* or a *puɤun*.

Malevolent *puɤun*, in addition to mosquitoes, snakes, and other undesirable creatures, were known to lurk in the bush, causing sickness and death to "trespassers" on "their" domain. To ward off malevolent spirits along the Muru River, the foreheads and chests of young children who visited the gardens for the first time were painted with lime. Firstborn children might be decked out in all of their feasting finery for this purpose. If a pregnant woman could not avoid the journey, she did avoid walking over a certain stone near the canoe docking place in Muru, which was believed to be the home of an especially malevolent *puɤun*. Walking over it was believed to cause a deformed or stillborn child. The Mandok also tried not to be wet with dewdrops falling from the trees along the Muru River, for in these dewdrops lay the concentrated malevolent substances of *puɣun*. Generally, these maladies were referred to as *morogoŋto su,* "bush sickness." No doubt these beliefs also rationalized the Mandok's more general dislike and fear of the bush, fears that were not completely unfounded. Malaria, for example, used to be blamed on *puɣun*. Although by the time of my fieldwork many Mandok knew more about the medical causes of malaria and other diseases, this knowledge did not appreciably alter their reluctance to go into the bush.

Puɣun and *mariam* were considered to be omens. If a person went to the gardens, for example, and saw a snake, a lizard, or a crocodile, he or she returned to the village immediately, for this was an omen that someone had died. Because reptiles shed their skin, the Mandok believed that there was a connection between reptiles and ancestral spirits. The new skin underneath was a kind of rebirth, which made the reptiles immortal. This was especially true of lizards, which were believed to be guardians of the men's area (*pulat*). When the *pulat* was consecrated, these guardians were said to have been given the power of sickness and death. In the Mandok *pulat* there used to be a great ficus tree in which many lizards lived (see Chapter 2 for a discussion of sacred trees). In 1968 the tree, rotten from age and weather, fell. The event, an important and sacred one in Mandok history, was marked by a great feast and a vigil that lasted for days. Deprived of their home, lizards roamed freely within the men's area. If a lizard appeared in the village, it was never harmed, and all activity stopped until the animal passed. "We can never know," said one of my "relatives," "who exactly that might be, but someone is watching us. If we harm it, we will die."

THE SEA VERSUS THE LAND

Although the Mandok lived on an island and used the surrounding sea extensively, they also needed and utilized the land. *Tan* ("land" or "ground") was distinguished from islands, *mutu*. The land (*tan*) contained broadly defined areas of villages (*panu*), gardens (*um*), or bush (*su*). Mainland New Guinea was referred to as *tan tiina,* "big ground." Umboi was not usually referred to as a whole but rather by specific area or village. Mountains, rivers, lakes, and other land features had generic terms, but in conversation each was also referred to by name. Although many of the myths and legends in the Mandok repertoire referred to gardening and bush activities (notably, cultivating taro and hunting wild boar), the Mandok did not engage in taro cultivation or organized pig hunts during my field stay. These stories were traded or carried to Mandok by immigrants from bush areas (Kilenge, Malasiga, Umboi Island, Tolokiwa Island, or Arop Island), where these activities were more prominent.

After pacification, the colonial government encouraged gardening (see Chapters 7 and 8). A variety of crops was introduced experimentally, including rice, coffee, pineapples, cocoa, onions, and peanuts. The islanders were urged to garden for themselves to gain independence from the trade system. Administrators also tried to mitigate the ever-present threat of famine in this marginal environment. In addition to gardening, government officers promoted cash cropping. In this way they hoped the Siassi would participate in a growing market economy. Over the years, Umboi horticulturalists expanded the variety of their crops with the help of the Lutheran mission. Although the Mandok did garden, at the time of my fieldwork they still depended on trade for their subsistence and for accumulating a surplus. We will consider these points more fully in subsequent chapters.

The Mandok cultivated a land tract of about 115 hectares (288 acres) on Umboi, adjacent to the Muru River. The area was called Muru, after the river (refer to Figure 1.4, p. 15).[2] Mandok Island was too small to spare garden land and had no fresh-water source.

The gardening was swidden cultivation. In this type of horticulture, bush is first burned off to clear the plot and to provide nutrients to the soil. Typically, new gardens are planted for a few years and then left fallow for one or two years to regain their fertility (times vary with land availability and soil fertility). The Mandok raised sweet potatoes, sweet manioc, yams, and Singapore taro. They supplemented these root crops with coconuts, bananas, and breadfruit. Some families grew limited quantities of aibika greens, tobacco, and additional treats of watermelon or cucumbers. Others owned rights to lemon or Malay apple trees. Areca palm and betel pepper were also grown.

The land on the east side of Umboi was not suitable for taro, apparently for several reason. One source (Patrol Report Finschhafen 17, 1961–62) listed the mountain barrier in Umboi's center as the cause; the mountain prevented any real division into wet/dry seasons on the southeast tip of Umboi. Another observer blamed the taro blight of the 1960s (Holzknecht 1980). Local interpretations stressed long-lasting feuds between the small islanders and the Simban River villagers from the early part of the 20th century through the 1940s. They claimed that sorcery, aimed at destroying rivals, instead ruined the land forever. The Mandok traded with Kowai communities on Umboi, and as far away as Kilenge, for taro. During my field stays, taro was rare and was eaten mostly on ceremonial occasions. Sago was processed along the Izon, Mambi, or Simban rivers, as well as in the swamps of the Muru River.

Agriculture did not maintain primary importance on Mandok, as it does in other parts of PNG, or even on Umboi. It was considered to be unpleasant work, and, from the elders' point of view, it constituted a major disruption to overseas trade (see Harding 1967; Allace 1976:18). The younger men realized that gardening was necessary for food and for "development" (i.e., cash cropping; see Chapters 8 and 9). All things considered, however, they preferred to go fishing and continue their long-standing tradition of "paying" for Umboi vegetables with their surplus fish. Once a Mandok garden was planted and the protective fences built, it was visited only two or three times a week for maintenance purposes. This work was done mainly by women and teenaged girls. Fathers continually nagged their sons to check to see that wild pigs had not destroyed the fences and eaten growing tubers. But gardening was regarded as a tedious chore and was often avoided.

An overriding pragmatism characterized the Mandok's attitudes toward gardening. A good garden, according to them, was the result of hard work; there was no indigenous garden magic. One man expressed his views to me this way:

> If you work hard during the dry season [October to December], when the rains come [May to August] you stay home and eat what you planted. If not, you go hungry.

Some men had the "luxury" of access to garden magic imported from Kilenge or Arawe through kinship and trade connections (noted also in Freedman 1967). One man was said to have magic that made the plants grow big and quickly; another man specialized in keeping wild pigs from eating the plants. Still another man, whose daughter married a Kilenge man, told me that she learned garden magic from the Kilenge, who were famed sorcerers noted for their magical spells (Zelenietz and Grant 1980). When the daughter visited Mandok she performed the spells for him; if not, then "we just plant."

The only strictly enforced taboo with respect to gardening was that a menstruating woman could not go to the gardens. Pregnant women were not barred from the gardens but avoided the bush during pregnancy because of fear of evil beings that inhabit it. Some informants mentioned that sexual intercourse in the gardens was forbidden; a man who had recently had sexual intercourse must not go into the gardens, either (although men followed these customs less strictly than did women). Men's feelings about garden taboos also contrasted greatly with the strictly observed taboos on sex before fishing with the large nets mentioned earlier.

GROWING UP ON THE SEA

Exploitation of the sea was critical to survival in the Vitiaz Strait. Children learned at a very early age to paddle their own canoes, both figuratively and literally. "They grow with the sea" is how one informant expressed it. So that a child got accustomed to being in the canoe, a mother would hold her toddler on her lap as she paddled to a nearby reef. By direct observation the child learned how to paddle. Children were generally free to roam, to fish, and to learn by experience. Young children of about four to six years placed in child-sized canoes in the small harbor off Mandok's main (north) beach. They poled their way along the beach, played at jumping on and off the canoes, and otherwise learned while frolicking in and around the water. I saw unsupervised eight-year-old children exercising their total freedom of movement some two hours of paddling away from Mandok. Children (and anthropologists) also learned reefing skills by accompanying older sisters who were charged with their care or by going out on the reefs with their own peer groups. They learned quickly. I spent many afternoons being humbled by the sharp eyes of pre-adolescents while we searched for different kinds of shellfish on the reefs. Their full baskets always seemed to mock my meager finds.

The sea lay at the center of Mandok's subsistence economy. For them, however, the value of the sea extended beyond "survival," for the sea also had psychological value—both cognitive and affective—in orienting individual Mandok in their culturally constituted behavioral environment. Knowledge of the sea and its resources was also an important criterion for leadership in traditional Mandok culture (see Chapter 6).

Now that we've heard the Mandok creation legend that explained to them how the universe operates and seen the importance of the sea in Mandok cosmology and general worldview, we turn to a discussion of Mandok ideas about personhood. Definitions of personhood obviously lie at the heart of anyone's identity. But what were they on Mandok? This is the topic of the next chapter.

CHAPTER FOUR

Firstborns: The Hereditary Basis of Social and Political Organization

All of your strength goes to your firstborn.

Mandok saying

Mandok social and political systems revolved around a principle of "firstness." The firstborn child was the most important because it was the first issue of a marriage. This importance was illustrated and symbolized in several aspects of Mandok life, including the largest portions of food, the most attention, and the least daily discipline. The birth of a firstborn solidified a marriage contract, harkened a new generation, and ensured a replacement for the social selves of the parents, particularly the father and paternal grandfather in the case of firstborn males.

All first accomplishments of firstborns had to be marked publicly by ceremonial distributions and rituals of varying complexity and fanfare. These ceremonies provided both a major competitive arena for proving "strength" for the father and paternal grandfather and a generational link to the ancestral/spirit world (see Chapter 6; see also Scaletta 1985). Firstborns thus provided the hereditary basis of Mandok social and political systems. The structural importance of firstness, the rules surrounding firstborn behavior, and the symbolism of firstborn ceremonials provide additional insight into Mandok notions of cultural and personal identity.

A "key symbol," in the simplest terms, is one that "summarizes" or "elaborates" core themes in any given culture (Ortner 1973). It is multivocal (literally, "many voiced"; Turner 1967), having many different meanings at the same time. For the Mandok, the firstborn represented above all a key symbol of what it meant to be human.

THOSE WHO CAME FIRST
AND THOSE WHO CAME BEHIND

Mandok kinship and social systems were organized primarily around three attributes: age, generation, and sex. The principle of "firstness" formed the apex of a conceptual pyramid that reckoned relative age and status through consanguineal and classificatory kin. The discussion that follows uses a hypothetical individual called "Ego" from whose perspective the system is being described, in accordance with general anthropological usage.

Within Ego's natal family, siblings were distinguished terminologically by age and sex. The firstborn was the *olman,* "elder." The rest were "those [who came] behind." The terminology for real siblings distinguished older/younger siblings of same/opposite sex with respect to the speaker. The terminology for same-generation kin was extended to include all of the children of Ego's parents' real and classificatory siblings. Thus, all kin included in the same generation were classified as "siblings." In order to find the exact relationship, one could trace back to an original sibling set, as if it were the apex of a pyramid. I call this original set an "apical sibling set."

"Firstness" in subsequent siblings became "relative age." The more precise application of classificatory sibling terms with respect to age was patterned on the original sibling pair to which any given two people traced common ancestry. The relative age principle was most important in determining seniority of any two siblings. For example, consider X and Y, apical siblings who were ancestors of A and B three generations back (see Figure 4.1). If X was older than Y, then X, and all of X's descendents, were senior siblings to Y and to all of Y's descendents, ad infinitum. If A was descended from X and B was descended from Y, then A was the senior classificatory sibling to B, regardless of the actual ages of A and B. This principle repeated itself throughout the kinship system and for all the generations, thereby enabling any individual to determine the proper term to be applied (and the proper behavior to be exhibited) by tracing back to a known relationship.

Relative seniority constituted the template for social relations by patterning the interactions between people in an individual's kin network. An older sibling (male or female) was in a socially superior position to a younger; this hierarchy was especially marked in the case of firstborns, but it was replicated throughout the system. Younger siblings showed deference to older siblings: they could not raise their voices or argue with them in public, and they were admonished never to raise their voices in anger to them. They were forbidden to step over a seated or reclining firstborn's legs (a more general form of respect usually accorded to elders, visitors, Europeans, and other people recognized as "important

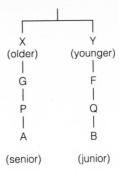

FIGURE 4.1 *Relative age of classificatory siblings.*

people"). They were generally supposed to obey the firstborn and to follow the firstborn's lead, whether on a bush path or in public discussions. They had to do the older's bidding and generally follow the older's lead in important decisions, such as when and how to hold certain feasts, who might or should not go to secondary school, and so on.

Older siblings, on the other hand, were charged generally with "looking out for" younger ones. At the time of my fieldwork, this responsibility often required older siblings who had an education and were employed to bear the burden of school fees for younger siblings. Writ large, the principles of firstness and relative age also organized a loose ranking of different *runai,* of *runai* elders, and of other social relationships such as trade partnerships (see Chapter 5).

The firstborn, whether male or female, was said on Mandok to "have a name." This meant that as the firstborn, the child enjoyed a status apart from the rest of the children of the marriage, receiving during childhood the most attention, the largest portions of food, and the least amount of informal discipline. The value of firstborn children in general was further dramatized by the fact that parents whose firstborn child had died received special mourning names: *kakam* for the mother, *mandaat* for the father.

The firstborn's special status did not come for free; it was "purchased" with a lifetime of investments in feasts and food and wealth distributions that started at birth. In the following sections we will examine some of the Mandok ceremonies, the rationales for these feasts, and how their symbolism illustrates Mandok ideas about being human.

LIFE CYCLE OF A FIRSTBORN

We have already learned that the general term for firstborns was *aidaba,* "head of the tree," deriving from the combined nouns *ai,* "tree" and *daba,* "head." The Mandok considered the firstborn to be the parents' *olya,* "replacement." This was especially important for firstborn sons because they continued the trade network and the canoe-building and carving industries, carrying the designs through the generations.

The commitment to a firstborn child began when its mother realized she was pregnant. From that moment onward, she observed many food and behavioral taboos, with increasing restrictions as the pregnancy progressed. When the time came, the older women of the village came to "help" the new mother deliver. A new mother would not have seen a childbirth, so the women came to "show her the work" of birthing children.[1] These attending women were given tobacco, betel nut, rice, and tea in exchange for their services. A successful first birth was marked publicly with a large distribution of betel nut, provided usually by the child's paternal grandfather.

In Mandok belief, biology might make a baby, but society made it human. Once the baby seemed viable, the process of creating a social person began. The life cycle of a firstborn illustrates the breadth and depth of this commitment.

A Named Being

The firstborn was usually named by its paternal grandfather, either after *his* father (or sister, in the case of a female child), or perhaps his firstborn sibling (if the grandfather was not a firstborn). Although there was no special naming ceremony, certain names were specifically designated to be "firstborn names." Each *runai* had its own list of possible names for males and females. A firstborn son in a long line of leaders would be named for one of his great ancestors, so that he might replace that ancestor's social personality and continue the name in the *runai*. The father/firstborn-son names of one great line of leaders, for example, was Sopol, Naŋas, Sopol, Naŋas. There was an informal rule on Mandok that for any generation of children in an extended family, a group of siblings could use a name only once when naming their children. The children of the firstborn or oldest brother had the first choice of names. These rules alleviated some of the confusion in what amounted to a cyclical naming system within extended families and *runai*s. When doubt existed, patronyms were used, such as *Sopol to Naŋas natu,* "Sopol, Naŋas's son." More recently the addition of Christian names also helped create more precision in names. For example, there might be five men named Kusso but only one named Lewis Kusso.

From the child's point of view, although food and behavioral taboos and food distributions would already have been offered on his/her behalf, receiving a name was the first step to personhood. By receiving a name, the child gained *runai* membership and all the rights and duties that accured therefrom. The name also connected the child consubstantially with its ancestors, for a substantial essence in the name enabled a newborn to share something fundamental with all of its ancestors of the same name (expressed in the notion that the child was an *olya*, "replacement" for the ancestor who previously bore the name). Such naming practices also conveyed a sense that the child inherited some maritime "substance" that made it specifically a Mandok child, as opposed to a child of any other small island, and especially in contrast to a child of bush areas (see Chapter 3 and Pomponio 1990a). Mandok women living in towns were often prevailed upon to travel back to Mandok to give birth on the island, especially for first births, an effort that ensured "the right stuff" for their children. Children whose matrilineal ancestors were from other places might receive a name from that place. Naming in this case linked the child with his/her matrilateral kin and ensured him/her rights in that place. My Mandok brother, Lewis Kusso-Alless, whose mother's mother came from Barim, is an example. The name "Alless," from Barim, connects him with his matrilateral relatives and matrilateral *runai* there.

From Baby to Human

As noted earlier, each first accomplishment of a firstborn was recognized publicly and ceremonially. These celebrations signified a subtle theory of child development as formulated in Siassi. A newborn's inner "self" (*anunu*) was not yet firmly anchored inside its body. Although it adhered to its mother, it also had a tendency to "follow its father," and for this reason both new parents observed many food and behavioral taboos after the birth of a child. A new mother was confined to the house until the postpartum blood flow ceased. After that, she was confined to the immediate area around the house. Although after a few months she could visit relatives across the village, she could not leave Mandok Island. New fathers were prohibited from going fishing in channels and in deep water, nor could they hull out canoes, carve, or chop down trees. Although these taboos applied to all births, they were strictest with the firstborn child. If the child cried inexplicably, the Mandok believed that one of the parents had violated a taboo that caused its *anunu* to leave. A ritual specialist was then called in to "call the baby back" (see Chapter 3).

As the child grew, the Mandok believed that the *anunu* gradually moved from "the surface of the skin" to the inside of the body, a common belief in other areas of Melanesia as well (Panoff 1968; Weiner 1976). The more the child showed evidence of independent action and self-reliance (what Westerners sometimes called "personality"), the more firmly its *anunu* was believed to be situated inside the body. As the child's capacity for learning (*ngar*) increased, the child was said to be "gaining *ngar*." In the Mandok view, each new proof of this process demonstrated the growth of the child's inner strength and personal power as a functioning individual and a decidedly human being.

Each stage of a child's development was viewed as an accomplishment, and each accomplishment was marked with a ceremoney appropriate to that stage. These ceremonies can be divided into (1) those that celebrated bodily decoration, with particular attention to adorning the skin (see Weiner 1976); (2) those that introduced the child to the socio-economic life of the village; and (3) those that formally initiated the child into Mandok ritual and spiritual life and recognized him or her as a moral person, legally bound by the tenets of Mandok custom, ideology, and law. (These categories are not mutually exclusive; they are listed separately for heuristic purposes.) Important aspects of the initiation process for all firstborns emphasize Mandok concepts of child development and the ways in which this development was related to maritime middleman trade. A full listing of Mandok firstborn first-accomplishment ceremonies is provided in Table 4.1.

An Adorned and Social Being

In the first year of its life, the firstborn child was presented with its first set of beads, usually small white shell beads that used to be used as money. Although this was no longer the case at the time of my fieldwork, they retained their value as important wealth objects. The beads were placed around the baby's neck, wrists, and legs. At this time the baby might also be presented with strands of shell beads, a dog's-tooth belt, pig's tusks, or other valuable ornaments obtained through trade. Its skin and hair were painted with red ochre, in designs specific to that child's *runai* and/or family line (see Chapter 5). When the baby was presented with these beads and other body decorations, its parents provided a small food distribution to the village. Until that time the baby remained unadorned (see Table 4.1, items 1–5).

With the presentation of these personal adornments—valuables given by close relatives—the Mandok demonstrated the "personal power" of the child. In fact, these relatives used the child to display their own personal power and "success" in trade, which they were "transferring" to the child. The child's personal power at this stage was limited to and by things "outside the skin," for the valuables adorning him/her were things *given to* rather than *produced by* the child. Their origin was external and they were therefore displayed on the skin (cf. Weiner 1976:121–136 for similar themes).

Once the child became a toddler and the father could afford a pig and other necessary food items, the women of the village performed a ceremony called *sake* (item 7, Table 4.1) at the new mother's house. The ceremony was named after the song they sang to the mother. Both the child and the new mother were ritually washed and decorated in their personal finery, and the mother's hair was cut in a motif resembling a sea urchin or other sea creature. The child was usually painted with red ochre and coconut oil (sometimes baby oil was substituted for coconut oil) and was dressed in new clothing and whatever shell valuables he or she possessed.

TABLE 4.1 *Firstborn first-accomplishment ceremonies.*[a]

NAME/PURPOSE	APPROXIMATE AGE	FOOD DISTRIBUTED	METHOD OF DISTRIBUTION
1. Birth of child[b]	At birth	Betel nut, tobacco	From new grandparents to attending women
2. *Ramoŋ*[b] Father's first fishing trip after birth of child	1–2 weeks	Fish, taro pudding, tea with sugar	*Baliŋwaro* distributes to village, by *runai*
3. *Gemgem*[b] First neck beads/body decoration	3–4 weeks	Taro/manioc pudding	*Baliŋwaro* to village, by *runai*
4. *Monoŋ* Presentation of ceremonial shrubs; shell beads on legs and arms	4–6 weeks	Taro/manioc pudding	*Baliŋwaro* to village, by *runai*
5. *Tipareureu*[c] Dugong or turtle figure constructed in sand; women's and men's mock battle	Infancy	Galip nut	*Baliŋwaro* to village, by *runai*

Table 4.1 (*Continued*)

NAME/PURPOSE	APPROXIMATE AGE	FOOD DISTRIBUTED	METHOD OF DISTRIBUTION
6. *Tiguz ai*[b] "They tie wood"; construction made "to help child stand quickly"	9–12 months	Manioc pudding, rice, tinned meat or fish, tea with sugar	Child's parents to male workers
7. *Sake*[c] *Tikot liva daba*[b] "They cut the woman's hair"; mother and child come down from house and reenter village life	1 year +	Pig[c] Manioc pudding, rice, tea	*Baliŋwaro* to attending women
8. *Pipi/Malo*[b] "Grass skirt/bark cloth"; first clothing	2–4 years	Pig, rice, tea with sugar	*Baliŋwaro* to village, by *runai*
9. *Soŋoŋ*[b] First betel nut chew	4–6 years?	*Sago, coconut solids,* betel nut, tobacco	*Baliŋwaro* to village, house by house
10. Ear/nose piercing[c]	4–6 years?	Pig, taro, rice, tea, betel nut, tobacco	*Baliŋwaro* to village, by *runai*
11. *Tiririu pani*[b] "They wash for/on him/her"; first sea crossing		Pig, rice, tea, betel nut, tobacco	*Baliŋwaro* to village, by *runai*

	Age	Food	Presenter
12. *Gol avo/uasoŋ*[b] "Mouth of the clam/net-fishing"; first canoe trip	5–6 years	Manioc/taro pudding, sea clams, fish, tea with sugar	Parents to village in five groupings
13. *Narogo*[b] First *singsing*	5–8 years	Taro/sweet potato manioc, pig, rice, tea, tobacco, betel nut	*Baliŋwaro* to village, by *runai*
14. *Nalaguŋa*[b] Superincision (boys)		Pig, rice, vegetables, tea, betel nut	*Baliŋwaro* to village, by *runai*
15. *Losiŋ*[b] "Beating"; *Nakamutmut* "beats" child	5–14 years	Pig, taro/sweet potato manioc, rice, tea, betel nut, tobacco	*Baliŋwaro* to village, by *runai*
16. *Ikanlai* Girl's first menses		Manioc pudding	*Baliŋwaro* to village, by *runai*
17. *Bodeŋ*[c] "Painting"		Taro/manioc pudding (?)	*Baliŋwaro* to attendants
18. *Rabuŋ*[c] "First tattoos"		Pig, vegetables, betel, tobacco	*Baliŋwaro* to village, by *runai*
19. *Vaiŋ*[b] Marriage		Extra food presented; more brideprice (boys), more trousseau (girls)	Parents of newlyweds
20. Birth of first child		Extra betel nut, tobacco	Parents to female attendants

TABLE 4.1 (*Continued*)

NAME/PURPOSE	APPROXIMATE AGE	FOOD DISTRIBUTED	METHOD OF DISTRIBUTION
21. Death			
(a) *Aisor* (song of mourning)[b]		Rice, tea	Family of deceased to village and attendants
(b) *Titun pelpel* "They burn the basket"		Pig, rice (after mourning period)	
22. Replacements/Additions[a]			
(a) Baptism[b]			
(b) Communion[b]			
(c) Confirmation[b]			
(d) School graduation[b]			
(e) High-school graduation			
(f) Birthday celebrations			Parents gave food for a party in village square

[a]For a full discussion of patterns of ceremonial distribution, see Pomponio (1983: 208–211).
[b]Witnessed by the author.
[c]No longer practiced by the time of fieldwork.
[d]In these ceremonies, the first three of which were Catholic, the baliŋwaro did not usually distribute food but served as godparent or witness, as appropriate. These services were paid for with carved wooden bowls, clay pots, laplaps, clothing, or money, according to the family's resources.

This ceremony was a "coming out" party for both child and parents. The child was exposed for the first time to people other than close kin, and the parents were freed from food and behavioral taboos. The father moved back home and resumed his fishing, carving, and hunting activities. The mother could once again go where she liked: she could leave Mandok Island to go on fishing or gathering expeditions or she could go to the garden. Most of the women I saw who underwent this ceremony left the instant it was finished (weather permitting) to "go pull"—that is, canoe paddling, with the implication of "going fishing." Their relief was evident in their broad smiles. New mothers also resumed normal eating patterns, which had been carefully monitored during their prenatal and postpartum periods.

By 1979 this ceremony had been altered so that a pig was no longer distributed and *sake* was no longer sung. Attending women were fed manioc pudding, rice, and sugared tea. Most people referred to the abbreviated ceremony with the phrase, *tikot liva daba,* "they cut the woman's hair."

An Economic and Social Being

The next series of ceremonies described here introduced the firstborn into those activities that created a productive member of Mandok society. The child, now usually between four and six years of age, was formally introduced to Mandok socioeconomic activities in two major celebrations concerned with maritime activity: the first canoe trip (item 12, Table 4.1) and the first sea crossing (item 11). The first canoe trip for boys was called *wasoŋ*, meaning the "first net-fishing expedition," or *totoɤoŋ*, the "first canoe poling" expedition, which means the first time the boy hunted dugong. The name *wasoŋ* derives from the verb *-was*, "to net fish." The term *totoɤoŋ* derives from the verb *-toto*, which describes the method of propelling a canoe with a pole, for example, across a reef or through other shallow waters. Dugong are caught on or near the reefs; hence the term for the ceremony. All the men of the village took the boy out and showed him how men catch fish or dugong in the large nets.

For girls, the ceremony was called *gol avo*, which means "mouth of the clam." A firstborn girl was taken out on the reefs by all of the women of the village and shown how to dive for sea clams or how to cull the two important mangrove clams *motak* and *tiwai*, mentioned earlier. When boys or girls returned from this initiatory outing, the entire village came to the beach to greet and pelt them with dried coconut husks. Villagers also splashed them with seawater, and eventually everyone got drenched.

The firstborn child was not permitted to travel indiscriminately. In the past, the child was not permitted to leave Mandok Island. By the time of my fieldwork the range of mobility had expanded a bit to include the immediate areas surrounding Mandok, Por (for school), and perhaps the garden area on Umboi. A firstborn's long-range travel was restricted until it was marked with a pig killing and a large food distribution (item 11, Table 4.1). The first sea crossing celebrated the child's first voyage across the Vitiaz or Dampier straits. At each stop, the father's trade partners organized the ritual for the child; the child's father "paid" for the ceremony with Siassi wooden bowls (traded for pigs; see Chapter 6 for a case description). Traditionally this ceremony marked the child's introduction to his or her father's overseas trade partnerships. It also symbolized the ability to overcome obstacles—in this case, the sea. For this ceremony on Mandok, the women of the opposite moiety from the child's (see Chapter 5) dressed up in ridiculous attire, some of which included their husbands' or brothers' trousers, normally improper attire for women on Mandok. They danced and clowned their way across the village and then doused the child and his or her entire extended family with buckets of seawater. The child's father provided a pig and a good distribution for the entire village.

The child was often too young to participate actively in these ceremonies. The important factor for the Mandok, however, was that through the rituals the child was publicly acknowledged to *have the right* to engage in those subsistence activities that were crucial to Mandok survival: fishing, boating, and trade. The precise timing of particular feasts varied according to the family's resources (especially that of the child's paternal grandfather). The motivation and symbolism of the feasts, however, demonstrate a fairly clear-cut pattern that reflects how Mandok notions of the physical, social, and moral development of an individual were related to the sea and maritime activities.

A Moral and Spiritual Being

After the child's physical and socioeconomic development was validated and officially marked—with rituals of personal adornment and development and with rites celebrating introduction into socioeconomic activities—the next formal stage in the growth of a child pertained to what I call moral/spiritual development (items 13 and 15 in Table 4.1). This next stage requires a brief description and explanation of the *nakamutmut*, masked figures that symbolized many things.[2] Most important for this discussion, they symbolized Mandok apical ancestry and were keystones of Mandok cultural identity.

Nakamutmut were one kind of *mariam* ("spirit"; see Chapter 3). They were named after significant environmental features of their derivative places, most often reefs, mangroves, sand cays, prominent boulders, or other distinctive *maritime* landmarks. Figures could also be named after significant historical events. One figure, for example, commemorated a shipwreck in which Mandok survivors were taken in by

FIGURE 4.2 Nakamutmut *dancing feast.*

Pomio people (south-central New Britain), who helped them to find their way home.

The physical form of the figures was that of a mask, with various plumes and significant decorations, attached to sago fronds (see Figure 4.2). The figure's face was painted white, with black outlines enclosing a long nose, stylized eyes, and a long, red, protruding tongue. The colors, feathers, flowers, and other leaf decorations were unique to each figure, following strict rules of "copyright." Some *nakamutmut* carried a ceremonial wooden sword; others carried rattles or rattan frames as emblems of their power and their identity within Mandok "law" (see Chapter 7 for an expanded discussion of "law"). As the figure danced, characteristically bobbing and weaving in rhythm to the beat of the drums, its fronds swished and swayed, much in the way reef grass undulates with the alternating currents of the sea.

As the figures entered the village plaza from the men's area, women danced up and back again to greet and escort them into the plaza. As they danced, their bobbing made their multicolored grass skirts rise and fall in a wavelike motion. At the height of each motion the plumes flicked, suggesting the bobbing tail of sandpipers as they comb the shoreline for food. Their synchronized waving of croton leaves both indicated reverence to the figures and marked a boundary between them and the dancers.

Rituals involving the *nakamutmut* were part of a feasting cycle that could last for many years. The cycle began at dawn of the day on which a *nakamutmut* was "pulled up." This phrase indicated that it was "pulled up" from the sea, much as canoes were "pulled up" onto a beach. The phrase also implied attraction, in the sense of "pulling *in*." Men "pulled in" trade partners and thus wealth to themselves. In this case, the "father" of the *nakamutmut* "pulled it up" with food and wealth, in the form of a village-wide distribution. As first light turned darkness into shadow, the figure "appeared" on the reef that lay off the village in the direction from which the *nakamutmut*'s roots were traced. For example, *nakamutmut* from Kilenge appeared on the reef off the northeast side of the island; those from Finschhafen or the New Guinea mainland appeared off the southeast or south reefs, and so on. Later in the day the firstborn child of that figure was painted, dressed in his or her feasting regalia, and then presented to the figure and introduced to the dance.[3]

The *nakamutmut* "brought food" to the village through the many feasts given in its honor. Whenever it was "pulled up" or "escorted out," the usual feasting foods of taro (or manioc) pudding, sweet potato, and pork had to be supplemented by *gol suru*, clam chowder. This soup was made from sea clams or from the two mangrove clams, *motak* and *tiwai*. When the cycle ended years later, the *nakamutmut* was escorted "out" in the same direction from which it came. The sago fronds that formed the body of the costume were saved by the feast's sponsor. Later he used them as "good luck charms" to attract fish into his fishnets, in much the same way as the old woman in the Legend of *Las, Naŋur,* and *Sup* instructed fishermen to do with a stone. The catch was then distributed to the whole village. Nonsponsors collected fallen fronds and used them to enhance their own fishing luck. If woven into bracelets and necklaces, they brought the wearer more general blessings.

"Pulling up" a *nakamutmut* implied more than performing a few ceremonies and offering food distributions. Each figure had its own demands and "customs." The "owners" (i.e., the parents and extended family of the child) could be committed to several years of distributions and spontaneous giving. A figure could come to the house at any time and demand "the child's excrement" (i.e., tobacco, tea, and other consumables) for the men's area. The figure could also come out and put a taboo on coconuts (e.g., until feasting season) or demand clam chowder. When the figures were "walking about," it was imperative that the village be completely peaceful. The child's parents had to be in harmony; they should not fight.

Although the *nakamutmut* were sources of ceremonial life, they were also dangerous. Their construction and their mysteries were the exclusive knowledge of men. Women and children were forbidden to see their construction or to touch the figures. During the dance, women averted their eyes. To look "into the mouth" of the figure was to risk death. During these feasts the entire village was "charged" with nervous and sexual energy. Mothers warned their daughters not to look into the "gaping mouth with the protruding tongue." The *nakamutmut* were also the symbolic repositories of traditional Mandok law and custom, as are other masked figures in Melanesia (see Sack 1972; Zelenietz and Grant 1981).

The *nakamutmut* served as constant reminders of the tenets of Mandok substance, morality, and law. The power of the *nakamutmut* was demonstrated dramatically when it ritually "beat" all children in a ceremony called *losiŋ,* "beating," usually referred to in the phrase *nakamutmut ilosi,* "*nakamutmut* beats him/her" (item 15 in Table 4.1). A pig was given in honor of the firstborn in whose name the *nakamutmut* had been "pulled up." The ritual beating was usually the last official ceremony the figure supervised before being escorted out. Latterborn real and classificatory siblings "followed the pig" of the firstborn in whose honor the ceremony was being performed; that is, the ceremony was performed for them along with the firstborn and was paid for with the firstborn's pig.

In most of these ceremonies, the child's paternal relatives provided all the food and wealth objects that were distributed. The actual ceremonies and distributions were performed by a ceremonial exchange partner called a *baliŋwaro* (*baliŋ,* "wealth" and *waro,* "vine" or "vein"). The role of the *baliŋwaro* in distributing wealth is discussed in greater depth in Chapter 6. At this point, note that the *baliŋwaro* was a member of the child's matrilateral extended kindred, usually classified as a "mother's brother."

FIGURE 4.3 Baliŋwaro *protects child as* nakamutmut *strikes.*

When the *nakamutmut* was to "beat" a child, a male *baliŋwaro* held the child while the figure slapped him/her with a switch made of croton leaves (Figure 4.3). Just before the blow, the *baliŋwaro* swung around and took the beating for the child. This ceremony reinforced the safety of the child in the hands of the *baliŋwaro*. He represented the importance of matrilateral kin and also symbolized Mandok writ large in the face of external dangers. If the firstborn was a troublesome child, the *baliŋwaro* turned more slowly, or not at all, to let him/her know that transgressors of the law stood alone to be punished. For girls, the ceremony ended when the *nakamutmut* returned to the men's area.

For a boy who had come of age (14–18), the ceremony was just beginning. The *nakamutmut* swept him up and carried him into the men's area, where he learned that the *nakamutmut* was really a masked figure with another of his *baliŋwaro* inside. He was initiated into the men's area, where both a taboo was lifted and secrets were revealed (cf. Fortes 1974). He was instructed formally in men's sacred knowledge and was "given the law" (*tutaŋ*). Thereafter he was publicly recognized as a man, and as a result he was expected to be more serious in life, to be responsible, and to begin his own garden, carving, and other activities in preparation for marriage and adult life.

The final ceremony for a firstborn was performed upon his/her death and had two parts (item 21, Table 4.1). In the first part, called *aisor* ("song of mourning"), the men of the village, particularly the elders, sat on the ground facing the deceased's house and chanted this mourning song all night. Women joined in later in the night, in a keening style characteristic of Siassi women's singing. Women also cooked food for all who kept the vigil over the deceased. A pig might be killed for the men who built the coffin and dug the grave. A year or so later, to end the official period of mourning, the man's sons (or parents, in the case of a young or middle-aged man) "burned his [betel nut] basket" in a ceremony called *titun pelpel*, "they burn the basket." At this ceremony a pig and other foods were also distributed, but by the family of the deceased, not by the *baliŋwaro*.

Aisor was most often performed only for firstborns. In special cases it was sung for other important people or for people who died under peculiar or auspicious circumstances. The ceremony officially bid farewell to the person and recognized a significant loss to the community.

A bereaved firstborn became a focal point of the mourning process. Though everyone mourned a family death, younger siblings observed a shorter period of mourning than did the firstborn and the parents. The latterborns took over the details of daily life while the firstborn "mourned for all." In the case of a lost sibling, a firstborn took a special "mourning name"; outside the village a firstborn was also referred to by another term meaning "firstborn who has lost a sibling of the same/opposite sex." The special name further underscored the logic of the sibling terminology discussed previously.

"PERSONS" PAR EXCELLENCE

Personhood among the Mandok was not a status ascribed as a consequence of birth, but rather an achievement that required the contributions of many people, both kin and nonkin, throughout a lifetime and even through death. The firstborn child was explicitly viewed as a trailblazer, literally and figuratively, for subsequent siblings (cf. Fortes 1974:94). As such he or she had to be "shown how" to be a person in Mandok terms. As we have seen, each first major accomplishment was publicly celebrated in the form of feasting cycles and food distributions.

Two ideas inherent in this conceptualization of personhood played a major role in Mandok cultural identity and in their subsequent experiences with development. First is the concept of limited good (cf. Foster 1965), which is widespread in Melanesia (see, for example, selections in Jorgensen 1983 and Miegs 1984). In this concept, children shared the "substance"—generally expressed as a combination of blood, food, and work (discussed in depth in Chapter 3)—of their parents and other kin. Also involved is the notion that parents, who transmitted their own internal substance(s) to the child (in the form of semen, menstrual blood, milk, and so on) did so to their own eventual detriment. The Mandok maintained that since firstborns had the first access to the intact "substance" of new parents, firstborns had more of this important sustenance of life than the other children.

The second important idea is that personhood was not a given at birth, but rather was achieved through a transfer of "substances" from kin to the child (in this case, a firstborn). The ideological emphasis on patrilineality favored the notion that children "belonged to" the *runai* and the extended patrilineal kindred, a notion that was dramatized in firstborn ceremonials. Maternal kin, however, could moderate these claims by also contributing wealth to be distributed at these ceremonies.[4] As was the case in Kaliai, West New Britain, Mandok maternal kin could "reverse the distribution of goods, giving in their own name to the father's kin" (Counts and Counts 1983:47). Moreover, if the child's mother was from a powerful family, the family could "mitigate claims of the father's group by putting forth their own" (1983:47). In 1989 my Mandok father sponsored a huge *Sia* dancing feast for his grandchildren and his one great-granddaughter. Some of these children, especially the great-granddaughter, were children of his daughters and granddaughters.

The transubstantial nature of Mandok personhood meant that firstborns (and others) could be "created" through adoption (see Chapter 5). Beliefs and customs surrounding adoption offer a clear contrast with Western concepts of personhood; for the Mandok, the important "substance" was not contained only in blood or semen, but also in food, work (i.e., caretaking), and important knowledge (including sacred knowledge). By feeding and caring for a child, the "substance" of the adult could be transferred to the child. In this context "substance" does not mean biogenetic material but rather refers to the fruits of human effort, close association, and enduring solidarity. This is part of the reason why knowledge is included in the list of "substances." Important knowledge was not defined in abstract terms but rather as concrete personal property. Capacity for knowledge was partly inherited and partly created, as the discussions below and in Chapters 5 and 6 illustrate.

A complete human person in Mandok terms was the product of many generations of transubstantial intercourse with human and other-than-human persons in the Mandok's culturally constituted behavioral environment. The role of the masked figures in the creation of a moral and spiritual person provided tangible and symbolic proof of the Mandok's continuity in and revitalization of their existence. This existence, by definition, was grounded in the sea. By undergoing these important ceremonies, the firstborn was not just a trailblazer for younger siblings (cf. Fortes 1974): he/she symbolically represented the continuation of the essential life forces that sustained life for the entire community. The precise timing of particular feasts varied according to the resources available to the child's father (or, more precisely, to the child's grandfather). The Mandok's motivating ideology, however, demonstrated a fairly clear-cut pattern that articulated Mandok notions of a person's physical, social, and moral development with the sea and maritime activities.

Firstborns who had been fêted properly were treated with more respect than firstborns who had not, and they had more privileges than latterborns. The Mandok summarized this state of affairs in the expression *saveŋ isob, pa tagan ngai toni wa*, meaning "Finish the talk, for we already ate [the child's] pig." Finally, in death, as in life, the firstborn as a person was set apart from other mortals and was shown the respect and reverence of the entire community. The community experienced a greater loss in a firstborn's death than in the death of latterborns, for more had been invested all along.

TRADITIONAL LEADERS: "THE RIGHT STUFF"

> The Great *Maron* ["traditional leader"] is in Heaven. The village *maron* was his "second-in-command."
>
> *Mandok and Aromot elders*

Beliefs about firstborns had important consequences for the Mandok's political system. Traditionally there were two overall leaders of Mandok: one in charge of the village as a whole and one overseer of the *pulat* ("men's area"). The first three *runai* to settle Mandok were *Mandog Sala*, *Simban*, and *Pandan Puɤu*. *Mandog Sala* members considered themselves to be the "founders" of Mandok and therefore enjoyed an elevated status vis-à-vis the other *runai*. *Tavov Puɤu*, derived from *Mandog Sala*, produced the village leaders, and *Mandog Sala* produced "the police."

The village leader, the *maron*, led the other elders in debates and in decision making. A *maron* was a peacemaker—a leader in the sense of seeing through conflict and finding peaceful solutions. Because he was a man of insight and wisdom (*ngar*) whose presence was felt and whose judgments were sought and respected, he was considered a spiritual guide. *Maron*s were also noted for their generosity. They had plenty and gave generously to those who did not. Having "plenty" was the only way in which a *maron* was distinguished economically from others. The notion of generosity was extended metaphorically to other people in the phrase *lolo [to] maron*, "he/she [has the] inside [of a] *maron*." Stingy people, in contrast, were called *lolo mbuza*, "rotting insides." The Catholic missionary translated "God" into the local language as *maron tiina*, "the great leader, peacemaker."[5]

The *maron*ship was hereditary; primogeniture ensured a genealogical pool of possible contenders (cf. Chowning 1979).[6] If there was no son, or if the firstborn was judged to lack the right temperament, other measures could be taken to ensure a successor (for example, adoption; see Chapter 5).

But adoption was not the only alternative for producing an heir. For example, some *marons* had firstborn daughters who could produce successors. Such women were called *(n)garawaat tidi*, a polysemous phrase that on Mandok meant either the daughter or the wife of the *maron*. On other islands it referred only to the firstborn daughter. The phrase combines a compound noun with an adjectival noun: *(n)garawaat* is composed of *(n)gar* ("wisdom," or "knowledge"); *-a* (third-person singular, inalienable possession marker); *waat* or *wat*, which could be an honorific applied to elders and ancestors, or a superlative, similar to the "-est" suffix in English; and *tidi*, which means "woman" or "women" as in the phrase "Mandok woman." In this case, glossing the concept into English gives us a "revered [because she is] /wisest/most knowledgeable-as-an-inherent-part-of-her-person woman." Understanding this label is important because it tells us descriptively why this woman could give birth to a *maron*: she was one herself. But because leadership on Mandok was always in the hands of men, she could not become a *maron*. The *maron*ship could, however, legitimately pass *through* her to her firstborn son, should he display the proper personality traits.

This is not to say that *(n)garawaat tidi* were without power. They had considerable power and influence, according to the islanders. Their power was not formal, but these women could (and did) participate in public debates. Most women did not. In this case, however, the *(n)garawaat tidi* was a "middleman" herself (Pomponio n.d.): she provided the bridge to leadership that "kept the line true."

A case from Aromot and Mandok history illustrates the possibilities. At the time of the political split that caused the settlement of Mandok (see Chapter 1), the *maron* for Aromot was Namu, from *Mandog Sila* (this *runai* was later renamed *Tavov Puʁu*). Namu married Abiaŋ (from *Pandan Puʁu?*). They had two daughters but no sons (see Figure 4.4). Their firstborn daughter, Apes, married Guau, a contender for the *maron*ship from *Mandog Sala runai* on Mandok, but at that time the *Mandog Sala* candidates were judged unfit to lead. Apes's son Sopol, although born into *Mandog Sala*, was groomed by *Tavov Puʁu* elders to become the *maron* on Mandok because through his matrilineage he had rights to *Tavov Puʁu*. As a firstborn in the *maron*'s extended family, he was eligible to be groomed to become *maron*. (This case has an additional twist to it. Later on, Sopol switched *runai* and "ate with" *Pandan Puʁu*. Today, his descendents still "eat there.")

The second example of flexibility in the *maron* system is the custom of *ndaab*, another polysemous term, which roughly means "wealth distributed at death." A related term could also be used to mean "seduction" or "enticement" (e.g., of a man's wife or of a *bigman*'s supporters). Mandok notions of personal power extended into an individual's creations. Thus, objects produced or owned by a powerful person were imbued with some of his or her power. When a *bigman* died, he was

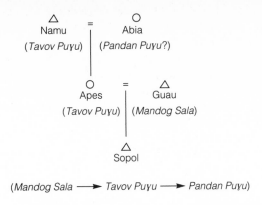

FIGURE 4.4 *Succession of* maronship *of Aromot/Mandok, ca. 1700.*

usually buried with his pig's tusks and other important objects of personal adornment. The rest of his worldly possessions were distributed through his kinship and trading relations as *ndaab*. When these possessions ran out, lesserborn individuals might be given as *ndaab*. These people became workers for the elders who claimed them. Alternately, castaways and refugees could be given asylum by a *maron*. A castaway could be adopted and become a full-fledged member of the *maron*'s family, with all the attendant privileges of that identity. Such a person was also called *ndaab*. Thus the term implied an outsider who was taken in for one reason or another. Although I cannot prove this, I suspect that Mala set the precedent for *ndaab* when he was invited by the elders to stay in Gom in Episode II of the Namor legend (see Chapter 2).

As Namu aged, he had no heirs on Aromot. One day, a man and two other people "drifted" from Umboi to Aromot on a raft made of coconuts lashed together. The man's name was Aluŋa. Namu "took him as *ndaab*" from someone at Marandige (now Marle). He later adopted him and gave him a name from his *runai*. The drifter was renamed Marimbu, after Namu's father. By doing this Namu "stole" another man's follower and created a male heir who could "replace" his father's identity (and social personality). The new Marimbu succeeded Namu and became the *maron* of Aromot.

As the example with Apes and Sopol shows, there has been in Mandok history a certain juggling and alternation between *Mandog Sala* and *Tavov Puɣu runais* for the position of *maron*. Generally, however, *Mandog Sala* were said to "police" Mandok and the *pulat* (men's area). More accurately, perhaps, they policed Mandok *via* the *pulat*. All the small islanders were adamant that the *maron* be a man of peace: "he could not have blood on his hands. He spoke, and people listened." Conversely, those with "dirty hands" could not be *maron*. The *maron* system declined after European colonial governments introduced a new system (see Chapter 7). As will become clear in subsequent chapters, however, its legacy remains.

The next rung of leaders included the seven *runai* elders, or *(d)olman to runai*. Ideally these positions also were held by firstborn sons, but the same kinds of juggling were sometimes necessary to fill a position. *Runai* elders made important decisions that affected the group, for they were the acknowledged repositories of certain forms of *runai* knowledge. For instance, they were the authorities consulted on matters of genealogical information and for their knowledge of certain spells and activities of *runai*-specific *mariam* ("spirits"; see Chapter 3). They were regulators of carving designs and served as the general spokesmen for *runai* members. Before European contact they organized and directed overseas trading expeditions. After the Australian colonial administration banned overseas sailing, the elder of each *runai* continued to organize and distribute food to the members of his group during ceremonial distributions.

Logicians speak of necessary and sufficient conditions in determining whether a statement is true or false. We can apply this same test to leadership and status in the Siassi status mobility system. Heredity was a necessary, but not a sufficient, condition for leadership; the rest depended on individual achievement. If a firstborn in line to be a *runai* elder or *maron* was not capable, he did not lead; he was passed over for perhaps a firstborn of a father's brother or of a father's sister. Heredity, moreover, could be created. In addition to a principle of firstness, the Mandok's social organization revolved around middleman trade. This is the subject of the next chapter.

CHAPTER FIVE

🐚 Casting the Fishnet: Social Relations Among Middlemen

Trade makes brothers. Once you sit down and eat with someone, you can't forget him. Later you part having exchanged and shared something. So once in a while you send him things, and he sends you things. If you give him something and he has nothing to give you in return, he has a debt. Later he repays it.

John Aibung, November 1979

Much of Mandok social and political process revolved around a struggle to balance heredity and achievement. This struggle came to the forefront when the Mandok tried to initiate their own development projects (discussed in Chapter 9). In order to understand the political processes at work in these enterprises and why these projects eventually failed, one must understand the significant social groupings and social process on Mandok.

The Mandok adapted to their windy maritime environment by maintaining social and economic relationships throughout the Vitiaz and Dampier straits. Along with Aromot, Mandok was a commercial hub in the precontact economic system that connected New Guinea with New Britain. Like firstborns in the previous chapter, middleman trade was a key symbol that organized, summarized, and elaborated the Siassi Island social system around long-term investments in people. Clearly, the goods acquired through trade were important in and of themselves. In the long run, however, they were at least as important for the social relationships they helped to create and maintain (see also Munn 1986), for such relationships were investments against future exchanges and relationships. This chapter characterizes important social relationships on Mandok as investments in trade.

KINSHIP AND SIGNIFICANT SOCIAL GROUPS

The Mandok reckoned kinship in a number of ways, but, most fundamentally, kinspeople shared blood, food, and work. This sharing was underscored by the additional recognition of a common "place." "Place" could have several referents. Common site of apical ancestry, common genealogical origin, and some things as immediate as the working household were common "places." Using these guiding premises about who kinspeople are and what they do, the Mandok manipulated their kinship terminology to include any and all potential contributors to the running of a household and to the establishment and maintenance of renown.

Throughout the Siassi region the village was the largest group to which people claimed common ties and ethnic identity. Especially on the small islands, each village was separated by geographic and ethnic boundaries (see Chapter 1 and Freedman 1970). Within a village, individual Mandok were members of different kinds of groups, including the *runai*, extended kin groups, the household (also described by Freedman 1967, 1970), and the *lain* (TP for "line," any categorical grouping of people based on various criteria). Our discussion here focuses on the rules for recruitment into these groups.

The Runai

Mandok village was subdivided into named, exogamous components called *runai*, which were nominally patrilineal descent groups that functioned primarily as food- and wealth-distributing units. The *runai* were localized corporate entities: they exchanged brideprice payments; controlled bestowal of personal names, canoe names, and large fishnets; and regulated rights to carving designs for canoes, houses, paddles, drums, and tattoo and body-painting designs. *Runai* did not, however, own garden land. In 1980 there were seven of them.[1]

Runai members traced their genealogies back to the same "place," often to one or more original settlers. In this we see the juncture between sharing "blood" and sharing "place." As already mentioned, the *runai* elder should ideally be a firstborn male. Thus, geographical *runai* foundations can be discovered by tracing the genealogy of the elder of each *runai*.

Runai origins revealed the social significance of "place" in determining and maintaining kinship ties.[2] As noted in Chapter 1, local historians specified that the first immigrants to settle Mandok came from Aromot. At that time, Aromot village was divided into two moieties: one called *Aromot*, the other *Mandoog*. The moiety system in the Siassi small islands was a fluid organizational grouping of related *runai*, and village settlement patterns reflected these groupings. The only discernable, formal function was in the firstborn, first-accomplishment celebration for the "first sea crossing" (see Table 4.1). Apart from this ritual function, moiety divisions served as a kind of shorthand for referring to grouped *runai*. These moiety groupings became important political factions on Mandok in the mid-1970s, during community debates about particular development projects (see Chapter 8).

The important point here is that the first settlers on Mandok (then called *Ove*) constituted a moiety called *Mandoog*, which was divided into three *runai*: *Mandog Sala* ("Upper Mandok"), *Pandan Puɤu* ("Base of the Pandanus Tree"), and *Simban* (possibly named for the southeast region of Umboi, along the Simban River). The original names of these groups are important because they were the groups from which Mandok village leaders, *maron* (see Chapter 4), were chosen. *Mandog Sala runai* was the lead group; in sociological terms, it was a "firstborn" *runai* on Mandok. It later split to form another *runai* called *Mandog Sila* ("Lower Mandok"). That *runai* split again: *Mandog Sila* was renamed *Tavov Puɤu* ("Base of the Callophyllum Tree"), and a new *runai*, *Panu Boga* ("Village Branch"), was established. *Panu Boga* and *Pandan Puɤu* also traced connections to Arop Island. *Taa Puɤu runai* seems to be the result of a separate migration from Kilenge. *Bedbedaŋ* stood alone as a *runai* that evolved through matrilineal ties to Barim (west Umboi). The timing of each group's immigration to Mandok, and the place from which the immigrants came, gave an unofficial ranking of these groups in the village. *Mandog Sala* and *Tavov Puɤu*, originally one *runai*, were said to "own" Mandok because they were the island's founders. These divisions were instrumental in the debates regarding development projects and a political schism within Mandok discussed in Chapter 9.

Though *runai*s were nominally patrilineal, relations through women were also important because they provided connections in virtually every direction of the trade route. Some matrilateral ties were stronger and carried higher status than others. For example, there were very strong ties to Tami Island and Malasiga on the mainland of the Huon Peninsula, to Kilenge and Pililo on New Britain, and to numerous points on Umboi (especially Barim). Ties to Sio, Gitua, and the Rai Coast, however, had declined since the 1960s (cf. Harding 1967). Commercial boats, the introduction of European goods, and trade stores made the Rai Coast less important to the Mandok than it had been before European contact. This was not the case on all the small islands, however. Genealogies of *runai* elders on Malai and Tuam display a different pattern. The people of these islands showed stronger ties to the entire New Guinea coast than did the Mandok or the Aromot. Their respective locations probably had a lot to do with these differences: both Malai and Tuam are closer to the New Guinea coast.

All male members of a *runai* were "brothers," and they shared ties in blood. Although there was no named apical ancestor for the formation of *runai*, members of each could name the first member of their particular group to immigrate to Mandok and where he came from. Thus they also shared common apical ties in "place."

A person belonged at birth to the *runai* of his or her father. Theoretically, upon marriage a woman went to her husband's *runai*, but in practice the rules for *runai* membership were flexible. A man could opt for membership in (or be adopted into) his mother's father's group, and a woman (or her father) could request that her husband come into her *runai*. In these cases, the Mandok said that the man was "pulled into" the new *runai*. It was also possible for an individual to switch *runai*. The Mandok exercised the flexibility of the system with practical adaptations designed to keep the *runai* at roughly equal sizes and to maintain lines of leadership within any particular *runai*.

When I returned to Mandok in 1986, *runai* membership had been reorganized to accommodate the rising population and several new houses built since 1981. Three of the larger groups had split to make three more groups, for a total of ten. People explained the split as a practical means by which ceremonial food distributions, the *runai*'s most visible function, could be accomplished more efficiently. (Feasts or other large food distributions were usually organized according to *runai* membership.) Several distribution combinations were possible, depending on the type of ceremony and the amount and kind of food to be distributed (Pomponio 1983:208–210). When asked "To which *runai* do you belong?" the common Mandok response was, "I eat in (*runai* name)." Group membership was thus expressed as food sharing.

In the past, *runai*s controlled various reefs and mangroves around Mandok, and *runai* members usually traveled together on overseas trading expeditions. Although they did not own garden land in Muru, *runai*s did control village land on Mandok. Houses were arranged into roughly two sets of two to three rows on either side of the *maran*, the central ceremonial plaza and meeting place. Housing ideally followed *runai* membership and *runai* property boundaries. Coincident with the land shortage created by a rising population on only four hectares (ten acres) of land, crosscutting kinship ties gave people rights to the resources of more than one *runai*.

Extended Kin Groups

On Mandok the extended kin group was composed of all of those people to whom any traceable connection, either consanguineal or affinal, could be established. These were kin who were related by real or putative ties in "blood" or through marriage. Such groups extended beyond the *runai* and included matrilateral and affinal kin.

The most explicit rules associated with marriage ruled out certain categories of people. First, people who could claim a common set of "grandparents" within three ascending generations on either side (i.e., "great grandparents") were forbidden to marry (cf. Freedman 1967:250). Second, people could not marry into the *runai* of either parent. The Mandok called these prohibited categories of people *siŋ ee moʁon* ("one blood") or, as appropriate, *runai ee moʁon* ("one *runai*"). "Sister exchange" was common in the past, and during my first fieldwork period it was still claimed by elders to be a preferred arrangement. It was less

probable by then, however, because arranged marriage was being replaced by marriages based on individual choice.

The levirate was practiced before pacification and missionization. Informants stated that if a man should die after paying the brideprice for
his wife, the woman was still considered to "belong to" the husband's
group. The group was charged with taking care of her and her children,
who were born into the man's *runai*. The "brother" category included
classificatory (i.e., *runai*) brothers. The levirate often involved polygyny,
which modern Christian Mandok considered to be sinful. By the 1980s,
a widow might marry a husband's "brother" if he were a widower or
a bachelor, but not if he were a married man. Efforts were made to
preserve the woman's affiliation with her deceased husband's extended
family, especially if she had young children.

The Household

The household was the most basic social unit on Mandok. The preferred
arrangement was for one nuclear family to live in its own house, but
in fact households often included any one of a number of extended
kinspeople as well, especially aged or widowed grandparents. Each
household was defined by a hearth; even if two families shared the same
house, they usually kept separate hearths. In addition to sharing "blood"
(recognized kinship ties) and food, household members usually worked
together in the gardens and often fished together. Members of a
household also shared rights to each other's property, such as canoes,
paddles, poles, fishnets, and so on.

Newly married couples established their own household after an initial period during which residence arrangements were variable. In the
first stage of marriage (betrothal), the groom went to the bride's house
to live. The couple was given a separate part of the house, but they
generally contributed to the bride's household work group. After the
final brideprice was paid, the couple moved in with the husband's family,
or, ideally, into their own house. In any case, the wife theoretically
"followed her husband" to his part of the village, and they both resided
within his *runai*. In actual practice, these rules were flexible, as noted
above, so that the couple might indeed remain with the wife's parents
or acquire rights to construct a house in an area belonging to another
runai.

The Lain

The Mandok also organized members of their nuclear, extended, and
affinal kin groups into differing Ego-based groups, depending upon the
particular project at hand. Freedman (1967:216–220) calls these flexible
groups "assemblages." This serves as an adequate "etic" construct, but

I prefer to follow the Mandok's use of the Tok Pisin term *lain* ("line"). *Lain* is a polysemous term that could mean any categorical grouping of people, whether this grouping was based on recognized bloodlines, age groups, household membership, or political affiliation. A man's *lain* comprised all of those people—"blood" relations, "trade" relations, friends, and political allies—upon whom he could call for help in his enterprises. They constituted what Lawrence (1967) calls his "security circle." The important aspects of a person's *lain* were its fluidity and flexibility.

The marriage rules extended a man's potential social network across other groups (including other communities across the Vitiaz and Dampier straits). An industrious man tried to incorporate into his *lain* as many people as possible, a strategy that reflects the underlying logic of a trading ideology in an environment of limited resources. The object of the system was to create and maintain as many social ties as possible with people who would be obliged to come to the aid of a *bigman* and help in the work for feasts. In short, the way to maximize one's access to scarce resources was to expand one's sources for those resources. Thus the expansion of social ties aided in the process of acquiring resources, which were then recycled back into the village exchange system (see Chapter 6). In this case, the "sources of resources" were people. The more people a *bigman* could attract to him through trade, kin exchanges, and sponsorship, the wider his future resource base. This is partly what Kilibob was doing when he created the *Sia* dancing feast on Arop (Episode I in Chapter 2): he attracted people to come and enticed them to stay by putting them in his debt, which was incurred through the food, personal decorations, houses, and so on, that he "gave" them.

TRADE AND THE CREATION OF KINSHIP

The overseas trade system declined drastically between about 1900 and 1979, especially since the early 1960s. Trade as a "cultural system," however, still framed the Mandok's self-identity and social relations. Kinship helped to form and maintain trade relationships and vice versa. Through time, trade relationships were converted into true kinship ties. The process illustrates Mandok concepts of personal investments in people.

The ideology of kinship could be extended to accommodate those people to whom an individual looked for support and labor in his or her enterprises. The ideal Mandok family contained a balance of males and females. An aspiring *bigman* could manipulate the basic principles of the kinship system (i.e., sharing "substances" of blood and food or sharing work) in order to maximize the number and balance of people in his *lain*. When nature confronted people with a gender mix that was less than optimal, they filled in the holes of an ever-expanding "social fishnet" by cultural means: through trade, marriage, and adoption.[3]

Trade Made Siblings

A common characteristic of small-scale societies is that, within the local group, social relations are predominantly kin relationships. People often express their relationships in the idiom of kinship regardless of actual genealogical connection. Beyond a certain geographic range, "all men are strangers" (de Lepervanche 1973:8). The Mandok expressed these universal social themes for small-scale societies both in the Legend of Namor and in their actual social relationships. For example, we have already seen that throughout the various episodes of the Namor legend, the protagonist disguised himself in order to disarm villagers. Instead of fearing and possibly killing a stranger, the villagers took pity on an old man and offered him food. This was the first step in changing strangers into kin: they shared food. This was partly what Malaka was doing when she offered me my first Mandok meal; it is also the message of the quotation that introduced this chapter.

The recipient of the food incurred a debt. Once strangers shared food and exchanged material items, they were no longer strangers but "trade friends" (*gurubadi*). In time they became "brothers" and shared putative ties in blood. When men were roughly the same age, the initiator became the "elder" sibling to the "younger." If one was much older, father-son terms were used, as Ambogim did with Mala in the Namor legend. The children of these men inherited the trade partnership and continued this classificatory terminology as if they were real siblings.

Trade Made Affines

Trading trips often inspired dancing feasts. The host village fed the Siassi traders, who in a sense "sang for their supper." In addition to their prowess as traders and navigators, Siassi men were famed for their dancing and singing talents. They were also infamous womanizers. In the course of the feasting and revelry, many women had their hearts "stolen," just as Ambogim demonstrated in the Legend of Namor (see Episode III in Chapter 2). These women married Siassi traders and came to live in Siassi.

An individual trader received several benefits by expanding his social network in this way. First, he got a wife. Second, he extended his kin network abroad. Not only did he have a "brother" in trade, he gained affines *through* trade. Third, marriages arranged through trade relations ensured protection in foreign lands (see Harding 1970) and dependable trade partnerships: the trader was now dealing with his "family," not with "strangers." Because his "trade friend" and his new wife might be from different *lains*, he had the opportunity, theoretically at least, to double his trade options abroad.

Fourth, marriage across the trade routes intermingled populations. Just as Mandok men brought in wives from other places in the trade system (notably Kilenge, Tami, Barim, and other points on Umboi and in Siassi), Mandok women married out. Finally, by transforming a trade relation into an affinal one, a man further increased the membership of his *lain.* The birth of his children guaranteed long-standing trade relations. In this manner, and from an individual's perspective, trade often generated kin, which further reinforced trade.

As the trading system deteriorated, the rate of village endogamy increased. A consequence of this change was that by 1980 it was virtually impossible for a Mandok to marry another Mandok without marrying a prohibited relative. The ideological value of marriage through trade persisted, however. By 1987 an entire group of women had married off the island.[4] This persistence reflects the elders' concern about marrying relatives who were too close; it also illustrates the relationships involved in trade (sharing "substance"), in "sister exchange" (sharing "blood"), in maintaining ties in ancestral "bloodlines," and in retaining rights in "place" through the generations.

For example, members of two families who traced their origins to the same place sometimes tried to arrange a marriage between two of their children. This was done to "keep the ["blood"] line true" and to consolidate further the camaraderie of apical ancestral "place." Thus "sister exchange" may not involve exchanging sisters (real or classificatory) at all, and the term *sister* could be extended to include "a woman of the place," as opposed to an in-marrying woman from another place. More likely, "sister exchange" in Siassi meant "child exchange" between "fathers." Men were obviously involved, for they made the arrangements and married the "sisters."

Trade Made Children

A third means of solidifying the transition from strangers to trade brothers and then into a true kin relationship was by adopting a child. People adopted children of either sex, often depending on the sex ratio of their own children. Children adopted through trade were raised as the trader's own. The child then grew up as a Mandok and married on Mandok. This is how my Mandok grandmother originally went to Mandok from Tami Island (Chapter 1). Her children were Mandok children. Through her they also retained rights of blood relations (e.g., to land, to *runai* designs, to names, etc.) on Tami Island. This was how my "father" Aibung learned to carve Tami bowls: he was sent to Tami to learn from his mother's brothers. Similarly, affinal relationships weakened through trade could be reinforced through adoption. If a woman married off the island, she sent at least one of her children back to her natal place, most often to her brother, as her "replacement." Her brother adopted the child and raised it as his own.

Adoption offers perhaps the clearest example of the transactional nature of Mandok social relationships. The use here of the term *adoption* in a general sense refers to "taking as one's own the child of other parents" (Carroll 1970:3). Howard et al. offer a more precise definition:

> We define "adoption" as the establishment of relationship rules appropriate to a specific set of kinsmen between persons not occupying those genealogical positions. (Howard et al. 1970:21)

This definition emphasizes the transactional aspects inherent in adoption as a structural manipulation of different categories of relatedness (Brady 1976).

The Mandok adopted children in a variety of ways, each of which carried different social, structural, and genealogical implications for the adopted child and its adoptive parents and siblings. The Mandok defined two broad categories of adoption. The first, *utuŋ* ("adoption"; *-ut* means "to adopt"), is formal adoption. The second, *paroŋ* ("succor"; *-par* means "to nurture, look after, provide for," etc.), is fosterage, which implies "temporarily taking care of another's child as an obligation of kinship" (Carroll 1970:7).

Results from a survey I conducted in 1981 indicated that over 22 percent of the total population of Mandok had participated in some form of adoption or fosterage (Pomponio 1983:187–189). The data include 81 cases of adopted people and 43 additional cases of parents adopting a child (five of which are included in the first group of adopted children). Of 77 adoption cases for which comprehensive information was obtained, 48 (62.3 percent) were adopted by real, classificatory, or adoptive siblings of one of their birth parents.

Of 79 explanations given for individual adoptions, *utuŋ* was the most popular with 69 (87.3 percent) respondents: 56 (81.2 percent) of these were *utuŋ* proper and 13 (18.8 percent) "in name" (see the next paragraph). Thirteen of the 79 people (16.5 percent) were adopted as firstborns, and 18 (22.8 percent) were adopted for a variety of reasons. By far the biggest reason to adopt was that the adopting parent(s) had no children: 17 (21.5 percent) people were adopted thusly. Thirteen (16.5 percent) were adoptions to create firstborns. Other reasons to adopt a child included evening out the sexes within the nuclear family (11.4 percent), taking in orphaned children (8.9 percent), pulling family lines closer (8.9 percent), replacing a mother given in marriage (7.6 percent), retaining ancestral rights in another place (5.1 percent), and keeping *runai* approximately equal in size (2.5 percent).

There were two subcategories of formal adoption: *utuŋ* proper and *iza* ("his/her/its name"). The most significant changes occurred within the general category of *utuŋ*: in family lines (i.e., recognized bloodlines), in *runai* membership, and in parental rights and duties. Through *utuŋ* the structural position of "firstborn child" was manipulated, creating the potential for twice the number of firstborn feasting cycles any parent normally had to sponsor. Manipulating the definition of "firstborn" maintained agnatic "blood" lines for *runai* and *maron* leadership positions.

When a child was adopted formally, several things happened. Most often the child was adopted as an infant and changed households soon after weaning. Children could even be claimed for adoption before birth. In the past, adopting parents gave the birth parents of the child a pig "to pay for the [mother's] milk" and to acknowledge formally the change in the child's natal family. Though discontinued on Mandok by the time of my fieldwork, this custom was still practiced in other parts of Siassi. One Aupwel man, remarking on the Mandok's discontinuation of the custom, felt that the mothers on Mandok who gave up their children "for nothing" were being shortchanged. Perhaps it was this aspect of formal adoption that led previous patrol officers to describe it as "a black market in children" (Patrol Report Finschhafen 17, 1961–62:11). During my fieldwork, adoptive parents continued to send food—especially fish and vegetables from their own garden—to the child's mother. In Mandok ideology, by feeding the nursing mother with food produced by their labor and by contributing to her breast milk, adoptive parents also fed the child. They transferred their own "substance" to the infant and established their own claims to its parentage (see Counts and Counts 1983 for similar themes in Kaliai, New Britain).

Adoption on Mandok was predominantly an agreement between individuals, not a decision of married couples. In fact, a person did not have to be married to adopt a child. If the adoptive parent was a man, he bestowed upon the child a name from his own *runai*. If the adoptive parent was a single woman, the child became a member of her (i.e., her father's) *runai*. If the woman later left Mandok in marriage, her adoptive child was usually given to one of her brothers to raise, which kept the child within the adoptive family lines and *runai*. The child also claimed the adoptive bloodline, thereby fitting into his/her new nuclear family in the appropriate birth order as if he or she had been borne by the adopting parent(s). If the adopting parent(s) had no children or was not yet married, then the child became a firstborn child and enjoyed all of the privileges and status of firstborn children. Children adopted in this situation had a dual status: they kept their biological birth order within their natal families but achieved a superior sociological birth order in their adoptive families. Legitimate firstborn children were rarely given in adoption.[5]

Adoptive parents provided all the feasts and food distributions necessary for public acknowledgment of the child's "name" (i.e., his or her status; see Chapters 4 and 6). They paid school fees and brideprice and fulfilled all other jural and social obligations of biological parents. Natal parents were free to contribute to any and all of these events, and they did. In many cases the child was not alienated from its natal parents but instead acquired an additional set. Once grown, an adopted child had multiple sets of primary parents who had claims to any surplus goods, money, and so on, that he or she might have. This situation became especially demanding for adopted children who later grew up and secured jobs in town. Such workers had multiple parental and sibling obligations that siphoned off their earnings.

The second type of formal adoption, *iza*, was similar to *utuŋ* in its jural and sociostructural aspects but did not necessarily entail changing households. I consider it to be in fact a subcategory of *utuŋ*. In discussing this form of adoption, Mandok say *tiwat iza moɤon*, "they call(ed) the name only." In this case, adopted children assumed (and thus *continued*) *runai* or family names but did not change households. A man who belonged to a *runai* that was dying out, for example, could adopt "in name" a male child to keep the *runai* going. A child so adopted took on the appropriate names, having been "adopted in name" as a newborn. A child could also receive a name from his natal *runai* or from his mother's father's *runai*, again without changing households.

Mandok kinship terminology merged "father" and "father's brother." If the adoptive parent was a father's brother, there was no great change in terminology or familial obligations. By both staying in its natal family and becoming a member of the adoptive family (and *runai*), the child retained rights of consanguinity in his (or her) natal family line and also gained rights and privileges in the *runai* lines of the adoptive family. As one man expressed it,

> if you adopt from a close brother [i.e., a true sibling], then it doesn't matter—they keep the smell of the line and later they know whom they belong to. But if you adopt from "a little way out," then you take them into your house so they lose the smell of their parents and they take on your smell. Otherwise when they grow up they won't know where they belong [i.e., where their obligations lie].

"Smell" here is an expression of "substance." The important point for the Mandok was that the child be incorporated into the family and become a productive member of the household. If the child were adopted from a close sibling of his/her parents, then the child would automatically be included as a member of the *lain* and would be assumed to be a dependable ally in household projects. The child was already recognized as being a "primary" kinsperson by virtue of sharing close kinship ties and food. If the adoption was between classificatory siblings with more tenuous "blood" ties, however, the child was physically brought into the adoptive household to become a true member of that family by sharing food and work and by gaining knowledge from the adoptive parents. The adoption provided additional incentive and obligation to contribute to work projects in the adoptive household.

The Mandok adopted most frequently within extended family and trade networks. Adoption thus "tightened" the bonds between lines that were already connected. Siblings through adoption might already have been classified as siblings, but through adoption they became "true" siblings (in a nuclear family). The parents involved in an adoption exchange thus filled in the holes in the "fishnet" of each other's kin network. An additional tightening of the lines could occur in the next generation, when an adopted sibling either took in a child from or offered a child to another adoptive sibling.

An adult who was adopted could also increase his or her kin network and strengthen ties with both his or her natal and adoptive extended families by adopting children from both groups. Classificatory siblings who thought that their family lines were growing too far apart sometimes "swapped" children, either in name or in fact (i.e., actually changing households). In other cases, an older parent might adopt a small child on behalf of his or her own (usually unmarried) child. This investment ensured for the future the presence of a worker for that person's household and enterprises. Adoption was also used as a lever into the village by outsiders. Teachers, for instance, might adopt or foster a Mandok child in order to integrate more personally with villagers and village life on Mandok.

Thus, adoption in its various forms served a variety of purposes on Mandok. Each implied various degrees of "blood" ties, *runai* affiliation, and name distributions. The predominance of adopting from a pre-established kin group (especially between real or classificatory siblings) ensured that the adopted child would be well taken care of. Adoption also had wider social functions. Illegitimate children were legitimized, orphaned children were absorbed into families, and marriages of a questionable nature or with inadequate brideprice payment could be righted by sending a child back to the woman's natal group. Similarly, the loss of a woman given in marriage was often compensated for with the return of a child in adoption. Just as trade made kin, kin made trade by expanding opportunities for marriage, adoption, and their resulting exchanges.

PEOPLE AS WEALTH

Up to this point, we have viewed the Mandok's social system as a system of investments among people who were related through kinship or trade. There was traditionally another way that people became a member of an island community: sponsorship of outsiders. Sponsorship could be the result of warfare, famine, plague, politics, an earthquake, or a death— any extraordinary circumstance that forced people to move.

The settlement of Mandok Island by wanderers, drifters, and mavericks (see Chapter 1) was typical of settlement throughout the Siassi region. If a drifter came ashore, the *maron* could grant him (and whomever was with him) asylum. Mala set the precedent for this custom in Episode II of the Namor legend (Chapter 2), when the village elders invited him to stay with them instead of killing him for violating their wives. People sponsored in this way became supporters of the headman and members of his large *lain*. They were also free, however, to establish themselves as leaders in their own right. Aluŋa from Marandige became Marimbu of Aromot and ascended to the *maron*ship of Aromot through Namu's sponsorship (see Chapter 4). The next chapter pursues these points in greater depth.

Each kind of manipulation—sponsoring refugees or acquiring trade partners, wives, or children—constituted a long-term investment in human capital. Each implied a future return of goods, people, and food, which continued the system. These manipulations served, in turn, to counteract or underscore hereditary givens (as, for example, in the case of adopting a firstborn). But there were limits to the manipulability of the system. The next chapters describe some of these limits.

CHAPTER SIX

Routes to "Success," Paths to Renown

A *bigman* gives many pigs.
A strong man knows many things. People respect him.
He talks, people listen [i.e., obey/follow his advice].
A *bigman* is generous. He gives many feasts and
distributes a lot of food. Then the whole village
eats, dances, and we are all happy.

Mandok children from composite grades 4 and 5, 1980

To be strong you have to work hard. You must have a big garden, plenty of trade partners; you must carve canoes, bowls, and have other wealth objects [*baliŋ*] to trade. So you give them your crafts, and they give you things. They give you pigs. Then you must hold big dancing feasts and give generously. You must not scrimp—you must give everything you can. You see all the people who hang around my house? They are hungry. They know I have plenty of food, so they come to me. They come and I feed them. That is all.

A Mandok bigman, 1980

In order to understand what happened to transform the Mandok's reputation for success into a cycle of frustration and failure, we must understand several things about their traditional system. First, what made the Mandok achieve? Second, what were the traditional arenas of achievement and definitions of success? Third, what were the desired qualities of Mandok leaders? Finally, what was the nature of the status mobility system, and how did it compare with that offered through "development"? These are the questions this chapter addresses.

Anthropologists and psychologists have long recognized a relationship between the dominant subsistence activity of a society and the personality attributes of its leaders.[1] Traditional systems often have been major factors influencing economic growth in the contemporary world. Development and modernization entail what LeVine calls a "psychological factor." Specifically, he refers to an acquired drive for excellence or need to achieve. An individual's need for achievement is patterned by the society's traditional social mobility system (LeVine 1966). LeVine defines need for achievement as an affective concern about, or preoccupation with:

> doing well in relation to achievement goals, unique accomplishment, long-term commitment to the attainment of such goals, instrumental acts directed toward their attainment, obstacles to be overcome, and prospects of success or failure. (LeVine 1966:12)[2]

A concern with achievement in this sense is a distinctively Western preoccupation. In order to understand and analyze non-Western people's achievement patterns, we must add to LeVine's theory the *culturally defined nature of achievement* and the *direction of goals*. The Mandok's subsistence economy differed from that of many Melanesian societies in its minimal horticulture and pig husbandry. Traditional patterns of leadership revolved around middleman trade and maritime fishing/gathering. It was in these matters that outside agencies went awry in their plans for and assessments of the Mandok.

The two-masted canoe made life possible for the small islanders by enabling them to expand their exploitable environment beyond the limits of Siassi, as we have already seen. The wealth they obtained abroad also supported their status mobility system. The Mandok subsidized their subsistence economy by trading for vegetable staples rather than growing them themselves. By contacting other cultures they also obtained other valuable forms of knowledge and customs that were not indigenous to the small islands, including various forms of magic; varieties of crops; carving, house, canoe, and *nakamutmut* designs; personal names; songs; entire dancing feasts; initiation rituals; and the Tami bowl-carving tradition. They wove these things into their own culture to create a pattern that was nonetheless distinctly their own. This chapter examines this cultural pattern by elucidating significant Mandok categories of achievement and traditional paths to leadership and renown. It also includes a synthesis of these different but related concepts into a general theory of "success."

CATEGORIES OF DISTINCTION

Achievement on Mandok was expressed in terms of "work," "wisdom," (*ngar*; see Chapter 3), and "strength." In Mutu, the familiar Melanesian *bigman* was called *ngeu tiina*, "big man," or *ngeu ariaŋa*, "strong man." A "strong man" had many trade connections through which he obtained the goods necessary to give feasts. In order to reach foreign shores for trading purposes, he had to be an efficient sailor and navigator. Men who were renowned sailors and good navigators were therefore highly regarded. Along with maritime knowlege, such a man would also possess magical incantations to control the weather, wind, and seas, and, in some cases, the sorcery by which to control or destroy his rivals.

The Mandok never had enough land for large-scale gardening or the space or vegetable resources for large-scale pig husbandry (see also Freedman 1967). Nevertheless, the traditional idea of a success in Mandok terms was someone who killed many pigs, distributed valuables (shells, pigs' tusks, wooden bowls, clay pots, and so on), and distributed manioc or taro pudding, the ceremonial vegetable accompaniment to pork. Such a man might be described literally as *ngeu to ingalngal ngai ve poroŋ*, "a man who spears pigs and [gives] taro or manioc pudding." This is an idiomatic expression. In fact, a Siassi *bigman gave* pigs; someone else killed and butchered them and distributed the pork on his behalf. Because it would weaken his power, a *bigman* "never got blood on his hands"; that was something a lesser man did. The opposite of a *bigman* was a *ngeu sorok*, a "nothing man" (TP, *rabisman*, "rubbish man").

The traditional Mandok "strong man" also strove to become a *ngeu to mos*, an "artisan." The term *mos* means "craft," "design," or "complex creation." A "man of complex creation" was a master craftsman, specifically a master carver or canoe builder. Artisans were respected for their works but not necessarily for their leadership. They were valued because they produced the major material objects of trade. In addition, they were revered because through them, the traditions of the ancestors were passed down and thus continued. When planning a marriage contract, families considered which potential affines were *mosa*, "artisans." From the perspective of a potential bride's family, marrying into a family of artisans ensured a large brideprice, which augmented her family's wealth. A marriage involving a *mos* on either side held the promise of future wealth in formal and informal exchanges, especially for firstborn ceremonials (see Chapter 4).

Beyond these particular skills there were several attributes of leaders on Mandok, each with subtle refinements. The attribute most central to our discussion is inherent in calling a man a *ngeu to ngar*, a "man of knowledge or wisdom." The concept of *ngar* included the notions of knowledge (both as a general category and as a specific body of information), morality, and law. As discussed in Chapter 3, the capacity for *ngar* separated humans from animals. It was believed to be a function of hearing. If one did not hear, one could not listen or understand; therefore, one could not learn. A "man of wisdom" was a man who knew the proper customs, important oral histories (*kamos*), and genealogies. He said the proper thing at the right time and generally displayed good judgment. To say of someone that he was a *ngeu to ngar* (or that she was a *liva to ngar*, "woman of knowledge") was a great compliment. To say the converse was an insult. To be a truly "strong man," and especially a *maron* (see Chapter 4), a man had to be a *ngeu to ngar*.

The term *ngar* carried the weight of traditional knowledge preserved through time in the memories, carvings, designs, and ceremonials of respected elders, and it involved the wisdom to observe properly the customs set forth by Mandok predecessors. A "man of knowledge" was a man of insight who could see through contradictions and problems to reach clear solutions. He was a good speaker and probably multilingual. He was a man of controlled and productive action. It was therefore possible for a child to do well in school and learn many "things" (i.e., "European things") yet still be classified as *ngar mao* ("no wisdom"). Conversely, a child could do poorly in school yet behave well, listen and obey his or her elders, and do the proper things at the proper times to the appropriate kin relations, and still be referred to by the positive appellation.

On Mandok, *ngar* was described as something that grew with the body, as is the case in other Melanesian cultures (Panoff 1968; Strathern and Strathern 1971). As a child developed and learned more about the environment and proper behavior, so did its *ngar* grow inside the body. People berated misbehaving children with the criticism "*le ngar mao*," "he/she/it has no *ngar*," which implied that the transgressor was poorly raised and had no sense of right and wrong.

"Men of knowledge" were thus usually elders. As we have already seen, the term for "elder" is *olman* (see Chapter 4), a polysemous term used to define relative age between two siblings (real or classificatory) or between any people of different ages in the kinship system. In a wider sense *olman* was applied to the general category of *bigman*, though its more precise meaning referred to the village elders (*dolman*, pl.). The term designated people with decision-making authority: village leaders, the powerful men who controlled much of what happened on Mandok. This kind of authority came with age. Thus, the term was also a general term of respect used to designate the heads of prominent families as a group.

A traditional *bigman* would combine as many elements as possible to produce many forms of wealth and enhance his renown. A particularly ambitious man who had many talents and who was also well-respected for his knowledge and social/political ties was called a *gorgoor* (also pronounced *ngorngoor*). This term derives from the verb *-ngor*, "to chop," as in "to chop [down] a tree" or to manufacture (chop down, hull out) canoes. To call a man a *(n)gorgoor* carried the sense of a "Renaissance man," one who knew and did a wide variety of valued things well. A particularly aggressive trader and active feast-giver might be called a *ngeu ee moron*, a "one of a kind." Middleman trade in the Vitiaz trade system entailed a style of entrepreneurship that required creative abilities, mental shrewdness, knowledge concerning economic investment/return ratios, multilingualism, and manipulation of social relationships. A *bigman* had to use his talents and so demonstrate his power continually.

PUBLIC DEMONSTRATIONS OF STRENGTH

Apart from leadership positions, there were several occasions on which a man publicly demonstrated his strength. The most important included competitive feasts, firstborn ceremonies, and brideprice payments. Brideprice payments were paraded ceremonially through the center of the village on the heads of the prospective groom's female kin. The accumulation of the necessary wooden bowls, clay pots, clothing, and money provided an additional example of the interdependency of the extended kin group. The following discussion focuses on the different forms of firstborn and competitive feasts.

"Raising the Name" of Those Who "Had a Name"

As described in Chapter 4, the firstborn child, whether male or female, "had a name." The phrase indicates high status. Before pacification and missionization, the Mandok traded for all their vegetables. Food was scarce, so the population was kept low. Genealogies and mission records support this claim. People told me that many men delayed marriage and that having children was the prerogative of *bigmen*. When a man finally did marry and have children, his entire extended family (*ditaa pida*; TP, *lain*) shared the responsibility for the feasts for his firstborn child.

Firstborn ceremonials formed the backbone of the Mandok's status mobility system. The relative extravagance of the feasts marked the respect and privileges the child would later enjoy in the community (Bamler, cited in Chinnery, n.d.:43–44). More accurately, the respect and privileges also extended to the child's father and paternal or maternal grandfather, depending on who actually sponsored the feasts (see also Harding 1967:156). The price for this status was very high, drawing upon all of a man's (and his wife's) consanguineal, affinal, and trade resources.

In Chapter 4 we outlined the social and symbolic significance of this complex series of ceremonies. The relative importance of each particular ceremony was communicated in the nature and amount of the food distributed and whether or not it required only a "food distribution" (*mailaŋ*) or a dancing feast (*narogo*) (cf. Zelenietz and Grant 1981). Generally, the required presence of a pig indicated the more important ceremonies (see Table 4.1, pp. 79–82).

But how did the system work? How did these maritime mavericks obtain the goods necessary to perform these complex and expensive ceremonies? The following case illustrates the interplay among maritime skills, craft production, and trade in the organization and performance of firstborn feasts. Amui Josephine (1926–) was the firstborn daughter of Sakael, a renowned *bigman* and respected leader from *Tavov Puru runai* (see Chapter 5). Before Amui was born, however, Sakael adopted a firstborn son, whom he named Akorare. Thus Sakael had two firstborn children: a son by adoption (see Chapter 5) and a daughter by birth.

He performed the cycle of firstborn feasts and ceremonials in duplicate (except, of course, for those ceremonies specific to either sex). Here is Amui's account of her first sea crossing. The original text has been edited to render it more flowing and logical in English.

▼ When I was a young teenager, my father made a two-masted canoe named *Numas Wat* [named after a large reef to the south of Mandok]. Then we sailed to Tainduba [southwest coast of New Britain]. They "washed for us" [*tiririu pa yei*], Akorare and me. [My parents] got him first so he came first, and then I followed. They made us both *aidaba*s. They celebrated us both at the same time, with one trip.

I was terrified! It was my first trip ever in a sailing canoe, and I was very seasick. I was afraid of sailing. When we arrived, all those people splashed us and stared at us on the canoe. When they finished splashing us, my father took two large *on* [ceremonial bowls]— one for each of us—and exchanged them for two pigs. They took the *on*, killed the pigs, and got additional [vegetable] food. Everyone ate. Then we got back on the canoe and sailed.

We beached at an off-shore island called Werom. This is a small uninhabited island like Por. From stores in the canoe's bow they took some coconuts and taro [obtained at Tainduba] and made taro pudding—enough for all of us. They also fished. We all ate this food and relaxed awhile. Then we set sail again.

Some of our "fathers" were on another canoe. They went ahead to tell everyone in the next village that we were coming. People in that village were from our *runai*. They were waiting for us. They gathered pigs and food, too, and made everything ready. They waited, saying, "Be patient, for Sakael and his children are coming." When we finally did arrive, we went to them. They speared pigs and distributed more food. Everyone ate.

We rested, slept, and then they reloaded the canoe. At dawn, we reboarded and sailed for another place. This time we went to the islands Autumate and Akumpwa. They killed pigs for us, gave us food, and so on. We ate the pork and the vegetables, took what they gave us, and moved on to the other island.

At dawn the next day, we left again, this time for Binsini. They "washed for us" again and they speared two more pigs. That makes six. We stayed there for quite awhile. They gave us food, they took my father's *on*, and they gave us pigs, this time live ones. They also gave us vegetable foods, shell beads, and other things. We loaded these things onto the canoe and we left.

We did not usually stay at these places long. One day we went to one place, another day we went someplace else. On the way back to Mandok, we stopped one night at a small uninhabited island to rest and to feed the pigs. At dawn the next day we resumed our journey. At each place, my father took *on*s and matched each pig with

▼ them. One large *on* for one pig, for each of us. In the end he received eight pigs in all for us. [This was a large number in Siassi at that time.] He also got taro, sweet potatoes, and yams. Eventually he returned another *on* for the live pigs.

Finally we returned to Mandok. They "washed for us" here, too. We arrived during the day. They threw coconut husks at us as we came to shore. [One woman] didn't have any husks, as she was returning from a sago-processing trip on Umboi. She threw her sago masher at us! There were so many people; they splashed us, they dunked us, and everyone got soaked! They were so happy, they kept throwing husks and splashing us to show their joy. When this was finished, the last two pigs were speared, the food was distributed, and the whole village ate it.

Later, my father made another canoe, *Bobom Kain*. The name and design for this canoe came from Tami Island. We sailed this canoe to Arop. There they "washed for us" again and speared two more pigs. We stayed awhile, and they gave us more pigs, live ones. Then we got back on the canoe and went to Tolokiwa. After that we returned home. On the way home we stopped at Barim to rest. [Sakael had matrilateral relations at Barim.] At dawn the next day we set sail for Mandok. By this time I was older, on the verge of adulthood. Then the war [World War II] broke out, and we couldn't sail.

Native sailing canoes used to go really fast. They negotiated the waves and the currents. The men held the great steering paddle and steered the canoe from the back. Now that is all finished. Now we take commercial boats. It's not the same.

Before, prices were good: one *on* for one pig. They also gave us taro. Today, since Europeans came, the prices have really gone up, and the things given have changed. Today, parents give many more things: rice, shell strands, *laplaps*, sweet potatoes, yams, manioc, clothes, money, all kinds of things. This is all very recent.

Though Amui concentrated on those exchanges that concerned her, one can assume that her father brought on these voyages more than wooden bowls—coconuts, sago, smoked fish and shellfish, and other wealth objects—for reexport. For example, besides pigs, southwest New Britain was a source of dogs' teeth and live dogs. Arop was a source of drums (or drum designs, for men who could carve), fruit-bat-tooth necklaces, tortoiseshell, and other items. Clay pots came from the Sio/Gitua area of the Rai Coast. More than likely some of these things got traded as well, by Sakael and by other men on the canoe, for this was the essence of the Mandok's middleman system: clay pots made on the Rai Coast ended up in New Britain; obsidian from northern New Britain ended up on the Huon Peninsula, and so on. This is how the Siassi hub connected the spokes, as it were, of the Vitiaz trade system (see Harding 1967:118–153 for an expanded discussion).

Here is a simple example of how it worked. A man took a basket of smoked fish to the Kowai people of Umboi and traded it for a large (approximately 23-kg or 50-lb) lump of red ochre. Back on Mandok he divided the ochre into smaller lumps, perhaps 0.5 kg (1 lb) each. On the next trip, the trader took these 50 lumps of ochre to Sio and traded one-for-one for Sio pots. Now he had 50 Sio pots, which he brought back to Mandok. Some pots he distributed locally—to repay Kaimanga trade partners for feeding his family while he was away, or to the owner of the sailing canoe to pay for the trip (if the canoe was not his), or to settle old debts, for instance. The rest were stored against future ritual exchanges or for reexport. In the next trade season (see Figure 3.2, p. 57) he took some of the stored pots to Kilenge and traded them for pigs. According to Harding (1967:139), ten or fewer clay pots bought one pig (prices varied according to place and size of the pig). This pig was then brought back to Mandok for formal distribution. In this way, the original basket of smoked fish was converted into a pig. The inflation at each step, caused by supply-and-demand ratios, became the trader's profit. The sum total of profits was recycled into the Mandok's status mobility system.

Amui's story recounts just one set of ceremonies. Others, like male superincision or any child's first dance, required much more material wealth. The information in Table 6.1 illustrates the variety of material goods and the costs for the finale of a *Sia* dancing feast performed over a three-day period around Christmas, 1986. European contact and subsequent employment for wages changed the financial realities surrounding these feasts (see Figure 6.1). The feast shown in Figure 6.1 was extravagant, even considering inflation, but it shows the contemporary possibilities. The entire cycle lasted about three years and celebrated three children's first dance. Its total estimated cost to the main sponsor was K10,000.

It is important to note that whereas some of the objects of exchange changed over the years, their importance and their implications for status were still judged at the local level. This was true even for Mandok who held careers in towns. For them, it could be argued, the ante had increased qualitatively as well as quantitatively. Because they earned more, they were expected to give more. Because they had outside opportunities (including travel abroad), they were expected (or motivated) to give more creatively. During my fieldwork period there was an additional competition among town workers for exotica: rum, wine (purchased in duty-free shops), beer, packaged cigarettes, additional items of clothing, and so on. Modern Mandok might have used a new deck of cards, perhaps, but they were still playing poker.

In addition to goods for distribution, sponsors also brought gifts to relatives and gave special gifts to kinspeople who helped them with various stages of the feasts. Often these latter gifts were tailored to specific requests or to known desires of their recipients. They might include

TABLE 6.1 *Cost of finale of a* Sia *dancing feast, 1986.*

ITEM	QUANTITY
Pigs	4
Fish	19 baskets (exchanged for vegetables)
Manioc pudding	40 enamel basins
Taro pudding	6 large ceremonial bowls (*on*)
Sweet potatoes	4 *on*
Rice	6 bails @ 25 kg 4 bails @ 20 kg
Canned mackerel	1 case
Sugar	3 bails @ 15 kg
Gasoline[a]	2 drums @ 40 gal.
Tobacco	8 native bundles (ea. @ 100 leaves)
Newspapers	to match tobacco
Coffee	1 case
Tea	1 case
Areca (betel) nut	10 branches
Betel pepper	to match areca (5 native bundles)
Fabric	2 bolts (made into 16 *laplap*s each)
Cordial	8 bottles
Manioc	K6-worth
Old clothing	10 bundles (traded for vegetables)
Cash	K30

[a]*To run an outboard dugout canoe and travel around the Siassi region for vegetable foods.*

wristwatches, pressure lamps, cassette radios, tapes, batteries, saucepans, pots and pans, nails, can openers, vegetable peelers, bedding, towels, clothing, children's toys, running shoes, soccer balls, guitars, guitar strings, and a plethora of other store-bought goods. It was not uncommon to see young people taping even the most solemn of these

FIGURE 6.1 *Abore's first* Singsing Sia, *1987.*

feasts on large cassette recorders (Figure 4.2, p. 85). More will be said about this in subsequent chapters.

Sponsors did not actually distribute the food and wealth items they gave in their feasts; a ritual exchange partner did this. In the precontact era, feasts for firstborns involved two types of ritual exchange relationships within the village. Each form provided public and material demonstration of strength, and each was held "in the name" of the firstborn child. The comparative goals of these relationships, however, were opposed. One type, the *atam*, used competitive feasting to disgrace rivals. The other, *baliŋwaro*, centered on the reciprocal and dyadic relationship between matrilateral kin who became ritual exchange partners through their children. We will consider each of these in turn.

Atam: *The Competitive Road to Renown*

The Mutu word *atam* means "door" or "path."[3] In the past, this meaning was extended metaphorically to denote ceremonial competitive exchange partners. In this sense, the "path" to which the term refers was the "path" to renown. The *atam* relationship was one of competitive feasting, analogous to Young's (1971) description of Goodenough Islanders' competitions, except that *atam* competitions were between individuals (and hence, family *lains*) within Mandok, not between village groups (cf. also Scaglion 1976). It could be extended overseas in the form of formal competitive feasts, often given for a man's trading partner in honor of his firstborn, thus conflating overseas trade and local exchange by extending the competition internationally. Although a feast was sometimes offered "in the name of the firstborn," the object of the feast was to increase the status of the giver and to shame the recipient. The earlier Lutheran missionaries focused on this custom in their attempts to abolish all feasting and all pig killings, with the exception of killing pigs for food.

Harding (1967:157) said that the *atam* relationship was limited mostly to *bigmen*, but Mandok historians insisted that every man had at least one ceremonial *atam* (also confirmed by Bamler, cited in Chinnery n.d.:44). Because the Mandok (as well as the rest of the islanders) had abandoned *atam* competitions by the time of my fieldwork, I had to rely on the scant literature available that addresses the practice and on the memories of older men who witnessed these feasts either as children or youths. The ethnographic details were, on the whole, consistent. The departures here from other descriptions of *atam* feasting competitions are primarily matters of interpreting the value of this custom to Mandok social mobility and ideology of production.

Atam competitions were executed as follows. A man, whom we will call the challenger, stood in the center of the *maran*, the village plaza. He called out to his *atam*, whom we will call the recipient. He threw into the center a dry coconut with sprouts growing out of the top, which symbolized a pig, and offered one of his pigs, citing the pig by name; for example, "Marimbu, Kanalabu is yours!" The recipient then came out into the village center and swatted the coconut with croton shrubs, signaling his acceptance of both the pig and the challenge. The challenger's wife then came out and supported her husband by vouching for the vast amounts of vegetable food (taro, manioc, sweet potato) that she could produce from her garden and process for the distribution. The challenger and his wife were further aided by their extended family members (*lain*), who by this time had lined up on either side of the *maran* to "cheer them on." This verbal challenging continued until all of the challenger's coconuts were tossed, symbolizing the number of pigs with which he challenged his opponent, and which the opponent accepted, supported by his *lain*.

The vegetable foods were amassed in two types of temporary silo (*bor* and *pok*) in the middle of the village for all to see, until the appointed day of the feast. The distributions were accompanied by a dance. The recipient of the feast was responsible for providing an adequate number of singers and dancers in honor of the donor, appropriate to the amount of food to be dispensed. The greater the number of pigs, the larger the quantity of vegetable foods and the greater the number of singers and dancers that would have to be summoned by the recipient—for a "command performance"—else the recipient would be shamed. Conversely, if the recipient gathered together more dancers than the original amount of food offered warranted, the challenger ran to his kin at the last moment to procure yet more food, lest his aggressive gesture backfire due to inadequate commensal compensation to the dancers. Because the recipient distributed the challenger's resources, direct and precise tallies were possible.

Accepting such a feast put the recipient in a politically subordinate position to the challenger. He was in debt until the precise number of pigs and amount of food (pigs, taro, betel nut, tobacco, etc.) were repaid or, ideally, surpassed. The debtor was in a "shame" relationship to the challenger until the debt was repaid and could not contradict or argue with him publicly. If he did, the challenger could retaliate with swift and devastating admonitions to "Shut up," declaring, "Who are you anyway? You eat my food and chew my betel nut, and your taro stands rotting because you cannot repay your debts."

The process was a never-ending one. Each man tried to outdo his rivals, and each man's sons were socialized to pick up where their father left off: either to make good on old debts, thereby "clearing his name," or, in the case of the superiors, to ensure that the opponents would never catch up. These feasts could be held in honor of a man's firstborn or provoked by rivalry (e.g., by adultery, a political disagreement, competition for prestige and power, etc.). An entire feast was not always necessary. Sometimes the presentation of a pig sent the message. Freedman (1967:290) records a contest between two Big-Men [*sic*], now deceased, motivated by adultery and slander. The injured party presented one pig; shortly thereafter his opponent produced two; and many months later the competition ended when the initiator blitzed his rival with five pigs.

Alternately, if a transgressor wanted to avoid a full-blown competition, he could admit his guilt and send a pig to the injured party as compensation. Even though the feasts were no longer performed by the time of Freedman's or my fieldwork, their shadows still lingered on social relationships between former *atam* families.

The Baliŋwaro: *Conduit for Wealth*

The second major means of formally distributing food and wealth within the village, and one still in practice during my stay, was through the *baliŋwaro* (*baliŋ*, "wealth" plus *waro*, "line," "vine," or "vein"). The *baliŋwaro* was a category that denoted an intravillage ceremonial exchange partner. People in this category were responsible for distributing large amounts of food and wealth (see also Freedman 1967:280). The relationship had important ramifications for the life of children and for Mandok sociopolitical process.

Baliŋwaro implied a reciprocal and dyadic relationship, ideally between married couples. The relationship thus linked nuclear families and, consequently, *runai* together. When people spoke of their *baliŋwaro*, they referred to a husband/wife pair (unless one had died) or to the entire nuclear family of that pair. The *baliŋwaro* performed many of the functions of the mother's brother elsewhere. Indeed, in the majority of cases it was in fact a "mother's brother" relationship. In any event, one's *baliŋwaro* was *always* a member of one's extended family, usually in the maternal line. The role and its function in distributing wealth might in some way have been related to the custom of "sister exchange" in the sense of "paying back" a loss, as with replacement either by returning a sister in marriage or a child in adoption (see Chapter 5). In contrast to *atam* competitions, exchanges between *baliŋwaro* were supposed to be complementary, "even swaps."

In addition to distributing food and wealth at firstborn ceremonies, the *baliŋwaro* had many other responsibilities. This category of person was also responsible for the formal education of firstborns, expressed in the phrase *-gam tutaŋ pa-*, "to give the law for/to" (e.g., to him or her). The *baliŋwaro* maintained the masked figures during the *nakamutmut* feast cycle. More recently, the *baliŋwaro* served as godparent for christening, communion, confirmation, and marriage ceremonies in church. The individual who performed the service was paid for his or her efforts with a carved bowl, clay pot, baskets filled with laplaps, money, or other material objects.

Thus, the *baliŋwaro* was directly involved with the distribution responsibilities for the firstborn feasts and had the additional responsibility of inculcating valued forms of knowledge to the firstborn child (e.g., Mandok law, genealogical information, procedural instruction, or observance of taboos during male superincision or female menstruation). It was a relationship within the extended family of the child; the child's parents or grandparents usually chose the actual partners.

Discussion: The Aidaba, *the* Atam, *and the* Baliŋwaro

In many instances, the only written records available to anthropologists are those of missionaries; of course, the records are written from that missionary's particular point of view. These accounts are often biased and ethnocentric, and they tend to assign "good" and "bad" labels to "native custom" according to the similarities or differences they display with respect to Christianity.

For example, the first Lutheran missionaries in Siassi were mostly children of frugal Bavarian farmers (see also Harding 1985:44–45). They viewed the conspicuous consumption of competitive feasts as wasteful. They also saw competitive feasting wreak total destruction on a village, sometimes causing terrible famine. The feasts always provoked a seemingly endless cycle of "counterattacks" through food. For example, Rev. Georg Bamler commented that

> a dancing feast . . . gives rise to enormous expense. It requires about 1 ton of taro, thousands of coconuts for the taro puddings, several pigs, betelnuts, tobacco, &c., which usually is beyond the means of one family. This forces people to borrow from others; and especially is this so in the smaller islands where there is practically no arable soil. (Chinnery n.d.:44)

The dancing and revelry during the feasts sometimes resulted in adultery, and more arguments ensued. These were the major justifications given by the Lutheran missionaries for the abolition of feasting in general (see Bamler's discussion in Chinnery n.d.:42–45).

This example provides a succinct illustration of my point. Where Rev. Bamler sees "borrowing," a "sin" in Christian ideology, an anthropologist sees "delayed reciprocal exchange," a fundamental principle of Melanesian socioeconomic life. Where a missionary would see evidence of "paganism," the anthropologist sees "reverence of the sacred ancestral past." Finally, the animosity displayed in many feasting competitions is interpreted anthropologically as a dramatic acting out of status relations between political rivals and a physical demonstration of "strength." Some of this animosity was very real: *atam* competitions were also used to settle disputes nonviolently (see also Scaglion 1976).

Another potential problem not mentioned by Rev. Bamler was noted by Mandok historians: sorcery. During feasts there were large food distributions, and many kinds of wealth items circulated. There might also be strangers in the village. During these times one had to be careful not to leave around any "personal rubbish"—such as hair or nail clippings or food leftovers—for would-be sorcerers to use in an attack. These beliefs might have had something to do with the invariable choice of relatives as *baliŋwaro*. The threat of sorcery was thereby diminished.

The Mandok I knew thought that the *atam* competitions were "un-Christian" because they fostered anger and competition between peers instead of brotherly love and cooperation. They compared the *atam* relationship with that of the *baliŋwaro* and judged the latter to be preferable because "it honors our children instead of shaming our brothers." The Mandok did not convert to Lutheranism largely because, from their point of view, the Lutherans tried to destroy a most valuable custom—the feasts involving the *nakamutmut* masked figures (discussed in Chapter 4). When the Roman Catholics missionized Mandok, however, the Mandok were willing to abandon competitive feasting and *atam* exchanges. In fact, they suggested it themselves.

In the process of banning *all* feasting, the Lutheran missionaries merged what were for the Mandok two different kinds of relationship. The *atam* relationship was between men who were not related and was based on rivalry. The *baliŋwaro* relationship, on the other hand, was always between kinspeople. It required (ideally) a husband-and-wife pair and had the explicit purpose of "raising the name of the child." Although in the course of "raising the child's name" the father and grandfather were also demonstrating their own strength and "raising their own names," the stated goal of this relationship was egalitarian reciprocity rather than competition. The *baliŋwaro* was the public validator of a new generation and of a family's fulfillment of its social obligations to its firstborn child. As the primary party in the first accomplishments of a firstborn child, the *baliŋwaro* heralded the child's official journey through all of the rites of passage, which were performed throughout childhood and into adulthood (see Chapter 4 and Table 4.1, pp. 79–82).

The negative aspects of the *atam* relationship have been well documented (see Bamler, in Chinnery n.d.:42–45) and are eagerly confirmed by the Mandok. On the other hand, let us consider for a moment the possible *motivational* aspects of the *atam* custom. For one thing, the presence of constant competition gave everyone in the village a constant *motivation to produce*. A man had to keep extending his trading network throughout the Vitiaz and Dampier straits if he was to keep his support system going and obtain the food, pigs, and wealth objects necessary to reciprocate his *atam*'s feasts. Children were socialized in an ambiance of fierce competition and became part of it at an early age. They were messengers for their fathers, they helped in the garden, and they fished on the reefs and sailed the trade routes. At the time of his

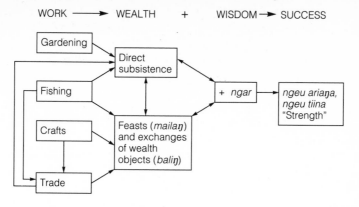

FIGURE 6.2 *"Cognitive equation" for "success."*

initiation into adult life, a youth was encouraged to "accumulate as much wealth as possible so as to be able to shame his rivals by exhibiting more possessions than they could exhibit" (Bamler, cited in Chinnery n.d.:42).

The *atam* system presented a coherent system of values and a cognitively clear route to achievement. The Mandok's underlying status mobility system reinforced both the value of the ultimate goals and the motivations to achieve them. Both of these were congruent with a *consistent standard of excellence* by which to evaluate success. The traditional route to success is summarized in Figure 6.2.

The actual achievement of renown and power in the traditional system was neither simple nor easy. "Strength" entailed a lifetime of managing people, relationships, material objects, and different kinds of specialized knowledge.

My first stay on Mandok occurred 50 years after *atam* feasting was abolished. Many factors were responsible for its abandonment. First, as mentioned above, were Christian moral considerations. Second, the increasing population, which came with pacification and missionization (see Chapter 7), put additional pressure on the island's food supply; competitive feasting became more burdensome. Population pressure also required more intensive gardening, which left less time for travel and overseas trade (see Chapter 3). Third, European contact contributed to the devaluation or replacement of certain trade and wealth items and an increasing dependence on cash (see Chapters 7 and 8). Fourth, plantation recruitment cut down on the male work force in the villages and throughout the trade system (see Chapters 7 and 8 and cf. Harding 1967:206). Nevertheless, certain aspects of the system endured. Commentators on more recent firstborn feasts, for example, warned that the sponsors of these feasts were "performing *atam* and not *baliŋwaro*" exchanges; that is, they were getting too competitive.

In any event, by the 1980s the only public obligations a family had to fulfill were *baliŋwaro* exchanges and firstborn feasts. The other children might have minor distributions to mark important life crises, but they were usually included with the larger distributions of a classificatory firstborn "brother" or "sister." For example, all boys were superincised and initiated into the men's area. Similarly, all boys and girls were ritually "beaten" by the *nakamutmut* masked figures (see Chapter 4). Only the firstborn was fêted, however; latterborns "followed the legs" of the firstborn.

In *atam* competitions, a man's debts continued even after his death. His children inherited his debt, his shame, or, conversely, his superior status. During my field stay, by the time a man's firstborn child was about 15 years old, most of his larger distributional requirements would have been fulfilled. No institutional sanction kept him on his toes, so to speak, and kept his family and himself producing at the same rate. Mandok children no longer saw this intense need to trade, produce, and distribute.[4] If *atam* was really abolished with the successful missionization of the island (which began in 1937), no one under the age of 50 has ever seen an *atam* feast. The "first-generation" children of the newly Christianized village were socialized in a different social and moral environment from that of their fathers, but they probably retained the moral codes of the previous generation. To the generation of school children I knew, however, accounts of the *atam* competitions were "just stories" with little contemporary relevance. This point is discussed in greater depth in Chapter 10.

MIDDLEMEN, TRADE, AND MANAGEMENT FOR SUCCESS

Middleman trade was the linchpin of the Mandok's status mobility system. It provided at once both routes to obtaining desired goods and arenas in which to display personal strength. A man who had many trading connections in different places, and who consistently traded successfully, had at his disposal a large support network of real and putative kin (his *lain*) upon whom he could depend for support (material support and labor) in his public distributions.

Another important characteristic of the Mandok (and Siassi) trade and exchange systems was their manipulative and distributive character. In contrast to other areas of Melanesia, the Mandok, as middlemen, never amassed the resources of other exchange systems (cf. Sahlins 1963; Strathern 1971). For example, instead of being a bank in which profits accrued, Mandok Island was more like a warehouse in which many wealth objects were stored for reexport. Though they produced many important exchange objects (canoes, carvings, trochus armlets, and so on), the overwhelming balance of trade consisted of consumables (e.g., pigs, marine products, coconuts) and reexports of items imported from endpoints of the Vitiaz trade system (Harding 1967, 1989). In this system goods kept moving or were accumulated for short periods and for specific purposes (e.g., for reexport, competitive and firstborn feasts, or brideprice).

Out of this constant travel and trade emerged a status mobility system oriented not toward accumulation of vast amounts of land and wealth in a sedentary environment, but instead toward manipulation and management of goods through mobility and trade—that is, toward control and *redistribution* of wealth (Sahlins 1963). This "middleman culture," though recognizably Melanesian, was distinct from the more familiar patterns of entrepreneurship studied to date in Melanesia in three crucial respects. First was the relative absence of land and of the use of land resources (horticulture and pig husbandry) as a basis for local economy. Second was the emphasis on trade both as a *primary* rather than a secondary feature of their subsistence economy and as a standard for evaluating entrepreneurial talents and achievements. A corollary point here is that "trade" specifically means "middleman trade"; it has different cultural implications than do one-way exchanges (see also Harding 1989). The Mandok felt that "we are great because others depend on us. If we weren't here, the Umbois [for example] could not marry" (because they depended on the islanders to supply their bridewealth items). Finally, the Mandok's centripetal social and distributive systems militated against long-term hoarding and reinvestment in larger ventures. The ultimate object of trade was to procure pigs, taro, and other items necessary for the Mandok's internal feasting and exchange systems.

Siassi *bigmen* were maritime men of knowledge, craftsmanship, and clever investment. They succeeded not by physically overpowering their adversaries but by outsmarting them; not by producing so much as by clever manipulation and management. Namor "showed them how." Through generations of trading they transformed a harsh environment and a land-poor society into a patterned system of seagoing salesmen, trading for profit their own and other societies' products throughout the Vitiaz and Dampier straits.

By connecting the geographical endpoints of this far-flung trade system to their own centralized location, they controlled the rates of exchange and also maintained, to a great extent, a monopoly of *access* to valued goods within the system (documented in Harding 1967). Profits were recycled back into the village distributive system, rather than accumulated or reinvested in other enterprises. Ceremonial feasts provided the public arena in which a man displayed all of his resources—the sum total of his work—and proved his strength over other men. These feasts also provided tangible evidence of achievement and a consistent standard of excellence by which to assess success. In this system, physical mobility and social mobility were interdependent requisites on the lifelong path to renown. These themes will reappear in the following chapters, as we see how new economic and status mobility systems were introduced to and understood by Mandok middlemen.

CHAPTER SEVEN

🌺 New Roads

The first time our elders saw white men, they were afraid. They
thought these strange creatures were spirits. But what kind of spirits?
Were they good or bad? They were like nothing our elders had ever
seen before. Their bodies were so covered they thought, "Ai—they
must not have any genitals. And how do they defecate with no anus?"
Because of the big boots on their feet, they thought, "Ai—they have
no toes!" The hats on their heads made it look like their heads were
bald and flat—cut off right at the forehead. What were they? But they
had many good things with them, and they seemed friendly. They
gave us stick tobacco and other good things our fathers had never
seen before. In time, our elders learned that they were not spirits,
but men, just like them. Their skin was white, just like yours, only
redder, for they had been in the sun. But underneath, we are all one
kind. God made us all the same.

Mandok and Aromot elders, 1987

The previous four chapters described Mandok cultural, economic, and
status mobility systems around the themes of mobility, the sea, and
middleman trade. The next two chapters describe the history of contact with Europeans and the political, economic, and social changes it
brought to Mandok.

By the time Europeans reached the Siassi area, it was already a major
sea lane and trade thoroughfare. Siassi populations came into contact
with peoples from as far away as eastern Indonesia, long before the first
Europeans landed on the shores of New Guinea. Contact could be
direct (through trade) or indirect (through exchanged artifacts). Contact with Europeans, however, was different, for it ushered in changes
that were dramatic and irreversible. Pacification, missionization, and the
introduction of a market economy brought changes to the Siassi area
that were radically different from previous contacts with "outsiders."
Each change was instituted by different agents; each agent had its own
set of goals and methods for achievement. From the Mandok perspective, however, all of these agents were in a sense "the same." Each exposed them, in common with other New Guinean populations, to
different types of European contact. However packaged, this contact

brought about fundamental changes in local culture and economic conditions that many Mandok are still struggling to understand.

PACIFICATION: NEW PEOPLE, NEW CARGO, NEW RULES

Siassi-European contacts had an economic aspect from the beginning. The first Europeans documented to have reached this area were traders and explorers. The English navigator William Dampier explored and charted the northern region of Siassi and named Arop Island Long Island in 1700. He took a northern route around Umboi, sailing through the strait that today bears his name (Figure 1.1, p. 7).[1] The French explorer J. S. C. Dumont D'Urville also took this route for his 1827 exploration of New Britain and Long Island. Neither of these explorers sailed around Umboi's southern point, so they never visited the small islands. This does not necessarily mean that the islanders were totally ignorant of the existence of these strangers, however, for news travels quickly through word of mouth, and material goods got retraded.

The earliest European records of contact with "natives" usually documented trade. For example, the German explorer Otto Finsch visited Long Island in 1885 and recorded these experiences:

> The people . . . were not greedy and were willing to barter. But they had nothing much, only things such as are found in Astrolabe Bay, e. g. woven armbands, breast decorations and the same kinds of bows and arrows. When they had sold almost everything . . . they gave the prow of their canoe and cut away even the painted sideboard. Among these [parts of canoe] were quite noteworthy little items, for example from the tip of the mast a triangle with crudely carved birds, a strange frame on the outrigger and so on; all objects which now may be seen in the Museum . . . in Berlin, which previously probably did not possess any pieces from Long Island. As provisions only some old coconuts and leaf tobacco were brought. The people did not appear to be familiar with trade tobacco, in contrast to glass beads and iron. . . . In the excitement of trading the newly acquired knife of one of the men fell into the water. Then one could see a grieved black, since for such a *child of nature* [emphasis added] this is scarcely something to laugh about. Now I like to see happy people, so I gave the man another knife, and one could again rejoice in a happy black face. Probably today I am still favorably remembered; for the blacks remember good as well as bad, and probably tales are still told of the strange ship without sails and the white man with the red beard. He must have been rich! (Finsch 1888: 188–189, cited in Ball 1982: 453)

This passage is particularly revealing, for it both documents specific items of trade and shows prevalent European attitudes of the 19th century. Europeans were generally ambivalent about other cultures, especially those they classified as "uncivilized." New Guinea was portrayed even then as a land of savages, head hunters, and cannibals. Even when Europeans had peaceful encounters, however, the best they could do was describe the islanders in such Rousseauist terms as "children of nature." Two attitudes thus dominated colonial policy, with its emphasis both on "pacification" (of the "savages") and on "civilizing" the "natives" ("children of nature") according to European standards of that time. From the Europeans' point of view, the exchange of goods constituted a sort of peace offering and an opportunity to interact with "natives," as well as a chance to collect both exotic souvenirs and artifacts for museums back home. From the local perspective, this peace offering was most likely interpreted as a prelude to longer-lasting exchange partnerships (see Chapter 5).

The Siassi area was part of the Old Protectorate of German New Guinea from 1884 to 1914. The New Guinea Company of Berlin administered the new colony, setting policy and conducting business from their mainland headquarters at Finschhafen. The headquarters was transferred to Rabaul in 1899, and administrative responsibility for the colony reverted to the German Imperial Government. Company agents traded along the Rai Coast and Huon Peninsula, including Siassi. One agent, a "Masta Pranis" (Mr. Prance) established a trading station on Mandok Island (1898–1899) for the purpose of collecting trepang (sea cucumber), tortoiseshell, and pearlshell (*Trochus niloticus*; see Sack and Clark 1979:165, 207).

Regional fighting was suppressed in 1907–08. A roving government steamer cruised the area from New Britain through Siassi to Salamaua, Sinogu, and Buka, training local police "to protect trade, promote recruitment and extend the area of public peace" (Sack and Clark 1979:278). Within Siassi peace came later: there were still outbreaks on the Kowai side of Umboi after World War II (Ploeg 1989). Australia gained control over northeast New Guinea in 1914. Thus the eastern half of the island of New Guinea was bisected horizontally. The "Territory of New Guinea" was governed by a separate administration from that of the "Territory of Papua."

MISSIONIZATION: NEW *LO* (LAW), NEW WAY

Mission history in Siassi is sporadic for its first 90 years. The first missionaries came from the Catholic Vicariate of Melanesia and Micronesia, established by Marists and headquartered on Woodlark Island. In 1847 Bishop Giovanni Collomb and three others left Woodlark for the northeast New Guinea region. They established a mission station at Nuru, on the northern tip of Umboi Island, in 1848 (Wiltgen 1979:474–487). Two missionaries died of disease within the first ten months; the survivors retreated to Woodlark Island to await further instructions. In 1852, one of these survivors accompanied three others from the Institute for Foreign Missionaries of Milan on their return to Nuru. They, too, were defeated, both by virulent malaria and by "natives' indifference."

The Woodlark Island mission station was abandoned after the violent deaths of some of its missionaries in 1855. The Marists retreated from Melanesia. In 1882, Catholics resumed activities in Melanesia through the Sacred Heart (MSC) missionaries working out of New Britain. Bishop Louis Couppé of the MSC mission visited Siassi in 1914, and because of boat trouble he visited Aromot Island (Mulderink 1989). None of these missionaries had any lasting success in converting Siassi villagers to Christianity. Nevertheless, Siassi Catholics of the 1980s revered them as "ancestors of the church." They were honored in the names of mission boats and motorized dugout canoes.

Although Roman Catholics were the first missionaries in Siassi, German Lutherans established control after German colonization of northeast New Guinea. The German colonial government divided German New Guinea into evangelical zones. Siassi was a satellite outstation of the Lutheran center near Finschhafen (at Sattelburg); New Britain was Catholic. Some of the early Lutheran missionaries feared Catholic encroachment on "their" territory. The Catholics, for their part, never recognized these divisions, as they felt that they had been there first. Siassi was, literally and figuratively, in the middle. Siassi peoples felt they had a choice, which made the missionaries who competed for them anxious.

Rev. Georg Bamler visited Siassi briefly in 1891 and 1908. He returned during 1911–19, then again in 1923 (Bamler 1892; Mulderink 1980:16). Beginning at Tami Island, most of Rev. Bamler's efforts were concentrated near Yangla on Umboi Island and on Tuam. He extended his evangelical network throughout the other islands by following Tami's trade connections. (This was much to the Tamis' chagrin, who felt that his superior array of cargo would ruin their trade advantage [Bamler 1892:1].)

Rev. Bamler and other Lutheran missionaries contacted the Mandok but were later rejected. The Mandok cited two events as instrumental in their decision. First, the Lutheran mission's policy at the time considered "native" feasting and dancing to be evidence of paganism and therefore detrimental to a Christian way of life. They tried to eradicate all evidence of this "paganism" by exposing all the men's sacred paraphernalia to the women and by prohibiting all pig killings except those for food (Bamler, cited in Chinnery n.d.:42–45); that is, they attempted to abolish traditional feasting customs (discussed in Chapter 6).

The other incident involved a Mandok girl who, around 1933, went (with three others) to the Lutheran school at Awelkon (west Umboi). She later married a Barim man and moved to Barim. She tried to keep up her reading but, according to her relatives, her husband was jealous of her knowledge. He beat her when she was in the later stages of pregnancy, and she died. Because this was a "Lutheran" village, the Mandok turned against all the Lutherans as a result of these two incidents (also documented in Mulderink 1980:16–17). After the latter incident, the Mandok sent a delegation of their leaders to Rabaul (then the seat of district government) to request that the government forbid any more missionaries from going to Mandok.

Soon afterward, some Mandok traders saw Catholic missions at Kilenge and Pililo. They learned that it was possible to have a mission, to get access to European knowledge, goods, and medicines, and to maintain their own sacred customs. In 1936 they sent another delegation of elders to Kilenge to request a Catholic mission. The first catechist arrived in 1937. The birth of a child named after this first catechist documented this historical event for the Mandok. Since then, Mandok has remained a Catholic island in a Lutheran sea. At the time of my fieldwork, the other small islands were all Lutheran, except for Aromot, which was half Roman Catholic and half Lutheran. Most Umboi villages were Lutheran, except for Aupwel, Kampalap, Opai, and Gomlonggon.

In Chapter 2 we explored the Legend of Namor, which explains from a Siassi perspective the creation of the world, the local environment, and the cultural charter for trade. In Chapter 5 we learned that Mandok social relationships had a definite economic component—that is, that they were long-term investments in people. In Chapters 4 to 6 we examined how the Mandok's prestige system emphasized trade, manipulation, and distribution of goods, food, and people; each new acquaintance became a potential new resource to be exploited and each implied a certain investment and return ratio. It should not be surprising, then, to learn that European contact was also viewed this way, once the islanders overcame their initial fears.

This understanding of European contact was not lost on the early missionaries. Most missionaries of this earliest period spoke of "tobacco Christians" and noted in utter frustration the apparent materialist motives of their prospective converts from their first interactions with them. In some ways, however, the missionaries themselves encouraged "materialist" thinking. When they visited potential converts, they traded for local crafts. For example, Rev. Bamler (1892:A3) wrote, "[When] we arrived at Aromot . . . [t]he people brought us a number of ornaments which we exchanged for iron and beads." His experience seems no different from Finsch's, from the same era. The items of trade were fairly constant; the differences would be seen in each man's long-range goals for the transaction:

> The Melanesian villager valued the missionary, at least initially, not for what he preached but for what he possessed, gave away or traded. In all but name the missionary on the frontier in New Guinea was a trader and land purchaser and his goods alone gave him access to pagan village communities. Before the German occupation

the Methodists paid for land in New Britain in axes, tomahawks, tobacco, cotton print, beads, boxes of matches, pipes, knives and even flasks of gunpowder. Except for the gunpowder, goods of this kind became the standard currency of land transactions between villagers and all missions.

Once permitted to stay, the missionary made himself indispensable to villagers by his constant supply of such material wealth. . . . (Firth 1986:156)

Firth's history is accurate; his wording, however, is judgmental. Although missionization was fraught with conflict in many areas of PNG, this seems not to have been true for the Mandok. Older Mandok described the coming of the missionaries like this:

▼ When the elders were in Kilenge they saw the Catholic missionaries. The missionaries doctored their sores, gave them medicine, and taught them the word of God. The elders saw that the Kilenge had their *singsing*s and could still get this medicine and learn many things from these white men. They thought, "This is something truly good," so they followed the road of the Catholic Mission.

The Mandok's accounts of their history synthesized over 150 years of European contact and over 50 years of missionization by means of important historical episodes. The following episode is excerpted from a longer historical account (*kamos*; see Chapter 2) of the first Europeans in Siassi.

▼ There was an old man on Aromot who was dying. He had a tropical ulcer on his leg, and he just sat under his house [i.e., waiting to die]. When the Europeans came to Siassi, they saw this man. They threw off his barkcloth [traditional dress] and bathed him. Then they re-dressed him in a clean new *laplap*. Next they threw away his old pandanus sleeping mat and gave him a new one. They also gave him medicine and doctored his sore. He was completely healed in no time, walking around as good as new.

In each of these vignettes the primary theme involves four considerations:

1. a view of Europeans as *wealthy*.
2. a view of Europeans as sympathetic, helpful, and possessed of powerful *knowledge* about many things beyond the capabilities of the Mandok of that time. This knowledge included *power* to heal (traditionally the prerogative of ritual specialists with personal/ancestral power).
3. the implication that this wealth, knowledge, and power (expressed in the number of material objects, medicines, and healing abilities at their disposal) implied and reflected Europeans' *personal power*.

4. a corollary tacit assumption on the part of these middlemen that by entering into social and economic relationships with the Europeans, they too could have access to these goods, these forms of knowledge, and hence this personal power.

This last assumption was widespread in Melanesia (see Lawrence 1964). This is not to suggest that European military might was ignored or was not a factor—quite the contrary. It was so overwhelming to basically peaceful people accustomed to spears and hand-to-hand conflict that, years later, it required little comment. But Siassi traders were accustomed to trading with potentially hostile clients and to sailing through hostile waters. It scared them, but it did not stop them.[2]

On Mandok, as elsewhere in Melanesia, the spiritual and material realms were intertwined. In Melanesian thinking, a man is powerful and successful when he lives within the *lo* (TP, "law"). The concept of "law" in this sense, however, has little to do with a judiciary system. Being "in the 'law' " had a religious connotation and a transcendent content. On Mandok it was subsumed under the concept of *ngar* or, more precisely, expressed as *tutaŋ*. *Tutaŋ* invoked the sacred ancestral past, the important "knowledge" that initiates received in the men's area (see Chapter 4). When the Mandok accepted Christianity, they had material expectations, to be sure; even the Mandok had their share of "tobacco Christians." For the Mandok's leaders of that time and for most of the Mandok I knew, however, the material concerns were part of a larger package that entailed a moral and spiritual "new way." These kinds of assumptions were summarized in the expression, " 'following the road' of the Europeans" in general and, in this case, of the Catholic mission in particular. These perceptions on Mandok spurred both a series of decisions and reorganizations of their social and political systems and active pursuit of new goals in a manner that was consistent with their cultural identities as maritime traders (see Chapters 8 and 9).

A MARKET ECONOMY: PLANTATIONS, WAR, COPRA, AND SHELLS

European contact in Siassi has always been sporadic and eclectic. Germans came from Madang and Finschhafen to buy shells, coconuts, and trepang. Occasional ships brought labor recruiters to the area, looking for plantation labor. In the last few years of the 19th century, a "Masta Pranis" from the New Guinea Company lived on Mandok. In 1913–14, a Mr. Weiss, another trader, made Mandok his base of operations and lived there. He hired two Mandok youths as cooks and helpers (Mulderink 1980:14; 1989). During the 1930s Japanese companies operating out of Manus Island collected trochus and trepang on Long Island (Ball

1982:457). It is reasonable to assume that they probably extended into Siassi: in the legend cited earlier the "Europeans" who treated the man's sores carved a red "mark of the sun" into a *taliz* tree.

A bit later the Lutheran mission underwent an administrative split that relinquished German control of Siassi. In 1936 the Australian Lutheran mission went to New Guinea and were given the Siassi parish. In 1937 they bought William Money's plantation at Gizarum to support the Awelkon mission station. Most Lutheran missionaries in Siassi from that time onward were Australian. In 1938–39 a Czech named Zyganek was in Siassi (Michael 1957:44). He lived on Aromot Island and taught the youths to pole vault (Mulderink 1987). During World War II, Japanese and later Allied forces used Umboi Island as a staging area for operations on New Britain and the New Guinea coast.

After the war, the Australians controlled northeast New Guinea as a United Nations Trust Territory. Private traders, most interested in their own profits, continued commerce on a sporadic basis. Siassi people distinguished the differences among government, mission, and business people by their behavior. They were never privy to the larger designs of colonial governments or mission headquarters.

Until the 1940s, few Mandok men migrated to find work. One or two became "native policemen" on New Britain. Occasionally a young man served as a cook, house servant, or ship's crewman, but only for specified contract periods: there was no massive labor recruitment campaign in which the Mandok participated, though other islanders did (Bamler 1892). But the notion that contact with Europeans meant opportunities to earn wealth persisted, most likely spawned by the presence both of trade goods acquired either through the trade system or brought home by returning migrants and by items introduced by roving traders, missionaries, and government officers.

World War II

Mission, business, and trade activities were suspended in Siassi during World War II with the exception of a temporary "black market" trade with American traders, exchanging cat's eyes (*Turbo petholatus*) for gelig nite toward the end of the war (Patrol Report Finschhafen, May 1945:3). Gelignite is an explosive that was used to blow up reefs as a method for catching fish. It caused many deaths and maimed many others in the hands of inexperienced villagers, however, so its use was outlawed.

World War II saw the first major Mandok cohort to migrate for "labor." I say "labor" because the Mandok never considered it "their fight" and saw no obvious stake in participating in this "white man's war." However, they did go and were paid in trade goods. (In 1985 the PNG government decided that this was insufficient and compensated war veterans K1,000 [about U.S. $1,200] for their services.) From 1942–45 over 30 percent of the active Siassi adult male population (mostly from Umboi) was recruited to serve with Allied forces. Twenty-three Mandok men served as soldiers, scouts, and cooks. All returned safely. Mandok villagers hid in their Umboi Island garden land at Muru. They dug a cave and hid during the day, and they came out at night to "get their wind back" (breathe fresh air). Only two people died during the war. One man was shot by Allied air strafing during the Japanese occupation of the area in late 1943, when he went outside to watch the airplanes; the other was an old man who died of illness in Muru.

The Japanese occupied Umboi Island (then called Rooke) for a short time in 1943. In anticipation of this invasion, Allied forces evacuated local populations to the Umboi bush areas between August 1943 and January 1944 (Patrol Report Finschhafen, May 1944:2–3). William Money,[3] former owner of the Gizarum plantation, became a coast watcher for Allied forces, supplying information on Japanese movements (Feldt 1946:334–338). The Japanese withdrew by mid-January 1944 (Feldt 1946:337).

The Japanese had minimal impact in Siassi:

> Demands for food and labour were made [and paid for with Japanese money], but there was no interference with native women. The greatest hardship was the order that no fires were to be made, and the usual method of burning off before planting was not allowed. The threat of beheading ensured obedience to Japanese demands. (Patrol Report Finschhafen, March 1944:6)

Older Mandok remembered the "hungry time" they spent hiding in the Muru gardens and recalled incredulously the severity of Japanese threats of punishment. No one, to my knowledge, actually witnessed an execution in Siassi, though many of the returning service veterans recounted gory stories about the Japanese.

Working for the Allies, whether as cooks, soldiers, or cargo bearers, gave Siassi men more direct contact with Europeans and their goods. One can still see evidence of abandoned government issue in Siassi, as in other parts of PNG. Empty shell casings served as cauldrons for large feasts, and spent mortar shells made handy buckets for pig slops. Tent-pole screwcaps, perfect for mashing betel nut, seemed to be everywhere. My Mandok mother proudly showed me her spoon stamped "U.S.A.," a gift from her classificatory brother-in-law, a returning war veteran.

The Postwar Period: 1945–52

After the war, concerted efforts were made to reestablish communications with the rural populations and to improve local living conditions. Patrols went through Siassi three or four times a year on short trips that took about one month to cover the entire district; they were usually hampered by wind and rough seas. Major concerns for the local populations at this time included food, health, curtailment of depopulation, and maintenance of traditional culture. Both American and Australian military patrols directly opposed the Lutheran missionaries and supported "native custom." One officer went so far as to recommend official intervention in maintaining the traditional feasting cycles (Patrol Report Finschhafen, May 1945).

In 1952, government administrators (Patrol Report Finschhafen 1, 1952:4) listed the following items as the "most urgent" administrative priorities in Siassi:

1. the enforced planting of sufficient subsistence gardens on the mainland (Umboi) by the Siassi Islanders
2. the establishment and maintenance of regular markets between coastal (Umboi) and Siassi Island people
3. the "price fixing" of trade articles
4. the encouragement and preservation of the canoe-building trade by the Siassi Islanders
5. the overcoming of the low birthrate in many villages
6. the improvement of subsistence gardens and the development of local industries and cash crops as an inducement to the people to seek money on their own island and to restrict overrecruiting

Food scarcity, always a major problem, was exacerbated by the wartime ban on fires. An increase in emigration of men seeking employment and a rise in abortion and infanticide (mostly on Umboi) resulted in a marked depopulation (Patrol Report 1, 1952, Part I). Patrol officers urged Siassi peoples to "re-populate" and closed the region to recruitment from 1952 to 1954 to encourage this process (Patrol Report Finschhafen 1, 1952, Part II:1).

Both government officers and missionaries saw cash cropping both as a means of limiting labor recruitment and as a route to self-sufficiency for local communities. In many cases Siassi missions were ahead of government planners in initiating projects. Though operating mainly from small outstations visited periodically by a single missionary priest, the Siassi Catholic congregation was buttressed by the Catholic mission center and plantation at Vunapope (near Rabaul). Mission centers of this era were self-sufficient villages. Vunapope had several kinds of school, a church, a hospital, workshops, joineries, "everything that was useful or necessary to carry on the work of evangelisation" (O'Neill 1961:11). After the war, Vunapope was rebuilt. The Australian Lutheran mission at Awelkon was larger than an outstation but smaller than a center. The Lutheran mission center remained at Sattelburg (near Finschhafen) for many years; it later moved to Lae. From the 1940s to the 1960s both the Catholic and Lutheran mission plantations remained Siassi's major and most consistent source of migrant labor.

Meanwhile, private traders, still trading predominantly for trepang, tortoiseshell, trochus, and cat's eyes, came and went (Patrol Report

Finschhafen 1, 1952:6–7). Some of these merchants financed their businesses with money earned through postwar salvaging efforts. After the war, the American military dumped most of its equipment into the sea or left it to rot in the tropical rainforest. Licensed Australian and American entrepreneurs salvaged some of this military refuse at Finschhafen. Copper wire, particularly valuable at that time, was salvaged from abandoned communications equipment. Ted Foad, one such entrepreneur, financed a landing craft called the *Beringa* with his salvaging profits and traded through Siassi and along the northeast New Guinea coast for copra and trochus. He later established trade stores at Sio and Wasu with Tomas Ola, a Sio man, in the late 1950s (Harding 1989).

Men like Foad kept the local Siassi market enterprise afloat. They made it attractive for island men to stay home, collect the desired shell species, and sell them for cash. Financed by salvaging profits, they could afford to collect small quantities at any given time, just to keep the market. The missions did some shell collecting, too. A temporary slump depressed the trochus market in 1952, but business picked up again within a few years. By 1955, the administration noted that the size of the collected shells was consistently getting smaller, indicating that the reefs were overexploited. Patrol officers recommended that trochus collecting be suspended for four years to allow the species to replenish (Patrol Report Finschhafen 3, 1955–56:2), but to no avail. Private traders continued to accept the smaller shells, only to discard them later for fear of losing the market altogether (Patrol Report Finschhafen 6, 1957–58:3). By the mid-1960s, Foad was collecting big shells again. At one point he sold 300 tons of trochus he had accumulated to a Japanese buyer (Harding 1989).

NEW STANDARDS OF LIVING

A government head tax, initiated by the Germans and continued under Australian rule, required rural New Guineans to earn cash. This tax was used to induce men to migrate and work on plantations. Plantation labor introduced Siassi men to new peoples, places, customs, and trade items, and European goods supplanted some traditional exchange objects. The desire to acquire these things in turn created new standards for achievement and inspired a variety of ideas about how to earn cash. Some men stayed away and took jobs as policemen, ship's crew, or plantation laborers. Others came home and tried to initiate changes based on what they had seen elsewhere.

The availability of wage labor after World War II brought still more material objects and expectations for earning cash. Compared to other small islands, Mandok and Aromot showed the smallest numbers of labor migrants up to 1963 (Harding 1967:205). From 1944 to 1963, Mandok sent 27 men, Aromot sent 14. Harding interprets the low absenteeism to be a measure of Mandok and Aromot conservatism and an indication of their economic commitment to canoe building, carving, and trade (Harding 1967:205). This is probably true, but two additional factors must be considered.

First, the 23 men Mandok sent into World War II constituted 50 percent of the male population of that time. Their absence disrupted an entire set of betrothals and marriage alliances. Deals were broken, new matches were made, and alliances were reshuffled. Families may have been hesitant to send off another cohort so soon. Later, Freedman (1967:112) calculated that 22 percent of the total resident male population of Mandok was absent while he was there in 1965–66.

Second, religion may have been a factor in recruitment differences among islands. Malai and Tuam were Lutheran islands; their migrants went to Gizarum Plantation on Umboi Island. Mandok men went to Vunapope in Rabaul, where they competed with New Britain Catholics who were closer to the plantation and therefore cheaper to hire. Ship's crew was always the most desirable job to get, but such opportunities were even scarcer than were plantation contracts.

Regardless of the numbers, however, the *percentages* of migrating males in relation to the total adult-male village populations were high. Such absenteeism affected the Vitiaz trade system in both positive and negative ways. Harding notes, for example, that

> with only meager earnings from copra production and the collection of trochus shell, wage labor [became] the primary means of acquiring cash, *laplaps*, and other European goods, which [became] essential ingredients of native trade. The profits of wage labor [helped] to fund and to sustain trading activity. What better way to maintain a family trading concern than by sending a son to work for a time in Rabaul? (Harding 1967:206)

Harding tempers this statement by noting the counterbalancing effects of wage-labor profits on the trade system—that is, that an increase in migrant labor caused concurrent suspension of a number of an individual's trade relations. Population increases absorbed trade profits. Moreover, increased mobility of other parties in the trade system led to more generalized knowledge about the indigenous economic system by *all* participants in the various trading spheres.

In the mid-1960s the government banned sailing in two-masted canoes because administrators judged the vessels to be too dangerous to sail safely in the precarious Vitiaz and Dampier straits. This ban placed additional constraints on the trade system and made the islanders more dependent on cash and on commercial boat schedules than they had been previously. Trading continued, but the scheduling and directions of trading trips were rearranged. These changes disintegrated Siassi's monopoly on control of access to valued trade items and reshuffled some trade alliances (see also Harding 1967:206–207).

Although some of the ethnographic details of the trade system changed, the "cultural system" that provided patterns for Mandok values, goals, and evaluations of personal and group achievement persisted. Trade relationships and networks were already established, whether or not they were being exploited at any particular time. They could be reactivated at any time and, when possible, were reactivated whenever it was necessary.

EDUCATION: THE NEW ROAD
TO WEALTH AND STATUS

Administrative Approaches

Rarely if ever does a developing nation omit formal schooling from its development plans. The content and peripheral linkages (e.g., education and technology, education and political or religious dogma, etc.) vary, but some linkage is fundamental. PNG is no exception. Even before World War II, education was a major administrative priority. How that priority was exercised is another matter. Throughout the history of PNG the government has changed several times, and government policies on education changed, too. Each policy shift described a different stage in the growth of the school system in PNG, and these stages of education policy had a direct impact on Mandok ideas about "development." They bear some description here.[4]

When the German colonial government divided northeast New Guinea between the Lutheran and Catholic missions, it allowed each mission to establish education as it saw fit. Between the world wars the Australian colonial government in the Mandated Territory of New Guinea took little interest in education as a policy rule, and it did not interfere with the missions, either. In the "mission phase," missions established and managed education through both colonial periods (see Pomponio n.d.; Pomponio and Lancy 1986). Approaches and emphases differed between the churches, but generally they taught rudimentary literacy, numeracy, and religious instruction for conversion to Christianity. Across the country the start of this phase varied with the earliest dates of European contact and the establishment of colonial rule. In areas controlled by missions, education was identified with and in practice linked to conversion to Christianity:

> The mission school was an extension of the trading relationship, a form of paid employment. The Marists and Sacred Heart missionaries paid openly for orphans and other children who could be brought to a boarding school, away from the distractions of the village, taught the fundamentals of the Faith and formed into the nucleus of the new Christian community. After a catechumenate of two or three years

pupils were paid off with tobacco and cloth and dispatched to their villages with news of the white man's wealth, literacy and beliefs. (Firth 1986:156)

Though interpreted cynically, Firth's documentation of mission activities sketched some of the evangelizing strategies used during the early days of mission activities. "Blackbirding" (a form of slavery used to procure labor forces throughout the Pacific) in New Britain left many orphaned children with no security. Many were killed or left to run wild. The Catholic mission took them in for humanitarian as well as recruitment reasons; by 1893 there were three orphanages on New Britain (Mulderink 1989).

Although the administration and the missions shared general goals, they differed subtly in their definitions of development. Government administrators viewed development in terms of the technological and economic changes necessary for adopting a market economy. The missions described development to rural villagers more in terms of changing their morality (i.e., "civilizing children of nature") and raising their standard of living. Hence, though defining it differently, both groups viewed formal education as the major agent of "development." For the most part, colonial administrators were content to let the missions do their work unmolested, for it made governance easier.

Mission and school activities were suspended during World War II. This period is thus rarely analyzed further in relation to education development history. But Mandok war veterans recounted with both great amusement and awe the variety of things they learned from Australian and American soldiers. This new knowledge ranged from eating new foods in metal packages to shooting guns and reading books. The men also learned a lot about European (specifically Australian and American) *thinking*, though they "focused" these lessons through their own "cultural lenses." They spoke of the soldiers with fondness and were proud to have served with them. By their nature, these very personal experiences set the stage for Mandok's later "boom" in schooling (see Chapter 8).

Australia assumed Trusteeship of northeast New Guinea in 1946. The postwar administration unified the territories of Papua and New Guinea. W. C. Groves became the first Director of Education in the new unified Territory. He tried to unite the various mission and administration schools in both regions of the country into one unified system. A trained anthropologist, Groves emphasized a "rural bias" and a "blending of cultures" in his approach to schooling. Language was a contentious issue in a country of from 700 to 1,000 different languages. The government schools used English as the language of instruction; mission schools used a variety of vernaculars and linguae francae, depending on the sect and locale.

By 1955, administrators realized that this approach was inadequate for economic and technical development. Paul Hasluck initiated a campaign for universal primary education (UPE) to achieve universal literacy in English in the Territory. UPE became the official goal of the education system of the 1950s and early 1960s. Fearing the rise of an indigenous (and potentially exploitative) elite, Hasluck provided for little education beyond the primary level. Even though this approach represented a major shift from Groves's educational philosophy, Hasluck's successors criticized his policy as paternalistic and potentially disastrous.

The approach of national independence (achieved in 1975) ushered in a third phase of education: "expansionism" (Pomponio n.d.; Pomponio and Lancy 1986). Expansionism lasted less than ten years, but it had a profound effect on the development of education both in the nation and on Mandok. Following the recommendations of a United Nations advisory committee (United Nations 1962), education was redesigned to produce an educated work force of Papua New Guineans to take over positions largely held by expatriates in a newly independent country. G. T. Roscoe orchestrated this comprehensive expansion and overhaul of primary schools using expatriate (especially Australian) teachers. During this phase, the motto of the Education Department was "Education for Development." "Development" here meant national development and presumed economic and technological change.

All levels of the education system blossomed during this phase. Rural areas not previously served by primary schools received them. Secondary education was expanded and tertiary education was created. The University of Papua New Guinea opened in Port Moresby in 1966, followed the next year by the University of Technology in Lae. Various other vocational, technical, teachers' training colleges, and subprofessional training institutions were also established during this period.

Education on Mandok, 1938–65

Schooling on Mandok was always in the hands of the Catholic mission. In 1938 the Mandok sent four young men to the Catholic mission in Rabaul in east New Britain. There they received basic literacy and catechistic training for the three years before World War II. The mission resumed its activities around 1948, with the same modest goals. The men who had gone to school before the war became catechists. They traveled around the Siassi area, teaching and evangelizing. Thus, Groves's "blending of cultures" approach and Hasluck's UPE policies were conflated into one long "mission phase."

In order to understand the profound changes education and missionization brought to Mandok, some background is necessary to describe the social and political climates of the times. At the time the mission was established (1937), the Mandok had strong, centralized leadership (described in Chapters 4 and 6). Village leaders were particularly strong individuals who had considerable personal power and influence. When they decided to admit the Catholic mission, these leaders implemented several changes almost immediately, not in itself a surprising development of mission contact. What is surprising, perhaps, is that the Mandok *themselves* instigated many of the changes, based on their understanding of what Christianity entailed. A few notable examples are pertinent to our consideration of subsequent developments on Mandok.

First, the feasting system was changed, as already mentioned (Chapter 6). Second, the Mandok discontinued using *rumai* houses in the village. (The *rumai* was the ceremonial or men's clubhouse; each *runai* had one.[5]) Before European contact, male initiation rituals and other ritual activities exclusive to males were held in each group's *rumai*. When the Mandok converted to Catholicism, they decided that initiation rituals would then be performed either in the village plaza or in the (newly consecrated) men's area (*pulat*). This was decided for three reasons. First, these buildings were enormous, and the rising population left less space for them. Second, every time a new *rumai* was built it had to be consecrated with a great feast. This required many pigs and tons of taro, sweet potato, manioc, and other resources. Third, Umboi Lutherans became less and less cooperative in planting new gardens for the Mandok's ceremonial consumption. Instead, Mandok villagers pooled these resources and applied them to building the mission. All of these projects were part of the "new road" brought by the missionaries and were designed to help the village "get ahead" and "grow" (i.e., "develop"). The last huge *rumai* house was built around 1920; after that, smaller ones were built. By the early 1940s the practice of building them had been abandoned.

Gradually, postpartum taboos were relaxed. Previously, when a woman was in about her fourth month of pregnancy, she moved back to her parents' house. After the birth (especially of a firstborn), she lived in virtual seclusion for at least a year, possibly more, depending on the time it took for her husband to organize a feast in the child's honor, after which most of the taboos were lifted (see Chapter 4). The couple was still not supposed to have sexual intercourse until the child was weaned and walking—about two to three years. The woman returned to her husband's house, but he usually slept in the *pulat*. According to middle-aged Mandok informants, patrol officers and the missionaries felt that a two- to three-year "separation" was not conducive to proper family life as they defined it because it led to philandering and broken marriages. They encouraged the men to return to their houses sooner. Consequently, by 1980 births were much closer together—about one to two years apart.

The population was rising, and with it rose the rate of population increase. Freedman (1967:36–37, App. 1) calculated that in the absence of population-limiting techniques, the annual rate of population increase was 2.2 percent. This figure was in line with the normal projected growth of 2.1 percent expected in the absence of any sort of population-controlling methods. By 1980 the rate of population increase was approaching 3.0 percent. Before European contact, families were limited to two or three children, but in two generations family size had tripled. (By 1987 the average family had ten children; over 75 percent of the population was under the age of 30.)

Perhaps the most drastic change was effected when the missionaries began a school in the village. All the children were taken off the reefs and put into school. By 1954, 51 children (33 male, 18 female) were enrolled in school. This constituted 22 percent of the total resident population for that year (Patrol Report Finschhafen 2, 1954–55:App. B). Because of this level of enrollment, a high percentage of the total potential labor force of the village was taken away from food-gathering activities. In a subsistence economy such as the Mandok's, in which older children and teenagers can catch enough fish or gather enough shellfish in one afternoon to provide the family's supper, this was a major change.

In 1960 the community built a permanent mission house and St. Finbar "Primary T" School[6] (grades K through 3) on Por Island, about 600 meters across a channel from Mandok. The school opened in 1961. Students went next to mission schools at Vunapope for grades 4 through 6, and then to high school or technical school in Rabaul. Although sending their children off to distant shores to attend high school involved fear of the unknown, parents' monetary investment was virtually nil. Moreover, each child sent to the mission school was one less mouth to feed on Mandok. The school children were in town centers and within reach of family trade relations or kinsmen who worked at the mission-owned plantations. These youths saw visible evidence of progress in town centers and, through their own experiences, became a part of the process of national development (explored in Chapter 8).

CHANGING PATTERNS OF LEADERSHIP

Luluais *and* tultuls

During the postwar period the primary evidence of colonial government in the rural areas was episodic, direct contact with government patrol officers. Following a system of local administrative representation initiated during the German era, native officers called *luluai*s and their assistants, *tultul*s, were appointed. (The terms *luluai* and *tultul* are Tolai words that have been incorporated into Tok Pisin vocabulary to mean "headman" and "assistant headman," respectively.) These officials were supposed to be selected on the basis of character and intelligence. On Mandok, most of the early *luluai*s and *tultul*s already were recognized to be people of social standing, often the next in line for the *maron*ship or a *runai* elder (see Chapter 4).[7]

*Tultul*s were required to speak Tok Pisin. This requirement implied that appointed officials had some previous exposure to Europeans, most likely the result of plantation labor experience. The infrequency of patrols, frequent transfers of patrol officers, and lack of clear direction from a central administration had "the result that administration [took] the form of a series of arbitrary and often conflicting orders from strangers rather than the expression of a considered policy" (Mair 1948:57). The colonial government instituted local patrol posts around 1948 as part of a move to consolidate guidance and make it possible for the same patrol officer to make repeated visits to the same villages (Mair 1948:58). But Siassi did not receive its own patrol post until 1963, when one was built at Semo (formerly Gom) on Umboi. The area was formerly administered from Subdistrict headquarters at Finschhafen.

Regulations had been introduced as early as 1903 "obliging native populations to plant specified numbers of coconut or other cash-yielding trees," but they were not taken seriously until 1912 (Mair 1948:84). From 1912 to 1930 administrators and missionaries expended considerable energy throughout the Territory to enforce them. In Siassi Subdistrict, administrators felt that more accessible supervision at the government level would encourage the indigenous population to develop and maintain cash-cropping activities and thus achieve self-sufficiency (Patrol Report Finschhafen 1, 1952:4). The Semo patrol station was part of this plan.

Local Government Councils

From the prewar period through the 1960s, patrol officers in Siassi observed that "most European contact comes from either recruiters or missionaries, and the attitude is that the administration is not interested in their [the Siassi's] well being" (Patrol Report Finschhafen 6, 1950:4).

Partially in preparation for independence, but more immediately in response to the number and diversity of languages, subsistence systems, and cultural groups in the country, the Australian colonial administration began introducing the concept of "Native Local Government Councils" (LGCs) during the late 1950s. Repeatedly, patrols noted the general apathy and suspicion villagers had toward administration programs and policies. The Siassi Local Government Council was established in 1964.

Village councillors were different from *luluai*s and *tultul*s. First, they were elected rather than appointed. Second, instead of representing the colonial government, they represented village needs and desires in localized monthly meetings and in an annual Siassi-wide conference. Various problems and solutions to the different communities' plights were discussed at these meetings, presumably in the hopes of achieving faster remedies. Because of rough wind and seas that predominate for about eight months of the year, attending "regular" meetings was virtually impossible for the islanders. In spite of these difficulties, they were eager to participate in the new council system. Much of this initial enthusiasm was generated by younger men who had worked on plantations and had seen LGCs benefiting communities on New Britain.

Initially, LGCs seemed to be a good idea and the logical next step after other "development projects" in which they were engaged by this time.

By the mid-1960s, the Mandok seemed poised for "development." Siassi peoples had their own LGC to look out for their interests and those of other islanders. Things looked promising from inside the village, too. The Mandok had expanded their gardens and planted coconuts for copra production. As more young men went off to earn cash on the mission plantation, those at home were encouraged by the promise of copra profits. A school had been built on Por, and children were being educated formally into the new way brought by Europeans. Villagers seemed eager and willing to try just about any project that was offered.

Unfortunately, this initial eagerness was short-lived. In its place grew a cynical skepticism, born of repeated "failures" and changing government definitions of and rules for "development." The reasons for this skepticism and Mandok's history of "failures" are the topics of the next chapter.

CHAPTER EIGHT

❧ Turning Tides of Development

The Siassi people are ambitious for development, although not too anxious to do anything constructive about their ambitions. They travel in considerable numbers, mainly to Lae and Finschhafen, whenever they can get space on a vessel. Many of them work in New Britain, mainly on plantations, but almost invariably recruiters come to Siassi with their own vessels. The Siassi people rarely go looking for work, principally because of the communications difficulty.

Patrol Report Finschhafen 11, 1961–62:9

Now, whenever I hear talk of "development," I flinch. I think, "Uh-oh, they're going to take something else away from us now."

Mandok man, 1980

For most Westerners, "development" means economic and technical change and participation in a market economy. In developing nations, "economic and technical change" implies cultural and social change, which requires education and has historically included missionization as well. If this sounds complicated and reminiscent of the refrain, "The knee bone's connected to the thigh bone," picture the confusion of rural villagers on an isolated four-hectare island!

Government, mission, and school administrators had different definitions of "development," and each definition influenced their notions of "development problems" in Siassi and the "solutions" they proposed. Businessmen and itinerant traders had no definition of, or interest in, "development"; their interests were strictly commercial. The Mandok interacted with all of them, however. Contact with each different kind of "European" carried different consequences for the Mandok. Each one also presented them with different ideas about how to earn cash.

By 1960 the administrative development priorities for the Siassi District were (1) cash cropping, (2) resettlement of overcrowded small islands, especially Aromot and Mandok, and (3) introduction and establishment of Native Local Government Councils (see Chapter 7) and election of representatives from each village (Patrol Reports Finschhafen 9 and 11, 1961–62). Except for a reversal in the importance ascribed to population, these priorities were no different from those noted in Chapter 7 for the period immediately following World War II. This chapter examines externally introduced development projects.

In 1979 there was no word or phrase in Mutu or Tok Pisin for "development." In Tok Pisin the idea had to be expressed in such phrases as *kirapim ples*, "to lift up, bring up the place or village," and *gohet*, "go ahead, forward." These phrases were usually followed by the promise of a better *nepoŋ*, Mutu for "lifestyle" or "standard of living" (TP, *sindaun*, "sit down"). By 1986, individual Mandok had picked up the word *divelipmen*, "development," probably from their children who worked in towns. I remain unconvinced, however, that villagers changed their understanding of what *divelipmen* meant. From the village perspective, all of these new roads introduced by Europeans—education, Christianity, cash cropping, and labor migration—led eventually to cash. Siassi people did not define "development" as an abstract concept of progress (itself a Western notion) but rather in terms of earning money to buy desired (mostly European-introduced, if not European-manufactured) things. "Development" for them meant "personal access to cash" and living within the new *lo* brought by national government, especially by mission representatives.

In time, doing unskilled migrant labor gave way to other routes to earning money that centered around three broad themes: cash cropping, cooperative businesses (trade stores), and secondary education. We will consider each in turn.

RELOCATION I: CASH CROPPING

Most patrol officers in Siassi defined "development" in terms of agricultural projects, especially cash cropping. Because the islanders lacked land and a fresh-water source, intensive cash cropping required resettlement to Umboi Island. We will consider these two aspects of "development" together.

During World War II the administration was worried about the possible extinction of Siassi populations. By the late 1950s and early 1960s, government concerns had turned instead to the overpopulation of the small islands, particularly Aromot, Mandok, and Tuam. The most obvious solution was to relocate these communities. The idea of relocating islanders was not new; nor was it limited to the government. As early as 1892, Rev. Bamler had used this notion as a battle cry for his evangelical enterprise:

> It is a pity to see the many large uninhabited stretches. Along the Simban banks there are so many coconuts that another 200 people could easily live there without subjecting the present inhabitants to any deprivation. But that is how things are here: On the little islands a great crowd is squatting on one heap, and since there is just no room

for the rising generation the babies are aborted or killed after birth. All the while on the mainland and on the large islands the ground is lying idle and the produce is rotting. And if one tells the people, "Why don't you emigrate there?" they answer, "The people there would sorcerize us." This shines a harsh spotlight on the text, "Leave the indigenes in their paradise and don't disturb them." In this situation only the Mission can help, and alongside of its noblest task to win souls for the Heavenly King, it will populate the land for the earthly ruler. (Bamler 1892:A5)

Residents of the small islands were encouraged to move to various points on Umboi. Starting in the early 1960s, patrol officers invoked the exercise of trade and marriage relations, and they approached different Umboi villages to propose that each sell land to the government for the purpose of resettling the islanders. In all, five blocks were considered. The northern tip of Umboi was, and still is, uninhabited, except for the small village of Mantagen. Officials attempted to purchase a parcel of land of some 2,000 hectares (5,000 acres) there for the Mandok and Aromot people (see Figure 1.4, p. 15). The Mantagen area seemed perfect for the Mandok because it gave them land and a reef-studded shoreline on which they could continue fishing and gathering. Long-standing trade and kinship ties connected the Mandok and some Mantagen people (via other relations in Barim), so they would not be total strangers. This area was, moreover, close to the ancient village site of Nuru, first landing place of the Marist missionaries; government officers and missionaries thus hoped it also had religious significance for the Mandok.

At first, both the Mandok and the Aromot entertained the idea with enthusiasm. It was not long, however, before administrators learned that resettlement was not a simple matter. The first problem they met was determining ownership of this land. Men from Mantagen, Mararamu, Aiyau, Barim, and Oropot all claimed ownership of land within the designated area. Put another way, people from five different villages and two separate language groups from different sides of Umboi claimed ownership of the proposed resettlement site.[1]

The second problem was more perplexing than the first:

ALL the people of these villages flatly refused to have anything to do with the idea of selling any of this northern land to the Administration for the purpose of resettling any of the Mandok and the Aramot [*sic*] people. The people loudly proclaimed that it was their land and they had all sorts of plans for developing it. When it was pointed out that no use had been made of the land for over 50 years many reasons were given, all of them extremely unconvincing. (Special Report, Patrol Report Finschhafen 5, No. II, 1961–62:App. B, p. 1)

Other land parcels in different areas were considered for each island community. Once again, by the time the projects got under way, both parties to the transactions had reneged.

Patrol officers initially blamed the missions for these continuing changes of heart:

> The two different faiths on Siassi allow their religious differences to overlap into their ordinary life, the Lutherans being worst in this respect and are in several villages very resentful of the Catholics. Examples of this are the difficulties the Mandok are having in getting land for subsistence purposes and the resentment at Kabib village because of the intrusion of the Catholics into nearby Kampalap village. The European missionaries themselves are mainly to blame for this situation as there is a certain amount of rivalry between them to convert the people to their particular faith, so it is natural that this feeling will extend to the natives under their influence. (Patrol Report Finschhafen 17, 1961–62:24)

Most of the time the antagonism manifested itself in petty squabbles and competition between villages, but occasionally it had serious consequences. Cadet Patrol Officer J. D. Martin noted that

> since [World War II] the Roman Catholic mission has slowly started to gain influence in many villages and the position has arisen where half a village are ardent Lutherans and half are ardent Catholics. This position reached a climax within the last year, when schoolboys from Gizarum central school burned down the house of the native Catholic mission teacher and he was forced to leave the area. . . . The [Lutheran] missionaries . . . quite naturally resent the intrusion but have told all natives that violence of any kind is to be deplored. (Patrol Report Finschhafen 6, 1950:7)

Many years earlier, in his 1927 report, Rev. Bamler had predicted that if the Catholic mission were to come to Siassi, they would enter via Kampalap (east Umboi). Some Awelkon students, passing by Kampalap in 1960, burned down the Catholic church there (Mulderink 1989). Problems persisted through the late 1960s, but afterward relations changed to an attitude of peaceful coexistence (Mulderink 1980; Kigasung 1976:11).

This explanation presumes, however, that missions dictated social and political relations between communities, who then accepted them passively. It thus denies Siassi peoples their own history. It is also too simplistic.

Religion correlated only superficially with the dissenting communities. The more telling cases involved the *exceptions* to the refusal pattern. Gauru and Yangla, both Lutheran communities, *did* sell their land to the island communities. Why? After they bought the land, the Mandok still stayed on their tiny island. Why? Since the respective missions have apparently resolved their differences, the question remains: why did these relocation problems persist 30 years later? There is an alternate explanation that considers both ethnic identities and the economic interdependence between communities that have land and those that do not.

Much of this friction reflected long-standing *atam* relationships (see Chapter 6), which stressed competition and one-upmanship between individuals and, consequently, groups (e.g., *lains*; see Chapter 5). Peoples' initial choice of missions may have echoed old rivalries from the outset. The different faiths may have provided a new focus for this competition, but did not cause it. The underlying competition between Siassi communities is better viewed as the product of long-standing social and political processes, rather than competition between introduced religions.

For the islanders, Gauru and Yangla were the most prominent of the Kaimanga communities. They were the closest Umboi communities to Aromot and Mandok, both geographically and socioculturally. They were also allied through trade and marriage ties (see Chapters 1 and 3). Their willingness to sell land to the Mandok (and the Aromot) reflects the long-standing kin-based relationships between them. They were interdependent, despite sporadic feuds and the gardeners' doubts about "the islanders' ability to work" (Patrol Report Finschhafen 17, 1961–62:App. E).[2] That is to say, not only had these two communities offered land to the Mandok before World War II (see Chapters 1 and 3), but they were obligated by the bonds of local trade, marriage, and adoption (i.e., obligations of "kinship") at least to entertain the notion of doing so again. Although similar kin relationships existed between the Mandok and the other Umboi communities, they were neither as numerous nor as strong as those with Gauru and Yangla. Genealogies that traced the network of relationships back to these villages showed over 100 years of kinship. Peaceful contacts and trade with the Kowai communities were recent; although officially noted since the first decade of the 20th century (Harding 1967:200–202), they actually occurred much later—after World War II (Ploeg 1989).

Though pacification increased trade and marriage alliances, the process was not always smooth. In 1912 some Gomlonggon men killed two brothers named Weber and their Malay cook. The islanders were sequestered on their islands while a German punitive expedition retaliated. The German Annual Report for 1912–13 recorded the incident:

In October the Weber brothers were murdered on the island of Umboi, where they had intended to establish themselves as planters. The south-eastern part of the island may be regarded as pacified, whereas the northwestern section is not yet under the control of the Administration. Disregarding all warnings, the Weber brothers chose that area for their venture. Although they believed they knew the character of the natives well, they fell victims to the rapacity of the mountain tribes. The guilty parties were killed in a fight against the police troop of the district office. One of the murderers was captured and shot in accordance with martial law. (Sack and Clark 1979:354)

What the report does not record is that the German punitive expedition used Mandok men to lure the Gomlonggons down to the beach near Bunsil on the pretext of trade (see also Harding 1967:193n.). During the fighting a few unmarried girls hid in the reeds along the river and escaped. They were later discovered by Mandok men, who took them back to Mandok as their wives.[3] Thus, although there was increased intermarriage and trade, and therefore increased interaction, the original impetus to the relationship occurred under less than optimal circumstances. Most Mandok did not have Kowai trade partners at this time; they met on the beach at Bunsil for a "market." Transactions were conducted in "silent trade"; that is, the Kowai presented their wares (e.g., vegetables), which were placed in a row of heaps, and then they retreated. The Mandok would then take the vegetables and leave their goods: fish or shellfish, or sometimes a wooden bowl or a set of trochus armlets. By the time of my fieldwork, people were able to communicate with each other in Tok Pisin, and relations were more amicable. Some young women knew each other from their school days at the Aupwel Vocational School. But people who had no kinship or friendship connections in nearby villages did not feel comfortable at Bunsil and could not wait, for the most part, to leave.

This kind of social relationship became important in subsequent Mandok discussions about "development." But initially, increased intermarriage with Kowai communities, however achieved, coupled with the new opportunity to earn money, did give the Mandok an increase in surplus vegetable foods and some additional land rights.

The uneasy alliance also created certain economic drawbacks. In accordance with traditional boundaries recognized by both parties, the reefs and sea belonged to the islanders, and the bush and gardens belonged to the bush people. Pacification, intermarriage, and government insistence that *all* "natives" garden changed these understandings. Crosscutting kinship ties, and the rights and obligations of kin to share, impinged on the distinctive economic pursuits of both groups. Now that individuals in these communities shared "blood" ties, the obligations of kinship demanded that they also share "substance" and material resources. By the early 1950s, some Kowai people were collecting on the reefs, and the islanders were "borrowing" sago from their newfound relatives. This resulted in many feuds, title disputes, and accusations of sago poaching. In 1952 the situation climaxed with a total breakdown of trade relations between the Kowai communities and the islanders (Patrol Report Finschhafen 1, 1952, Part II:7). The disruption of local trade and the "wildness" of the Kowai became additional Mandok excuses for resisting relocation.

Perhaps the real problem lay deeper, embedded in the Mandok's (and other islanders') perceptions of themselves as mobile sea people, not sedentary horticulturalists. Patrol Officer Parrish further noted that, though Gauru and Yangla people gave the islanders land for gardens, the islanders made only half-hearted attempts at horticulture that were inadequate to develop horticulture as a means of subsistence. The problem, as he interpreted it, was that "islanders claim they are fishermen and as such cannot be expected to toil in gardens in the same way as 'bush natives'" (Patrol Report Finschhafen 1, 1952:7). This interpretation better explains why the same problems regarding relocation persisted through the 1980s, despite the good relations then between the missions and the resumption of local trade among Siassi communities. Add to this the islanders' deep-seated fear of the bush, with its evil spirits and diseases, their fears of local sorcerers, and their belief that life on the sea is inherently better than life in the bush. Relocation then looks less and less appealing to an islander.

Agricultural projects initiated on Umboi had varying results. In general, Umboi Islanders widened their horticultural base to include cash crops. Kaimanga communities tried copra, Robusta coffee, and cocoa. Kowai gardeners also tried rice and Arabica coffee. These latter two failed, due to neglect (Patrol Report Finschhafen 9, 1961–62:7). By 1970 the major "development projects" in progress in Siassi included coconuts (copra), cocoa (bearing fruit by 1974), and robusta coffee. A few cows were also purchased to test a herding project. The major obstacles to Umboi gardeners seemed to be the amount of attention required to grow a particular crop and the perennial Siassi-wide problem of transporting their products to market (Ploeg 1984).

The Mandok, and most of the other islanders, cultivated more coconut trees for copra production. The Mandok had 1,525 mature and 920 immature trees by 1970 (Patrol Report Siassi 1, 1970–71:6–7). Three years later they had 1,617 mature and 1,799 immature trees (Patrol Report Siassi 2, 1973–74, App. B). Patrol officers were never impressed with Mandok's copra output, however; nor were they ever convinced that Mandok gardening efforts were sincere. But the Mandok never had the land to support large-scale cash cropping. Even when they did cash-crop, most of these projects were *communal projects*; the proceeds from copra production were used to stock the village trade store. Trade-store profits, in turn, were used to build and repair the church and school buildings and to provide parents educational loans for their children's secondary-school fees. These projects provided the individual with little if any personal revenue.

LOCAL COOPERATIVES

The Mandok's communal projects were part of a larger government program. Starting in 1958, the national government offered rural communities financial incentives to establish local cooperative businesses. These efforts were also encouraged by the missions, who used them to inspire villagers to "love thy neighbor as thy *wantok*" (TP, "one talk," "speaker of the same language," or "countryman," with the implication of in-group membership and mutual support). Missionaries stressed that Christian teachings were already extant in, for instance, Mandok's kinship obligations, *runai* membership, and allegiance to the *lain*. Cooperative projects were described as an effort to expand the notion of *lain* to include the whole village.

When trade stores came to Siassi in the mid-1960s, the mission helped to establish a store and counseled its clerks in order to prepare the Mandok for independence and self-sufficiency. The villagers pooled their capital to form the Mandok Society, a community business society that controlled a copra drier and the village trade store. Coconut trees for the production of copra were planted on the limited land in Muru. Proceeds from copra sales were used to stock the trade store with desired goods previously obtainable only in town centers. These goods included canned meats and fish, rice, razor blades, biscuits, pens, paper, envelopes, fish hooks, and fishing tackle. Profits from the trade store were deposited into a communal fund from which villagers could draw short-term loans, especially for school fees.

Outside of Mandok Island, several attempts were made to develop cooperative business societies that would integrate the entire Siassi region into a single network. The Finschhafen Marketing Development Society (FMDS) was established in 1958, and Siassi was included within its sphere of influence. Though its establishment did alleviate some transport difficulties for a while, its services were not adequate for the times. It ran a boat, the *M.V. Vitiaz*, in which Siassi people bought shares. Although the boat was solid enough for Siassi conditions, it was too small for the job of hauling the various Siassi products to market.

In 1970 the Siassi Cooperative, Ltd. was established, again to promote local businesses (Patrol Report Siassi 1, 1970–71:2). This organization also ran a ship, the *M.V. Siassi*, to haul local products to market. But the organization suffered from two perennial problems in Siassi. The first was boat trouble. The *M.V. Siassi* was too small and had no freezer, and it never fulfilled its intended purpose, either. Islanders were thus precluded from fishing commercially. The second problem was that the people sold their goods to the first buyer rather than waiting for the Cooperative's agent. Given the undependability of transport and trade and the dangerous sea and weather patterns in this region, this sales decision was probably sound business practice in Siassi. It provided a quick cash return, but it did nothing to nurture cooperative market enterprises.

All development projects in Siassi suffered from problems with "communications," a term Australian patrol officers used in several senses, from the exchange of messages (e.g., by mail, radio, or telegraph) to transportation of supplies and people. Transportation required both roads on Umboi and boat service to wharves on all the islands at which supply boats could dock. The colonial administration built a road on Umboi to connect the Kowai and Kaimanga halves of the island; it also built a permanent wharf at Lablab. Mandok and Aromot islands built rickety jetties (see Chapter 1) in the mid-1970s with the help of the Catholic mission. Malai Island had no anchorage and thus remained without a wharf. Malai Islanders paddled their outrigger canoes out to waiting boats to receive or ship their cargo and passengers, much like my first guide wanted me to do when I first went to Mandok. The Catholic mission ran two boats: first the *M.V. Collomb,* which ran aground in the early 1970s, and then the *M.V. Yawani* (see Chapter 9 for an in-depth discussion of the *Yawani*). The Lutheran mission also had two boats: a large one called the *M.V. Umboi* and a small pinnace called the *M.V. Karapo.* Two airstrips were also built in Siassi. The Australian Lutheran mission built and maintained an airstrip at Lablab, and the government built one near the Semo patrol post, which was maintained by the Siassi Local Government Council (see Chapter 7). All of these projects were designed to increase "communications" and to transport produce to markets in Lae and Madang.

With national independence (1975) came decentralization of governmental authority. The local administrative system was once again reshuffled. The old FMDS was remodeled and renamed the Finschhafen-Kabwuum Planning and Development Authority (FKPDA). This organization built more roads on Umboi and cement wharves on Aromot and Tuam. The Lutheran mission had built a temporary wharf at Lablab; after independence the administration built a permanent one. Gizarum (on the west side of Umboi) already had a wharf, which belonged to the Gizarum plantation.

The FKPDA was renamed again in 1984 to the Finschhafen-Siassi-Kabwuum Development Corporation, known as FISIKA. This change incorporated Siassi formally in its name, though Siassi had always been within its sphere of operations. FISIKA, which functioned as an umbrella corporation that financed local businesses, got its working capital from two sources: government contracts and sales of shares to villagers. Because FISIKA's first executive officer was a Mandok, the Mandok bought a significant number of shares. (This man's family was the largest single shareholder.) Many Mandok supported this organization and looked to it for "development." Because one of their own sons was in a position of authority and power, they felt that finally someone was looking out for their interests.

EDUCATION *IS* DEVELOPMENT

If you go to school, then later [when you grow up] you will have a better life in the village.

Sign painted on the wall of the Por-Mandok Community School, 1979

The Mandok's understanding of and values ascribed to education must be understood within the wider economic, political, and historical context in which schooling became available. Administrative predictions estimated that labor needs between 1968 and 1973 would climb to between 20,000 and 35,000 "for people with some secondary education" (McKinnon 1968:102). Students were pushed through the education system in anticipation of national independence and were able to get well-paying jobs in towns immediately after their school training. This training could be in high school or in various tertiary and vocational schools. Skilled and ambitious graduates of the school system had ample opportunities for rapid upward mobility and high-paying positions.

As the population of Mandok started to rise dramatically, Mandok parents searched for ways to increase their economic resource base. G. T. Roscoe's education expansion program of the 1960s (see Chapter 7) was perfectly timed for Mandok adolescents, some of whom were children of war veterans. Girls as well as boys were educated beyond the primary level. In 1964, two boys were sent to Vunapope for grades 4 through 6. They were followed in 1965 by seven children; three of them were girls. These two cohorts mark a critical juncture in Mandok education and development history. With them, migratory labor changed *qualitatively*. Migrants who had secondary and tertiary training were no longer "laborers"; they became part of the highly paid "educated elite" of the nation. The civil service replaced plantations as the largest employer in the country. This group of students was the "first generation" of Mandok's educated elite. They were "elite" for two reasons. First, they were the first group to be educated beyond primary school and therefore beyond the "3 Rs" of the "mission phase" of schooling. Second, all were children of Mandok *bigmen*: they were elite to begin with.

Table 8.1 shows the occupational distributions of Mandok born in five-year spans between 1900 and 1960. The distribution of occupations shows a pronounced shift away from plantation labor and toward skilled career employment. A sex difference is evident in some careers. High-school attendance usually led to careers as civil servants or teachers for both males and females, but males generally went farther in both occupations, gaining middle-level mangement or high-school teaching positions. Attendance at technical and vocational schools was divided between the sexes. Males went to technical schools and became carpenters and mechanics; vocational schools were usually attended by females, who became secretaries, cooks, and nurses. People of either sex could become clerks. Carpenters, mechanics, teachers, nurses, and clerks accounted for the majority of graduates in part because the training periods for these occupations were short: two years was the minimum, and then the student was employable. The rest could be accomplished as "in-service training."

As the seat of local government and mission headquarters changed, the high schools that Mandok students attended changed accordingly. Depending on the year of entry into Form I (grade 7), Mandok students attended secondary school in Rabaul, Dregerhafen, Madang, or Lae. All

TABLE 8.1 *Occupational distribution for people born between 1900 and 1960 (in five-year spans)*

OCCUPATION	1900–05 M	1900–05 F	1906–10 M	1906–10 F	1911–15 M	1911–15 F	1916–20 M	1916–20 F	1921–25 M	1921–25 F	1926–30 M	1926–30 F	1931–35 M	1931–35 F	1936–40 M	1936–40 F	1941–45 M	1941–45 F	1946–50 M	1946–50 F	1951–55 M	1951–55 F	1956–60 M	1956–60 F	ALL YEARS M	ALL YEARS F	ALL YEARS TOTAL
Plantation laborer	1				3		1		4		3		5		8		4								29	–	29
Military							22														3		2		27	–	27
Ship's crew	1				1								2		2		1		4		3		3		17	–	17
Carpenter									1								3		3		5		5		17	–	17
Teacher (K–6)																			1	1	3	1	5	1	9	3	12
Clerk, typist, secretary																					2	2	2	3	4	5	9
Cook																		1	1	2		4		1	1	8	9
Nurse																				2		3		4	–	9	9
Catechist							2		1				1		1										5	–	5
Administrator																			2				1		3	–	3
Teacher (7–12)																			2		1				3	–	3
Teacher at teacher training college																				1		1			–	2	2
Nun																						1		3	–	4	4
Mission carver																										4	4

						Total		
Sign writer/painter		1				2	–	2
Librarian		1	1			2	–	2
Mechanic		1				1	–	1
Detective, CIB		3	3			6	–	6
Tailor			1			1	–	1
Engineer			1			1	–	1
Architect		1	1			2	–	2
Air traffic controller		1	1			1	–	1
Bank worker		1	1			1	–	1
Plumber		1	1	1		2	1	3
Welder		1	1			1	–	1
Driver		2	2			2	–	2
Asst. catechist		1	1			1	–	1
Stevedore		1	1			1	–	1
Ship's capt.	1	1	1		1	3	–	3
(see "Ship's crew")	1	1	1			4	–	4
						146	32	178

these locations were town centers along traditional trade routes, except for Lae, which was by this time accessible by commercial boat. Dregerhafen was the only government high school Mandok students attended: all the others were run by the Catholic mission. The children, although far from home, were never far from a support group. The first students to go to school were accompanied by a male kinsman who cared for them while they were away from home. Other relatives worked at Vunapope plantation.

The administrative motto at this time (the mid- to late 1960s) was "Education for National Development." Students attended high school in a political and emotional climate of hope and promise. Most of their teachers at all levels were expatriate congregation members and lay missionaries from Germany, Holland, and Australia; all were dedicated to helping New Guineans "develop" in a Western sense of the term.

Mandok ideas about valued knowledge stressed acquisition of knowledge through an extended apprenticeship with a specialist. The school experiences of Mandok students were thus very much in line with their own traditions of learning and achievement. By attending school at mission and town centers they were at the source of the knowledge they sought. They went on to acquire well-paying town jobs and enjoyed rapid upward mobility.

Mandok traders were able to increase their trade networks in two ways. First, by visiting children at schools, they also visited towns and established new connections. Second, through remittances they sent to their village families, *the employed children themselves* became "new trade partners." This new wealth was absorbed into the traditional system of formal distributions and status mobility. These remittances, moreover, subsidized the declining trade system. Education, in essence, created a "new trade route." By educating their children who got town jobs and then sent money home, Mandok parents increased their economic base and staved off the demise of the trade system. They also evaded what they felt were intrusive government attempts both to relocate the village to Umboi and turn them into sedentary horticulturalists.

This, too, was short-lived. As self-government approached, the job market became flooded. Employment qualifications became more restrictive as opportunities declined. The "Weeden Report" (Weeden et al. 1969) became the guiding document for the education system of the 1970s. Primary schools were renamed "community schools" and were reorganized. This period was one of general "retrenchment" (Pomponio n.d.; Pomponio and Lancy 1986). The goals of the education department were to operate the system within the limitations of an internal budget and to wean PNG off the "massive infusions of foreign aid" (Lancy 1979b:1) that sustained it.

The Education Department's motto changed from "Education for National Development" to "Education for Better Community Living." No longer were children to be educated for town jobs; now they were supposed to return home and develop their communities from within. St. Finbar's school was renamed the "Por-Mandok Community School." Along with other PNG communities, Mandok was expected to maintain its own school through the payment of school fees and through community labor. A School Board of Managers, elected from the parents of school children, was in charge of the nonacademic management of the school.

The government's reduction of education resources, beginning with the Education Ordinance of 1970, hit the Mandok hard for several reasons. Education that had been free or had required a token payment of fees now cost a great deal in tuition, clothing, and transportation. The School Nationalization Program pushed Papua New Guineans out of school and into teaching service with six to ten years less education than their European predecessors. Teachers with less education and less firsthand knowledge of "European things" came to Mandok. They were no longer symbols of achievement in European domains, and the presence of strangers in the village caused many unanticipated problems (see Pomponio 1985).

Rising school fees and declining employment opportunities combined to make secondary education a more distant dream. The institution of a quota system for high-school entrance meant that as the number of children qualifying for high school increased, some children "failed" to make it. This system introduced a new concept of failure that had heretofore been absent (or at least less obvious). Many who did enroll soon returned home as jobless "school leavers." They were considered in the village to be "school failures." The mission worked against the notion of "failure," but the label persisted in parents' minds and influenced their approach to the whole process.

The proverbial "last straw" seems to have been the School Localization Program. High schools were built in rural areas in order to stem the flow of emigration from village life. The program was also designed to lessen the alienation felt by some previous boarding-school students by keeping them close to their home villages. Designed originally to encourage children to stay *in* school, it had the opposite effect on Mandok students. Instead of going to high school in town centers, they attended high school in two different parts of the Umboi "bush." The first was Gelem High School on the west side of Umboi. But the Kowai people who sold the land to the Lutheran mission (in the 1930s) kept asking for more money. They became so bothersome that in 1977 the missionaries moved the high school to Lablab on the east side of Umboi and renamed it Siassi High School (Ploeg 1989).[4] The students were no longer surrounded by kinsmen, no longer in urban centers, and no longer supported by the Catholic mission. Moreover, the high school, originally a Lutheran mission high school, was government-subsidized and controlled, as were most mission schools by this time, but the missions maintained an "advisory" capacity. To Mandok Catholics, Lutherans still ran Siassi High School.

Worse still, from the students' point of view, was that they now had to work in the school gardens. To children raised in a maritime environment, gardening was unpleasant and demeaning. The "first-generation" Mandok students who went to Vunapope during the mid-1960s were 17 to 19 years old at the time they entered Form I (grade 7). According to Mandok concepts of physical and moral development, they were on the verge of adulthood. In contrast, students attending school in Gelem and Lablab from 1970 onward were only between 12 and 14—too young, by Mandok standards, to be expected to do hard garden work. The students complained that they were being overworked and underfed in their bush high schools. Their parents, already wary of this new policy, felt both sorry for them and angry at the teachers for what they felt was unreasonable and cruel exploitation of "mere children." The students came home.

These changing attitudes are reflected in the total number of Mandok children sent off the island to secondary school (Figure 8.1). From 1964 to 1969, an increasing number of boys *and* girls went to a variety of secondary schools (including technical/vocational schools). This number peaked in 1970 and then dropped to zero within six years. No students were sent off the island (or remained in school if sent) between 1976 and 1978. At the end of 1979, nine students were chosen to start high school in the 1980 school year; five went (one to Dregerhafen). Of the four who went to Siassi High School in Lablab, two remained at year's end and only one returned for the second school year (grade 8).

Attendance at the Por-Mandok Community School (see Figure 8.2) showed a similar pattern of dropouts. For example, in 1979, 20 children dropped out of the community school, and none were sent back and made to finish the year.[5] The next year (1980) it took the teachers from January until the end of May to get a majority of parents to pay the K3 annual school fees for the community school.

The Catholic mission tried to channel the increasing flow of "school leavers" into other activities. It opened a vocational center for girls at its Aupwel (north Umboi) station in 1970. Many parents sent their daughters to this center after the daughters had completed the 6th grade, if they did not get into high school.

The priest on Por started a carving school for the boys. They learned from all the *mosa* ("artisans") in a concentrated program, each artisan focusing on a particular stage of the carving process. They also worked to convert the carving tradition into a cash-producing industry. This process went against traditional customs regarding the distribution of knowledge: a man was supposed to teach certain *runai* and family designs only to his son (real or classificatory) or to his sister's son. Apprentices were future allies upon whom he could draw for help when

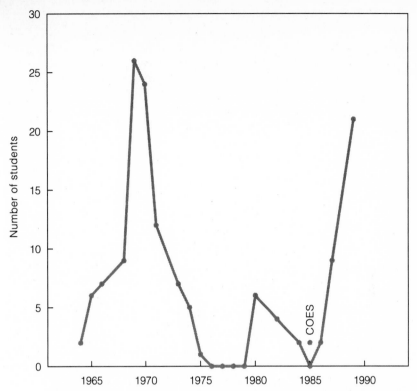

NOTE: Most year gaps represent cohort gaps—there is not a solid progression of grades. Because of the small number of students, and especially since Independence, the Education Department begins a 1st-grade class about every two years.

F I G U R E 8.1 *Students sent to secondary education, 1964–89 (includes vocational and teaching schools).*

he needed it. One could not be sure about "another man's son," for he was really a competitor. Many of the master carvers overcame these apprehensions, however, and went along with the school as an attempt to salvage what for them was a sacred tradition.[6]

Each solution to the "school leaver" problem met its downfall. As mentioned above, when the Aupwel Vocational School first opened in 1970, parents were eager to send their daughters there, and many did so. The school fees were minimal, and the girls cultivated a large part of their own food in vocational-school gardens. They learned to bake bread and to sew on machines. They also continued their education in English, mathematics, health, and religious instruction. Although the missionaries told the girls' parents that the school's objectives were to teach them practical domestic skills to be used back in the village for "better community living," they still expected the girls to secure wage

FIGURE 8.2 *Por-Mandok Community School, classroom of composite grades 4 and 5, 1981. Note the models of two-masted canoes hanging from the ceiling.*

employment upon completion of the two-year program. When they returned to the village, the only "skill" the girls could use was sewing. (The mission had several treadle sewing machines at this time as part of their Women's Club projects.) They got no jobs in town, and there were no ovens or stoves on Mandok in which to bake bread. Each girl received packets of peanuts, pawpaw seeds, rice, and other seeds for planting in their own gardens when they left Aupwel. By 1979 there was no evidence of any of those crops in Mandok gardens. The sewing machines were inoperative, rusting in the salt air on Por. This pattern was a condensed version of a more general decline in interest in "rural development" and secondary schooling.

Technical- and vocational-school attendance also started to decline sharply between 1970 and 1972. Whereas in 1969 20 teens attended (8 boys and 12 girls), by 1972 most of them had returned to Mandok. In the mid- to late 1960s, technical-school graduates found employment easily. As universal literacy became more of a reality, however, capability requirements escalated and the job market shrank. Minimal quotas were set for the allocation of teacher positions to rural schools. Children were sent to school earlier than they had been previously in order to keep the school open. Parents who were eager to educate their children in school sent younger children willingly. The student population shifted gradually until as a group it was much younger than before. Not only did this cause problems in garden work for high-school students, it also prevented many aspiring young tradesmen from completing their technical programs. They were too short to reach the work benches and too small to lift the materials required in the technical curricula. These students were sent home, to wait and to grow.

Once again, the mission tried to counterbalance these frustrations. The carving school on Por was a part of this effort and could have accommodated the first large class of "school leavers." But this too was short-lived. The carving program fell apart by 1977, due partly to the priest's leave of absence, but especially to a political split in the village. The results of this schism are still felt on Mandok and remain a divisive element in the process of community development (see Chapter 9 for a full discussion).

By 1972, education had become a "losing investment." Parents initiated their own retrenchment policy regarding education: interest in schooling at all levels plummeted. The comparative achievement levels of past and present Mandok graduates was especially telling. The early graduates in the work force quickly earned a reputation for being bright, highly motivated, and upwardly mobile. In a battery of cognitive tests administered by the Education Department in 1978, the children demonstrated a high level of cognitive development (Lancy 1983). The actual achievement levels of those children in the national grade 6 exam, however, declined sharply between 1975 and 1980, reaching an all-time low average score of 42.22 percent in 1979 (Isoaimo 1980). Such scores no doubt reflect lower motivation to perform, *not* cognitive capacity.

The Mandok were not alone in their concerns. By the late 1970s and early 1980s, achievement scores all over the nation had dropped. The focus of the Education Department became "standards" (Kenehe 1981). Early Mandok graduates noted that the standards of excellence, even at the elementary level, had declined drastically since they were in school. They blamed this condition on the removal of expatriates from the teaching staff during the nationalization program.

The worldwide inflation of the late 1970s also had an impact on the cost of education. Parents recounted bitterly that in 1964 there were no school fees; in 1970 they paid K40; in 1981, K150; and by 1988 the fee had risen to K250 (approximately U.S. $325).[7] In 1980, the price of staples such as rice, sugar, tea, milk, and coffee more than doubled in less than 12 months. In contrast to rising expenses, the access of the average Mandok family to money either remained constant (for carvings sold in Lae or to occasional tourists arriving by boat) or declined (for men migrating for temporary employment). Villagers depended on remittances of employed relatives in town to make up the deficit. By 1986 the Mandok had raised the prices of local crafts, sometimes by as much as 100 percent. But 100 percent of K1 is only another K1: school fees rocketed by comparison.

The Mandok's disillusionment with schooling was cogently summed up for me in 1980 by one Mandok woman who was a member of the "first generation" of educated Mandok. Early in her career she taught on Por; later she taught in a teacher's college. Here is her perspective:

▼ Before, when I was going to school, if a child was tardy, one of the *bigmen* went out to the plaza and yelled to that child's parents, "Who are you that your child does not have to go to school? Do you know so much about white man's things that your child does not have to go to school?" And that parent was quick to take the child over to Por. Today, many parents have already seen their older children go to school, and not get into high school, and come back to the village, or go to high school and then quit and come home. Either way, the children are back in the village, living as their parents are living. Money is so hard to get, the parents figure, "Why should I spend my money and send them to high school at all if the kids come home and live the same way I do anyway, in the end?" The smart kids are pushed, so they are more motivated. The not-so-smart ones are left alone because the parents know they'll wind up back in the village anyway.

It would seem that the Mandok adjusted their participation in schooling to reflect the likely return on their investment. It would also seem that these attitudes were transmitted to the children, who moderated their classroom performance in a similar fashion.

PROMISES, PROMISES

From 1960 to about 1974, several attempts were made to create appropriate business projects specifically for the islanders. Throughout the 1960s patrol officers commented on the islanders' willingness to participate in "development." They noted repeatedly the need for close supervision of development projects to help the Siassi peoples make the transition to a market economy. One of the first projects was the establishment of village trade stores, discussed above. There was also talk of initiating a fishing industry in Siassi specifically for the islanders.

The Fisheries Department conducted some feasibility surveys for commercial fishing operations in 1970, but nothing ever came of them (Patrol Report Siassi 2, 1970–71:7). From 1972 to 1973, two different private enterprises started fishing businesses in Siassi. In one enterprise, a retired Australian sea captain named Grant, who lived on Mandok, supervised the islanders as they fished in his two dinghies and stored the catch in his three freezers. He told patrol officers that his aim was to teach the Mandok how to fish commercially, and that later he would hand the business over to them as a communal enterprise (Patrol Report Siassi 2, 1971–72). It never happened. There is nothing in the patrol reports about the other business, except that it, too, was initiated by an Australian as an exploratory project (Mulderink 1980). Both businesses were bankrupt by 1973.

A rural development officer suggested that the Siassi LGC buy freezers and put them at Lablab for the islanders' use. This suggestion was rejected for two reasons. First, there was no clear "owner" of these freezers who would assume responsibility and manage their use and upkeep. Second, no clear market was identified for the fish (Patrol Report Siassi 1, 1973–74). Meanwhile, this same report notes that "Island people" (unnamed, but probably Aromot; Mulderink 1989) took A$500 of their own and requested Rural Improvement Plan (RIP) money to buy their own small freezer and a generator to run it.

Patrol officers also considered developing Siassi as a tourist attraction in order to preserve the carving and crafts industries (Patrol Report Finschhafen 5, 1963–64:17). This was part of the impetus for the carving school of the 1970s. Additional encouragement came from a visiting research officer from the Education Department, who suggested a museum/store combination business. The LGC representative liked the idea, for it promised to bring in income. The idea became a project supported by both parents and school; they built a house for the purpose. The school headmaster was in favor of the project because it would help to preserve "local culture." (This was during the era of "education for better community living.") The Mandok were excited both about the prospect of being the first island with its own museum and being a tourist attraction.

The plan did not come to much. Tourists did go to Mandok, but the "museum"—a shack with some mediocre carvings and other artifacts on shelves—was built on Por. The average tourist visit lasted 30 minutes—just long enough for the tourists to get a tour of Mandok and for the Mandok to gather their crafts for a quick sale. In 1980, the remnants of Mandok's "museum" of local carvings and other artifacts was still keeping its silent vigil on Por, awaiting the tourists' arrival.

From the Mandok perspective the important point was not that these "promises" were never realized, but that they were made in the first place and at this particular moment in their history: during the government campaign to relocate them to Umboi. At this time, too, children were in secondary schools and obtaining town jobs, single men were still migrating to do contract labor, and married men and stay-at-homes were diving for shells for quick cash. Under these circumstances, why *should* they garden?

Even if the islanders did wish to relocate to Umboi and produce cash crops, the transience and ineptitude of government officers worked *against* a successful transition. Patrol officers were not permanent residents of Siassi; they were expatriates who spent less than two years there. The lack of centralized authority and consistent guidance—cited as a major impetus to the establishment of patrol posts—was not overcome in Siassi. The following frustrated commentary summarizes cogently the local people's reactions to erratic outside governance:

> The native people have been so "fooled around" in the past with cash crops that they are becoming very cynical of suggestions made by officers now. Within the past ten years the crops advocated by various officers have been rice, cocoa, arabica coffee, and now robusta coffee which is not off to a very good start. They are becoming sick of being told by one officer to plant a certain crop, and being told by the next one to pull it out and plant a new one which he states has numerous advantages over the former. Their only comment is "something bilong [sic] government" [TP, *samting bilong gavman*, "the government's problem"], but there are probably much deeper thoughts underneath. (Patrol Report Finschhafen 17, 1962:4)

Even the LGC seemed to be collapsing. By 1970 patrol officers noticed that village councillors were getting younger. Instead of men aged 40 to 60, councillors were now younger men aged 24 to 36 (Patrol Report Siassi 2, 1970–71). Administrators viewed this as a good sign that indicated both an expanded involvement of younger men in village affairs and an increase in high-school-educated councillors. They thought that these younger men would also be capable of participating in a representative form of democratic government.

To Mandok villagers, however, the shift indicated something very different. Mandok's pattern of responses to LGCs was similar to that recorded for many other areas of PNG. The village councillor in 1979 was a young man in his late 20s. This was much too young, by Mandok standards, for a man to hold any position of real authority. The Mandok perceived the situation and the nature of the role, however, to be one that necessitated an educated youth who was literate and knew something of European ways of doing things. His value was that of a "translator" more than a "leader." All this leads me to believe that the election of younger men to LGCs reflected an increasing lack of perceived *relevance* of LGCs to village life.

The many reversals of government policy were exasperating to Mandok parents and children alike, who were frankly disillusioned with this downward turn in their fortunes. But their interest in "development" did not wane; it was replaced by other opportunities.

CHAPTER NINE

🌺 Bikhets and Bisnis

Siassi people are not always *bikhet* [TP, "contrary"], they are happy and hospitable people. But one thing they always like to do is to compete with each other to gain prestige or fame.

Pastor Jasaking Jawal from Tuam, cited in Kigasung 1976:2

The Mandok were not just passive recipients of externally introduced development projects. While the government was encouraging relocation and cash cropping and the mission was facilitating secondary education, villagers found other opportunities to earn cash. They also tried to initiate their own development projects. The design of these ventures, and their fates, illustrate the Mandok's views of themselves and their interpretations of "development." When things went wrong, as they often did, each party involved blamed the other. From the perspective of outside agencies (mission, government, school), the Mandok were quickly earning a reputation for being *bikhet*; from the Mandok perspective, these agencies were unreliable. Mandok people looked for other ways to earn money.

In the midst of government attempts to encourage cash cropping were other opportunities for cash accumulation that were often preferable and produced cash more quickly. Shell diving, for example, remained a popular, if sporadic, means of local employment through the early 1970s.[1] Shell diving was a profitable activity from the islanders' point of view because they could "have their cake and eat it too," in a sense. They stayed at home and "repopulated," which initially pleased the government, and they earned cash, which pleased themselves. Traditionally considered "women's work," shell diving became viewed as "easy money." Even though it failed in the end, the Australian Captain Grant's fishing project, while it lasted, paid the Mandok to do what they liked best: fish. There was no real incentive, other than government and mission urging and portents of future doom, to relocate or to cash-crop.

In the meantime, the Mandok were formulating their own plans for development. In 1964, during Marshall Sahlins's field visit to Thomas Harding (see Chapter 1), one man approached Sahlins and, speaking for the Mandok, asked him to buy them a ship. "We are a trading people," he said, "all we need is a ship" (Harding 1989). The Mandok eventually got their "ship," but not from Sahlins or Harding.

THE BOAT THAT SANK THE VILLAGE

In the mid-1970s, the Catholic mission wanted to sell their boat, the *M.V. Yawani*. The Mandok bought the mission boat, intending to haul copra and other produce from the entire Siassi area to market. The project became a fault line for a village schism in 1977–78. This example illustrates several characteristic aspects of the Mandok's encounters with economic and political change, both on and off the island. In order to bring these encounters into their proper context, some reiteration of village social organization, and an account of circumstances at this time, are necessary.

Mandok village was divided into two moieties, Mata and Sangup, representing the east and west sides of the village, respectively. Though always differentiated, during the 1970s these moieties became synonymous with the eventual split of the island into two competing "business societies" called the Sunrise Society (Mata) and the Mandok Society (Sangup). (School children sometimes called the Mandok Society the "Sundown Society.") Important bloodlines and *runai* origins came from Arop, Kilenge, and Aromot, all locations on or near the sea and all locations from whence the founding fathers of Mandok came. Ties to Barim and Malasiga/Tami were also important, but these were matrilateral ties. If one combines these genealogical connections (through marriages and adoptions) with patrilineal *runai* origins outlined in Chapter 5, one sees not "west side/east side" divisions of Mandok, but rather "sea/bush" origins of the first settler of any given *lain*. Mandok notions of transmission of "blood" and heritability of personality, intelligence, and leadership qualities through "bloodlines" retained these distinctions through the generations. Thus, those *lain*s that derived from "sea" locations were more valued than those from "bush" locations.

Each moiety included specific groups of *runai*. Though the Mandok insisted that the *runai* were all "equal," in times of stress or other unusual circumstances one learned otherwise. Specifically, those *runai* whose Mandok founders were the first lot of settlers to the island "owned" and therefore "bossed" the village. The other groups were considered, as one young man whispered to me during a village debate, to be "just so much driftwood." That is, their ancestry was less valued, and therefore they were not considered to be rightfully eligible to assume leadership positions within the village.[2] Hence, most, if not all, Mandok *maron* were from *Tavov Puxu* or from another *runai* within Sangup with ties to *Tavov Puxu*. Phrased simply, the Sangup side "owned" Mandok.

By the mid-1970s, the cumulative effects of secondary education, labor migration, the frequency of rural development proposals made to date, and approaching national independence produced a unique situation for the Mandok. The generation holding power was growing old. The elders were assessing the available future leaders of the village and considering the changes wrought by contact with European culture. Men in the 30–45 age group had received only minimal literacy training during the "mission phase" of educational development. Some had had experience as (primarily unskilled) migrant laborers on mission plantations. Younger men who might have been capable of leadership were instead away in towns, either advancing their education or pursuing careers. Consequently, there were no eligible leaders to take over when those then in power died. The combined perception of a village "brain drain" and the swiftness of the changes brought about by European contact prompted a serious reevaluation of the village's future.

Among the plantation migrants, the Catholic mission had trained several Mandok to crew mission boats and a few to captain them. Their extensive knowledge of the reef system, the winds, and their general orientation to the sea was invaluable in the treacherous straits that separated the Siassi parishes from each other and from the mission's mainland headquarters then in Rabaul (it later moved to Lae). The first boat was the *M.V. Collomb*, named for Bishop Giovanni Collomb, the first missionary to Siassi (see Chapter 7). It ran aground in 1970 and was replaced with the *M.V. Yawani* in 1971. The name *Yawani* comes from a waterway or reef near Morobe. The missionaries used the *Yawani* to haul supplies for the mission and to shuttle cargo and personnel between the widely scattered Siassi mission posts.

From the Mandok's perspective, one of the perhaps unexpected consequences of the new way brought by mission and government, and especially by the great expansion of the Education Department, was the number of Mandok children from lower-status families succeeding in the "Europeans' world." As more education was offered on a merit basis to more children, lower-status families could also increase their cash incomes by sending their children off to schools. Though the first-generation Mandok students were from the higher-status families, those attending by 1970 were from a much wider status spectrum. Those young men who had migrated for wage labor on plantations learned a different set of achievement standards from the ones by which they would have been judged at home.

When the mission expressed its wish to sell the *Yawani*, the Mandok planned to buy it. Instead of relying on the mission or on commercial boat services, they hoped to be self-sufficient and run their own business hauling copra and cargo produced by other communities in Siassi to markets in Lae and Rabaul. In this way, they could once again control commerce in the region. They also gained a promising alternative to relocating the village to the Umboi bush. This particular alternative reproduced, with new technology, their perceived historical prominence as Siassi middlemen. But this time the connecting market on the other end of Siassi was a commercial market in Lae, not a barter market on the New Guinea or New Britain coast.

Even though the prospect of buying the mission boat and running a village business was very tempting, some of the elders felt that the village was not ready for such a large-scale enterprise. They raised practical issues, such as: "Suppose the boat breaks down; who will fix it?" "We need fuel; where do we get it?" "We hire a crew, but how can we pay them?" After much deliberation and many public village meetings, however, the Mandok community bought the boat. They used about K4,000 of the Mandok Society's funds, which had been earned from the trade store and saved in the village communal fund (see Chapter 8). They borrowed the balance from the PNG Banking Corporation and the Development Bank.

Now that they had a boat, they needed a captain. This position became a metaphor for a new style of leadership in the village. There were two captains available on Mandok who were capable of running the boat for the village. Each had gained literacy and numeracy training in the mission school, each had worked on plantations, and each had some experience with running boats, also for the mission. However, the two men happened to be from different bloodlines and from each of the now-competing factions of the village. The first, whom I will call A, was from a long line of respected leaders and *maron*s of Mandok. He was not a firstborn child, but he was the son of a very prominent *maron* and *runai* elder. There was a tacit expectation among the elders that he would continue the family tradition and follow his father's example. The second man, B, was from Mata. Though also from a respectable lineage, he was neither a firstborn nor from the "right side of the village" to lead. He was therefore not considered to be as strong a contender, in Mandok terms, as a potential *maron* (see Chapter 4). He did, however, have more experience in handling motorized boats and in working on plantations than did A. B, who initiated the proposal to buy the boat, also had many young educated kinsmen who could serve as his crew. Although A was one of those who asked all the "What if?" questions, he was ready and able to captain the boat if the village elders decided that he should lead.

The purchase of the *Yawani* as a village enterprise now took on heightened political overtones. The Mata moiety, which had organized itself into the Sunrise Society years earlier as a direct competitor to the Mandok Society, escalated the competition. Members constructed a second copra drier to support the Sunrise Society's new trade store. The competition for the purchase and subsequent control of the boat became a focal point for longer-standing rivalries between the village moieties. The boat controversy escalated the competition into a village schism. Extended families split, so that children were forbidden to visit or use possessions (canoes, paddles, poles, etc.) of certain extended kinsmen. Customary exchanges of food and betel nut between relatives from different factions ceased. Violent threats went back and forth. In the end, the boat broke down mechanically, the community (by this time mainly represented by the Mandok Society) defaulted on loan payments, and the bank repossessed and resold the boat in December 1979.

For years afterward, the issue of the boat resurfaced every time either faction in the village initiated any new project. Generally two interpretations existed for "what happened" to create the tension and eventual schism. These two views were not contradictory; they merely represented different levels of analysis of a complex event. They also, however, revealed significant emotional investments of the interpreters.

The first view stated simply that the village was trying to go from a fishing and gardening community to a "business" overnight. Purchasing the boat and initiating a village business constituted a trial period during which the village was in transition from a communal, subsistence-oriented economy into a market economy. Never having had any business experience, they could not handle this switch, and things fell apart. The key word in this explanation is "communal," for this view assumed that the village *was* in fact a communal society to begin with. That assumption was historically inaccurate. Rather than describing reality, it reflected the wishful thinking of and mission influence on the younger, school-educated Mandok. Their parents knew different.

The second view pointed to long-standing political and status differences in the village. According to this theory, the boat offered a focal point for a "revolt of underlings." That is to say, now that the Mata side of the village had access to European knowledge, cash, and goods, they tried to gain local power by manipulating their control over the *Yawani*. By using *B*'s experience and knowledge of boatsmanship, they tried to rewrite the laws of Mandok leadership and loosen Sangup's stronghold on village politics. They failed.

When I arrived on Mandok in October 1979, there were two business societies, two copra driers, two trade stores, and no communal fund. After three years of conflict, the missionary priest and the church councillors were trying futilely to reunite the village, but the wounds were still too fresh. In some ways the situation worsened. Just before Christmas of 1979, one family *lain* erected a third copra drier for their own use and profit. This caused a stir that climaxed at a public meeting in the village plaza. Many Mandok feared another schism. Accusations then came from Gauru that the owners of the new copra drier were poaching coconuts. Things were so tense that it was difficult even to ask questions about the situation. Finally the church elders decided not to have the copra drier blessed until the matter was settled. This seemed to make a statement that everyone accepted for the time being. When I left Mandok in February 1981, the unblessed copra drier remained, as one church councillor had described it in 1979, "a building with sin."

RELOCATION II: MOVING THE SCHOOL TO MURU

> It is the same old story. When Fr. Sido was here, they built a house
> for him, then a school building. He moved to Muru, but the villagers
> stayed on Mandok. So he came back to Por. The house started rot-
> ting and falling apart, and they patched up the roof. Then Fr. Anton
> came, and it was the same story. Now Fr. Francis is here, and they
> are *still* talking about moving. Everyone knows that there is no food
> on the island [Mandok], and they all agree that life would be better
> in Muru, but does anybody listen?
>
> *A Mandok woman, after a village meeting regarding*
> *moving the school to Muru, 1980.*

The education system's emphasis on rural development and "better community life" required teachers to sponsor community projects in their
schools. In 1980, Por's two teachers were from bush areas; they both
felt more comfortable inland. To them, community development meant
land development. The Por-Mandok Community School was physically
detached from the community. Both islands lacked land, so community development was virtually impossible. A major problem, cited
repeatedly by all teachers who have ever worked on Por, was *food*: they
had no means of getting any, other than in the trade store(s) on Mandok. Because they were supplementary, Mandok gardens rarely produced enough to support extra mouths. Villagers did not even have
enough for themselves. Therefore, unlike teachers in other areas of PNG,
the teachers on Por could not expect to be fed by the community. During 1978 and 1979 the gardens were ravaged by heavy rains and maraud-
ing wild pigs. Food was a big problem for everyone. Toward the end
of 1980 the teachers initiated a "community project" to move the school
to the Muru garden area. The teachers felt that moving the school to
Muru would help the children learn to garden and grow their own food,
and there would be land there on which to develop other future community projects.

Once again, many community meetings were held and the villagers
made a firm decision to move—but not without several reformulations
of and references to past failures. The first decision was whether only
the school or the entire village was to move. Clearly the teachers' aim
was to get the village to move and thereby "develop." But the bad feelings that had accumulated over the past 20 years, and especially since
the incident with the *Yawani*, made the younger men who led this campaign tread softly. Only the school would move.

The second decision was how to feed the children. Organizers recalled that some families had moved to Muru during the late 1960s and
had even built houses there. In the early 1970s they had also built a
permanent house for the priest and an aid station for medical treatment.
The remnants of these buildings were still standing in 1980, and they

even appeared on the government's map of the area (Papua New Guinea Map Series T601, Sheet 8486). Yet they had no inhabitants. When the parents returned to the village, they claimed that they came back because their children were in school on Por and no one was there to take care of them.

Spurred on by educated and employed Mandok who had returned for the Christmas holidays, the elders decided to start building the new school in late November 1980. The Christmas feasting cycles soon began, however, and the buildings were abandoned half finished. The village councillor had declared the new school a project for *paua dei* (TP, "power day"), one day per week set aside for community work. Villagers used only four out of six possible work days allotted for the project. The 1981 school year opened in the school on Por.

FISHING FOR CASH

It would seem that the Mandok decided against the project to move the school to Muru. The village did decide, however, to buy an icebox to start a fishing business, and people pooled their money for that. The business lasted approximately five months. It suffered from equipment problems: the freezers purchased were not designed for industrial purposes, and the islanders had insufficient experience in packing and storing fish.

In 1984 a Tuam man, who also served in the provincial government in Lae, started a company called "Siassi Sea Food." He put a freezer with a generator on Mutumala Island, where fisherfolk could deposit fish that were later air-freighted to Lae via the airstrip in Lablab. This project made the Mandok venture less profitable. There was talk of joining forces with this "new" project, but old tensions between Aromot and Mandok prevented either side from encouraging such a merger. This project ran aground as a result of disputes over ownership rights to Mutumala land among people from Aromot, Tuam, and Mandok. It also had boat and money-management problems. The competition heightened as each island tried to outdo the others and become the one to run the area's first successful fishing business.

The Mandok responded with another fishing business of their own. Encouraged by the return of some of their educated "youths"—now men in their mid-to-late 30s and early 40s—they decided to buy a brand-new boat. In February 1985 they applied to the Investors Scheme Fund for a K78,000 grant to buy a new workboat and a new, big generator. They called themselves the "Mandok Fishing Group" and took pains in their application to separate themselves from "Siassi Sea Food." Villagers reunited in the face of an outside competitor and formed one inclusive business society. They named this new society "Matasangup" to underscore (symbolically) their new unity. In addition, the group's management committee combined the two previously competing sea captains (from the *Yawani* project) with younger, town-experienced men. The village proposed spending K41,560 of their own money to buy a generator, a generator shed, a deep-freezer shed, a wooden freezer unit (for ice blocks), six *mons* ("outboard dugout canoes"), one plywood boat, one aluminum boat, 20 fishing nets, eight outboard motors, three open-chest deep freezers, a trade store, and an office.

The establishment of the "fish business" and the commitment of the villagers to "really do it this time" inspired the opening of several new trade stores on Mandok. These too were short-lived for the most part, "rising and falling like the tide," leaving "always a debt" (Lenssen 1982).

When I returned to Mandok in October 1986, the freezers lay in the men's area, protected under a skeleton shed that had a green corrugated-fiberglass roof. They provided a strategic seat from which men could watch the channel facing Por and supervise docking boats at Mandok's wharf, but no one was using them as freezers. The village had one small generator, but it was owned privately. The application for the K78,000 grant was still pending. In short, there was no community fishing business.

INDEPENDENT INVESTMENTS

Copra, Trade Stores, Kerosene, and Gasoline

The construction of the independently owned copra drier that caused the uproar in December 1979 marked a turning point in Mandok business enterprises. Several other ventures were initiated between 1979 and 1989, each abandoning the idea of "communal business." Copra production became an individual/family activity run by individual family *lains* (see Chapter 5). Many families used the old village system for their own profit: they sold copra for cash, stocked a trade store, and then sold the goods on Mandok.

In addition, some enterprising *lains* started importing kerosene and later gasoline. All these businesses operated as follows: I (and my *lain*) buy a 44-gallon drum of kerosene (or gasoline) and pay to transport it from Lae. When it arrives on Mandok, I raise the price (not always consistently) to cover my costs and provide a profit, and you buy it from me. Trade stores worked the same way. By 1990 there were five trade stores still in operation, two of which also sold gasoline. I have no recent figures for kerosene sales, but my impression is that the number of businesses remained small, involving only a couple of family groups.

The Canoe Revolution

In 1980 the Mandok constructed their first motorized dugout canoe (*mon*). It started out as a village project. The technology came from the Kombe area of New Britain via kinship connections on Aromot Island. The introduction of this new canoe revitalized the declining trade system by allowing the islanders more independent transportation and the freedom to choose where to go. It started a revolution in the canoe industry and inspired three new business ideas: selling canoes to overseas trade partners, renting them out locally, and establishing gasoline depots. Previously, the Catholic mission had been the only depot in the small islands. There was a depot at Lablab, but its owner charged exorbitant prices, and one had to get there to do business. The mission sold gasoline at the mission's cost, as a community service. When this service started, the Mandok's *mon* was the second *mon* in Siassi, the first being the one on Aromot. Soon other islanders started building or buying them, and some islanders (mostly Mandok) started selling the gas, too.

As a business, renting out *mon*s was slightly different from selling gasoline, kerosene, and trade-store goods because the commodity sold was a service, not a consumable good, although gasoline was a consumable required for *mon* operation. The service required a significant initial investment by the *mon* owner. First, a tree had to be chopped down on Umboi and the canoe constructed. This process usually required a group of men to go to Umboi, and it also entailed exploiting traditional Umboi trade relations to get the tree trunk. These stages required food payments to workers and sometimes involved expenditure of additional cash (for rice, canned fish, tea, sugar, and so on). Some owners hired the Boys' Youth Club for these initial stages at a flat rate for each day's work. Next the owner needed to buy an outboard motor and fuel. All these expenses required cash.

As mentioned earlier, in 1985 veterans of World War II received from the PNG government K1,000 in compensation for their efforts in the war. Some of these veterans, now in their 60s and 70s, bought outboard motors with their money and built *mon*s. Most, however, received *mon*s either as gifts from their children working in towns or as the result of purchases by a larger *lain*. In either case, younger men usually operated the motors most of the time, but the old men controlled them. Control was important because the "father" of the canoe (and of the engine) not only controlled it, but also received the profits to disperse as he pleased. This arrangement also continued traditional leadership patterns in which elders kept control and younger men worked for them. Older men also had the rights to sell their expertise in the form of knowledge of how to build *mon*s.

In many ways the construction of *mon*s revived the ailing canoe-manufacture industry for which Mandok and Aromot had gained historical prominence. Martin Zelenietz reported Mandok attempts to sell *mon*s to their Kilenge trade partners, for instance (Zelenietz 1986). Building and buying *mon*s was not enough to run the business, however; the owner (or younger male relative) needed some mechanical knowledge to keep the *mon* running. In 1987 there were 13 *mon*s and nine functioning engines on Mandok. The need for skilled mechanics stimulated a new cohort of young men to go to St. Joseph's Technical School in Lae for training.

Some men rented their *mon*s to people who needed transportation for whatever reason. When I visited the other islands, I paid as follows. First, the *mon* rental cost K5 to K10 per day, depending on my relationship to its owner. Next, there was a K5-per-day charge for the "head of the engine," which presumably was saved against future maintenance expenses. Finally, I paid K3 per gallon of gas. The cost of gasoline raised the price of transportation considerably in Siassi so that, for example, to go to Lablab from Mandok (a distance of about 16 kilometers or 10 miles) to meet or catch a plane or go to the clinic it cost from K21 to K26. In contrast, to ride the *M.V. Salamander* to Lae (about 128 kilometers or 80 miles) cost K14. Needless to say, many Mandok found Lae much more appealing than Lablab.

Siassi Sea Cucumbers

In late 1986 a new business started on Mandok to collect, process, and sell sea cucumbers (also called *bêche de mer* or trepang). The business, called Panu Enterprises (*panu* means "village" in Mutu), was notable for several reasons, not the least of which was that it represented a series of "firsts" in Mandok commercial enterprise. First among the "firsts" was that the business was conceived, owned, and operated by a woman. Agnes Keke was the daughter of a *bigman* and a "first-generation" graduate of the expansionist era of education. She formerly had taught at a teacher-training college in Port Moresby. She had some tertiary education in Australia and had also lived for three years with her husband in Japan.

The second "first" was that most of the laborers were female. At the time of my fieldwork, 208 Mandok were employed by this project; 148 (71 percent) were females and 60 (29 percent) were males. Males (especially teenagers) did some diving, and they collected and cut firewood. Youths and young men supervised the overnight smoking phase and bagged the dried sea cucumbers. Women did the rest: most of the diving and all of the cooking, cleaning, burying, and sun drying. Third, the owner had a clear road to a market: she dealt directly with buyers first in Taiwan and later in Hong Kong as well. Fourth, she herself supplied the start-up capital with a personal bank loan. As of July 1990, though she had not yet shown a profit, she had good credit at the bank, was still in business, and was very hopeful about the future (Keke 1990).

Another interesting characteristic of this business was that it did not earn money off the Mandok; the Mandok earned money by being paid for their labor. In 1986, most everyone was excited about this business, particularly the women. Some of the elders were dubious at first and complained that this business was another born of personal greed, not communal beneficence, but their wives and daughters usually overruled them. Even if the elders could not quell their anxieties, the owner, as a daughter of a *bigman*, could not be dismissed lightly. The work force tripled within months. Within a short time, most of the original dissenting elders had changed their thinking, and several actively encouraged their wives and daughters to work for Panu Enterprises.

Sea cucumbers lie on the reef; all one had to do to harvest many species was bend over and pick them up. Other species required deeper diving, but Mandok women were accustomed to diving for sea clams (see Chapter 3). (The commercially important species of sea cucumber can be found as deep as 30–50 meters, but as of this writing divers were not going deeper than about six meters [Keke 1990].) Although it was time-consuming and tiring to dive all day, the process was not especially dangerous, except perhaps for the presence of stonefish and other dangerous reef creatures. But these were commonplace dangers of daily life in the Vitiaz Strait. Collecting sea cucumbers required no training, no talent, and no special equipment. Other stages required more tedious work, but none required special skill: anyone could do it. In general, younger women and teenagers did most of the diving and the heavier, more physical work. Older women did the more tedious village jobs: watching the boiling trepang and scraping the cooked ones.

Different stages of the process took longer than others, and workers were paid accordingly. Collecting and other full-day jobs earned them K1 (about U.S. $1.10), whereas boiling and other half-day processes earned them 50 toea (about U.S. $0.55). Heretofore only skilled women earned cash, and only through the tedious and time-consuming craft specialties of making trochus-shell and beaded armlets and weaving betel-nut baskets and grass skirts. These brought a price of between K1 and K4 for several weeks' work. Although some species required deep diving and some stages involved in processing trepang were time-consuming and tedious, women were still earning money more quickly and in larger quantities than they would have by producing traditional crafts. The newness of the project, and its promise of still more money, made it very popular with Mandok women.

The success of Panu Enterprises seemed assured, for virtually nothing was consumed locally and all participants were motivated by the same incentive: personal access to cash. However, the story was not over yet. Mandok commentators noted that because of previous trade in sea cucumbers with Kowai communities, Mandok reefs were depleted. This was not so with Aromot reefs, which remained well stocked. The Aromot, however, were jealous of this Mandok venture and wanted to be

TABLE 9.1 *Market price of sea cucumbers, May 1987.*

SIZE	COST
Large	K6.00/kg
Medium	4.50/kg
Small	3.00/kg

TABLE 9.2 *Size distribution and expected returns for sea cucumbers shipped in May 1987.*

SIZE	NO. OF BAGS	EXPECTED RETURN
Large	9	K2,700
Medium	7	1,575
Small	1	150
TOTAL		K4,425

included. Aromot women were hired under the same terms as Mandok women, but only for the culling stage, and all processing was done on Mandok. In 1987, a Mandok man married to an Aromot woman tried to process a batch to compete with Panu Enterprises for the business on Aromot, but the batch failed.

The initial loan for this business was K2,000, with which the owner paid for processing equipment, operating a *mon*,[3] gasoline, personal travel, and wages. The market price of sea cucumbers in May 1987 is shown in Table 9.1; Table 9.2 contains the size distribution and expected returns of the May 1987 shipment.

The initial contract was for a monthly shipment, but in fact from 1987 to 1989 Keke averaged only two shipments per year, partly because of her desire to limit the time she spent away from her family. Each shipment consisted of about 1.5 tons of mixed species, valued at K8,000 (about U.S. $8,800). She expected this figure to more than double for 1990, owing both to a rise in market prices in general and the addition of a market in Hong Kong, which was considerably better than the one in Taiwan. As time went on, workers became more efficient, and Keke borrowed more money to improve her equipment. In 1989 she bought an outboard motor and an 18-foot (5.5-meter) boat for collection; in 1990 she built a new drier made of more permanent materials than the bush materials she had used previously. These changes, combined with increased worker efficiency at the various jobs, allowed her to decrease her labor force (and, consequently, her labor costs) by half, though the ratio of females to males remained the same.

ALL FOR ONE OR ONE FOR ALL?

It should be evident by now that over the years the Mandok have tried a variety of *bisnis* enterprises. The larger ones that involved the entire community failed. Some of the smaller ones organized around family *lains* seemed to be succeeding, but even these had many failures for each recent (and perhaps temporary) success. Why? How could these intrepid sailors and shrewd middlemen keep failing at commercial enterprises? The answer involves a consideration of business, trade, and kinship obligations as viewed from inside Mandok society. In Chapter 5 we examined the Mandok's social system as a network of long-range investments in people that worked on a principle of delayed reciprocal exchange (Sahlins 1972). That is, if I am successful fishing today, I give you some; if you harvest sweet potatoes tomorrow, you give me some. There was no precise reckoning, for participants expected the exchange of food to continue ad infinitum. Gregory (1980) calls this kind of debt "gift debt," and he defines it as an interest-free exchange of objects that keeps the parties in a state of "mutual reciprocal dependence."[4] The motivation of any individual transactor is to maximize net outgoings (Gregory 1980:636). In Mandok terms, this meant to "give freely." This type of system supports a subsistence existence by distributing resources more equitably. Trade partnerships, while cast in an idiom of kinship, kept a somewhat closer reckoning of who had given what to whom, over how much time, and under what circumstances. Both these systems, however, were flexible; both presumed value equivalence in the objects traded, mutual interdependence of the traders, and equitable access to resources.

The etiquette of kinship obliged kin to give generously to one another. If someone had something he or she did not wish to give away, a request to give would be answered with the lie, "Sorry, I have no more," rather than by rebuke or refusal (see Kahn 1986 for similar themes, especially regarding food). Children were drilled in this sense of sharing from early childhood. When they became adults and married, the same value system was reinforced. Young brides, for example, were admonished never to cook in a small pot, for a hungry kinsperson passing by would feel rejected. I call this the "*Marimari* Rule." *Marimari* is a Tok Pisin term that means "mercy," "pity," or "sympathy." Missionaries introduced the term, as might be surmised from its meaning. In Mutu this idea was expressed idiomatically in the phrase, *lolo isamini*, "his/her insides are dirty for him/her," meaning "he/she is sorry for him/her." The Mandok adopted the shorter Tok Pisin term into their language.

Marimari broke down with purchased goods, unless there was a previously understood equivalence. Such equivalence was not usually stated. Individual Mandok did not have equal access to kerosene, gasoline, or trade-store goods because among the Mandok, individual access to cash varied greatly. This was also partly why the larger investments (trade stores, the village boat purchase) failed. In a capitalist system, debts incurred are of the sort Gregory calls "commodity debt." Commodity debt stands in opposition to "gift debt" because the former accrues interest and keeps the participants in a state of "mutual reciprocal independence." The motivation of an individual transactor is to maximize net incomings, especially to accrue capital (Gregory 1980:636). When the Mandok Society or the owner of Panu Enterprises took out their respective bank loans, they incurred commodity debt. When a relative asked for food, money, or material items, he or she was incurring gift debt. The business owners were therefore faced with the impossible paradox of having to maximize both income and expenditure.

Many Mandok personal businesses failed partially as a result of unfamiliarity with standard business practice. Much of this failure, however, also entailed a conflation of gift debt with commodity debt. The Mandok did not distinguish business assets from personal hoards; they were therefore subject to the *Marimari* Rule of the kinship system. This placed any business owner in a dilemma: those who were most likely to support the business (e.g., kin) were also the most likely to undermine it by exacerbating the owner's commodity debt while incurring their own gift debt. They bought things on credit or "borrowed" things according to their kinship rights and then never repaid them under the commercial obligations of commodity debt. Personally owned trade stores went bankrupt because relatives "ate the profits." What good son or daughter could stand by and watch an older relative and his or her family go hungry for want of a bag of rice and a can of fish?

In 1986–87, Mandok Trading (run by Sangup) was the most solvent store on the island. By 1989, however, a dispute had resulted in one manager forming his own business involving his own portable sawmill and another manager going to another store, called Ovesoso. (The name "Ovesoso" is an old one in Mandok history; it describes the channel between Mandok and Por islands.) Mandok Trading changed its name to Panu Lupung ("United Village"), but the name change does not seem to have helped business: Ovesoso was edging out Panu Lupung as of the end of 1989 (Mulderink 1989).

Most kerosene and gasoline businesses went bankrupt because of the *Marimari* Rule as well.[5] What good child could allow a loving parent to sit in the dark for want of ten cents' worth of kerosene? In cases of physical emergency (e.g., sickness, difficult childbirth, accidents), what good relative or citizen could allow someone to die rather than advance on credit a tankful of gas to rush the patient to the clinic at Lablab? Even without emergencies, the kinship net that supported every Mandok individual entangled their businesses. When the sea was calm and windless, the entire village wanted to go fishing. By using a *mon*, many more people could go and could venture farther out to the best fishing grounds, and the larger group gave a festive atmosphere to the outing.

On a hot, windless day when the sunshine was brilliant and the sea was glass-smooth, the temptation was overwhelming. If an older sibling or parent asked, the younger had to give. This giving absorbed profits and, eventually, inventories.

Politics also had to be considered. The old Mandok Society was a business incarnation of the village *maron* system. Sangup moiety controlled it through the *runai* elders, who made up the core of the decision-making body of the village (see Chapter 4). Any community business was therefore subjected to the authority of the village elders. No clear separation of political, judicial, or economic authority existed. Some of the actors changed, but the system was essentially reworked and subdivided from the one outlined in previous chapters. Any new business was, by definition, a competitor. Moreover, during feasting cycles or other extenuating circumstances, the elders could theoretically override "business sense" and demand that the goods be consumed for "community benefit." This was largely what happened with the community projects. Owners of independent family *lain* businesses, many of whom were younger and high-school educated, hoped to sidestep political maneuvering by preempting the elders' authority.

New wealth caused other problems as well. In the past, high status visibility and ostentatious displays of wealth were limited largely to feasting and other ceremonial exchanges (and controlled by fears of sorcery). On a daily basis, "wealthy" families did not look very different from "poor" ones. Moreover, the former needed the latter to work for them in order to maintain their standing. Families remained interdependent. A cash economy has produced, in contrast, a higher level of status visibility. Outboard motors, guitars, metal roofing, water tanks, cassette recorders, radios, and other items are more visible and enduring than feasting foods and distributed wealth (stored hidden from view on rafters deep inside individual houses). The possession of many and valuable material objects further reinforces the possessor's *independence* from others and becomes a source of ill will. This is partly what the elders objected to, though their objections were expressed in more general accusations of stinginess, selfishness, and a general lack of *marimari*.

Keke's trepang business was the only exception to the general pattern of defeat experienced by other independent businesses. Her project was immune to the *Marimari* Rule for several reasons. First, there was nothing to beg, borrow, or steal. Eating dry-roasted sea cucumbers struck me, with my Western palate, as somewhat like chewing on the sole of a rubber thong marinated in sea water. Most Mandok shared my appraisal. Older men and women told me that in the past sea cucumbers were a "famine food." They also recounted with great bellows of laughter how their parents and grandparents sold them (literally and figuratively) to the Kowai bush people as a "specialty food" in order to get a better exchange value against Kowai vegetable staples.

Second, rather than work against or in spite of the kinship system, Keke used it to her financial benefit. Anyone who wanted to work could work, and would be paid. The project soon had enough labor to support three complete and distinct work crews, each from a different part of the village and each, therefore, organized around extended family groups. The crews rotated, so that each group went in turn for different stages of production. Thus, individual women could organize their own family's activities around a larger group's schedule and work according to their own abilities and time constraints (e.g., sharing babysitting, gathering food for their own families, etc.). From a business perspective this ensured a constant work force, smooth interaction, and happier workers.

Third, as a former school teacher, Keke had some practical skills. She knew how to plan ahead and organize people into work groups. She took attendance in a roll book and kept accurate records both of each worker's wages and her own costs. She understood the basic concepts of supply, demand, overhead, and profit margin.

Finally, she parried the elders' reservations about her community spirit by recycling some wealth back into the village. In 1990 she had supplied ten houses with sheet metal for roofing—at a personal cost of K4,500—and was hoping to get a loan to supply ten more. This is partly why, after almost three years in business, she had yet to show a profit. She seemed content, however, as the following excerpt from a recent letter shows:

▼ Because of all the expenses, the loan and the wages, I still have not managed to make a profit and I have continuously large overdrafts. Though I would love to make a small profit, I am satisfied that because of my efforts, especially the women in the village have, for the first time, an opportunity to earn some cash. This enables them to be partially independent. I have calculated that those families which work for me can earn more than K200 [about U.S. $220] per year. As you know, until last year this was the only way to make some money [on Mandok]. Only recently have the people from Siassi started selling fish to the Siassi Development Corporation in Lablab through its agent on Mandok.

Still, obstacles of three types were in store for this business: ecological, market, and political problems. The ecological problems were twofold: species depletion and weather conditions. The species collected reproduce in about two years. By collecting only two shipments per year from only the shallower depths in Mandok waters, Keke seems to be managing this problem already. As she pointed out to me, if the shallow waters start looking depleted, the divers are willing and able to go deeper. She could even rotate depths as well as reefs, or negotiate with other islanders for harvesting rights in their waters. The weather problem was more difficult to predict or control: the northwest monsoon (January to March) of 1990 was not a kind season to her, and this limited the number of good diving days for collection.

The market paid well but was foreign and variable. Keke started the business by answering a newspaper advertisement for a company in Taiwan. All business thereafter was conducted by mail and by wire. She did not know the buyers, and they did not know her. Each party therefore depended on the good faith of the other to fulfill contract obligations. But it worked. In 1987 the market prices were, she thought, high. Since then she had found an even better market in Hong Kong that offered higher prices for a wider range of species. Keke was also well versed in Siassi history. She knew that trepang had long been a popular commodity for external markets, and she was learning from her business predecessors: she paid for labor rather than the product. In this way she controlled its quality.

Next was the political problem. Within Mandok there was potential competition from other business projects and the frustration of the elders, who had no control over this business and no way to obtain control. Outside of Mandok Keke encountered competition and the potential problems of harvesting rights and the overstepping of fishing-territory boundaries of the other small islands (see Figure 3.1, p. 56). At the time of my fieldwork, Keke had been quite successful in managing local politics with the adroitness of a *liva to ngar* ("woman of knowledge"; see Chapter 6).

Finally, the last potential problem for this business is that of absentee ownership. Keke was a married woman with a family who lived in Port Moresby. Every time there was a shipment to prepare, she flew from Port Moresby to Lae and then traveled by boat or plane to Mandok. The traveling was expensive, time-consuming, disruptive for her family, and debilitating for her. An elder kinsman managed the business in her absence. Historically, absentee managers and owners have not prospered in Siassi. However, by going to Mandok twice per year for two months each trip (Keke 1990), she seemed to be managing this, too.

Whereas the owners of independent businesses were generally hopeful, village elders were initially miffed. They complained that these businesses were motivated by greed and were therefore un-Christian. There was no sense of helping the village "develop," they charged, expressing their sense of development in the Tok Pisin phrases *gohet* ("go ahead") and *kirapim ples* ("lift up, get up the place/village"). Some tried to appeal to the Mandok's sense of community, but to no avail. Villagers, especially those experienced in town living, had already figured out the real game. What the elders really meant was this: the Mandok Society (and by default, the Sangup moiety) had no *control* over family *lain*s and hence over their businesses.

Viewed from the outside, the consequences of these kinds of problems often get lumped under the label "mismanagement." There was a lot of that, too. Few Mandok received educations in business admini-stration. But "mismanagement" is not just a deficiency or a cognitive problem; it does not result only from a lack of education, intelligence, dedication, or will power, as an outside observer might conclude. In small-scale, noncapitalist, kin-based societies, "mismanagement" be-comes a *cultural* problem. Any Mandok business that revolved around a consumable commodity would suffer the same fate.

The trepang business avoided this pitfall in two important ways. First, it produced a locally undesirable commodity. Second, it maintained cen-tralized authority: the owner made all the decisions; they were not sub-ject to a "committee consensus." This was just what the elders did not like about it. All the workers, however, seemed happy, productive, and hopeful. As far as they were concerned, this business *was* helping villagers to *gohet* and to *kirapim ples* by providing them with a way of earning money without leaving home. Big cash projects were previously controlled by men: Panu Enterprises offered women the op-portunity to earn their own money and thereby enjoy a certain degree of independence from men.

Once again, individual Mandok seem to have snatched victory from the jaws of defeat. Once again, they countered externally initiated projects with projects of their own. Once again, they found a way to avoid reloca-tion and cash cropping. But how long could this tide rise? What would be the next "development"?

CHAPTER TEN

❧ Conclusions: Negotiating Development

If you want to have money, you have to get your hands dirty. White people have a lot of money and many good things. Why? Because they *work* for it—they get their hands dirty.

"We are [sea]birds"—it is finished. We cannot think of ourselves this way anymore. We must look to our mothers and remember we are of the land as well as of the sea.

Men who have land are rich. They have money, they have a name. But you and I of the island will soon be rubbish. I have never heard of a rich islander.

Comments made at a village meeting at Muru, February 1987

Anthropological analyses of European contact and colonial rule have offered many perspectives from which to view cultural change. For example, Geertz, taking a cultural systems approach, suggests that in times of change a dynamic tension exists between the traditional ideational system and experiences people have in actual social situations (Geertz 1957). This tension provides the major vector in sociocultural change. On a more individual, psychological level, LeVine (1966) has found that there is a time lapse of several generations between structural changes in status mobility systems and the statistical frequency with which certain (unconscious) personality characteristics are exhibited. LeVine calls this time lapse "psychocultural lag." Both models offer insights into cultural dynamics that are generalized and abstracted from the ethnographic record.

The Mandok case suggests that the tensions placed on the traditional ideational system by the colonial situation provided an impetus to change, in the manner discussed by Geertz. On the other hand, there were also elements that reflected psychocultural lag as defined by LeVine. The differential applicability of these respective approaches seems to depend on which categories or cultural institutions a given community is *willing or able to change.*

The Mandok were willing to reorganize their economic, social, and political systems in response to pacification, missionization, and market and educational opportunities, but only to a point. They took their children (even the girls) out of the food-gathering work force and put them into schools. Time and again the Mandok were reported to be eager to develop and willing to participate in several different types of development projects. Their subsequent behavior vis-à-vis schooling and other development projects that came to Siassi reveals, however, a critical evaluation of relative investments and expected returns that dictated their choices of activities.

These evaluations were rational and were based on more than "economic" considerations. They reflected as well the Mandok's sense of identity, which, it seems, they were not willing or able to change. Moreover, as the failure of the *Yawani* project illustrates, the inherent tensions in the Mandok's political and social systems were exacerbated by the increase in market economics and the education of children from a wider spectrum of statuses. These were not yet resolved at the time of this writing—if, indeed, they will ever be. Lack of strong leadership and the unhealed scars of the village schism of the late 1970s inhibited any attempts in that direction. No one dominating personality (a *bigman*) was present on Mandok who could unite the village factions and rally a sufficient following to carry out such a project. Old competitions between individuals, *lain*s, and even islands prevented them from succeeding in joint ventures. The village was simply unable, at that moment in history, to act as a group. They acted instead in traditionally defined *lain*s.

Mandok subsistence activities, mythology, ritual life, and status and prestige systems bespoke the Mandok's maritime middleman culture. The Legend of Namor codified this worldview for the Mandok by illustrating that "success" was the result of the manipulation of people and situations for personal gain, and that social mobility was contingent on physical mobility in order to sustain control of social and economic networks. But the legend did not impose an imperative charter that prescribed behavioral norms (cf. Malinowski 1922, 1948).

Individual Mandok seemed to choose selectively those aspects of the hero's identity—models *for* behavior—that they wanted to emulate as it suited them. Some of these models were altered to embrace syncretically introduced Christian values and behavioral norms of the Catholic missionaries. The image of birds—seagulls and sea eagles in particular—served as a metaphor for their maritime subsistence activities and suited their self-perceptions (models *of* behavior) as middlemen who were important to a wide variety of culturally diverse groups. For many years these birds exploited the high seas and enjoyed a more cosmopolitan status than their Umboi bush neighbors. While the overseas trade system was thriving, the major means by which a man achieved renown was through *trade* and the *manipulation* and *redistribution* of material goods for profit. Carving and canoe building were major industries for the Mandok and constituted the major items of trade. They traded primarily nonedible objects for subsistence goods. Before European contact, Siassi was the commercial hub of the entire Vitiaz trade system.

With colonial inclusion, however, the commercial hub of northeast New Guinea moved to Rabaul, Lae, and Madang. Siassi became a peripheral link to commerce and an optional partner in trade. European contact and market economics changed the definitions of success in many sectors of life. Government head taxes, the creation and enforcement of regulations to "oblige" universal land productivity, and especially cash cropping disrupted trade and introduced a new variable into the system—cash. Opportunities to emigrate and work further disrupted regular trade, though this situation also offered opportunities to expand trade networks and supplant traditional items of exchange with European substitutes purchased in towns and in local trade stores.

The Mandok were eager for what they perceived to be the material and spiritual benefits of development, but they were not willing or able to sacrifice their mobile, maritime, middleman way of life to acquire them. The introduction of gardening was seen as an intrusion rather than a relief and was identified by many Mandok as the beginning of the decline of overseas sailing and trading. Supplementary gardening did not alter the way the Mandok perceived their environment or their cultural identities; nor did it reorient their basic assumptions, motivations, and goals for achieving renown or their social relationships with others. The profits of trade subsidized the feasting cycles that supported the Mandok's *bigman* status mobility system.

Throughout their development history the Mandok reformulated their choices based on preexisting models of achievement and status mobility. The colonial governments that controlled Siassi over time used their power to impose Western definitions of "development" and "success." In addition to external pressures to engage in cash cropping and in wage labor, these governments generally promoted European social and spiritual mores through the missions and through formal schooling. The Mandok society's achievement system, geared as it was to a maritime middleman existence, had no contemporary counterpart. *Atam* competitive feasting went underground, but it did not go away. Competition still underlay social interaction in Siassi, but it was not the sort of competition that would foster commercial enterprise, and it impeded the cooperative effort necessary for "community development."

The colonial system offered few dissenting choices other than recalcitrance. In a system in which they were otherwise powerless, Mandok people's responses to the various programs and projects became in essence behavioral negotiations of "development." At each critical juncture, they chose an alternative project or business that kept at least part of the population mobile and the rest of it on Mandok Island. They

evaded several attempts from different sectors (especially from government and school officials) to convince them to relocate to Umboi Island,
and they replaced these efforts with hopeful projects of their own
design. These projects mostly failed, for reasons already discussed.

The nationwide emphasis on cash cropping did more than threaten
the Mandok with relocation: it reversed the status relationships within
Siassi. Now that land was valuable, the people on the small islands "had
nothing." Umboi bush people, on the other hand, had land; therefore,
they "had something." Specifically, they had a clearer "road" to wealth
through cash cropping.

CULTURAL CONSTRAINTS ON DEVELOPMENT

Freedman (1967, 1970) characterized the Mandok status mobility system
as a "mini-man" system, owing to environmental constraints. Mandok
reactions to development projects introduced in Siassi indicate that
cultural constraints limited commercial exploitation of the land and sea
resources they did have. On the other hand, "more efficient" exploitation of resources in a Western sense could lead to resource depletion,
as the fluctuations in the size of trochus shells illustrate. Clearly, analysis
of the physical environment is not sufficient for predicting behavioral
patterns in times of change. An approach that takes into account the
indigenous categories and values associated with particular features of
the "behavioral environment" is necessary to understand apparently contradictory behavior. In effect, the Mandok were opting to maintain their
traditional values over what they acknowledged to represent a potential for material benefit. Over the years they had developed a pragmatic
skepticism and a "wait-and-see" attitude toward development as conceived and executed in Siassi. They also were very much aware of and
explicit about their choices.

Anthropological studies in Melanesia in which the focus has been
political leadership, entrepreneurship, trade, or "modern success" in cash
cropping or other business ventures have isolated three fundamental
elements in the traditional systems that stand out as being "pre-adaptive"
to a market economy: (1) productivity of the land and pig husbandry
as primary features of the indigenous economic system, (2) a status
mobility system that requires long-term accumulation of wealth and its
reinvestment in much larger enterprises, and (3) trade as a secondary
feature of the local subsistence economy (see Epstein 1968; Finney 1973;
Salisbury 1970). Trade supports the political system, but not the subsistence economies of most Melanesian societies.

In these pages we have seen that the Mandok system did not share
these characteristics. The Mandok were a land-poor society of mavericks
and drifters who became local entrepreneurs, making a living off others'
produce through craft production and middleman trade. The profits of

trade were either reexported and traded against larger stakes or circulated in village-based exchanges. They were not reinvested into larger, group-oriented endeavors, but instead were recycled into the local, individualized, and centripetal status mobility system. With the possible exception of the trepang business, the Mandok did not compete in commercial markets in the same ways that, for example, coffee growers in Goroka did (cf. Finney 1973).

The persisting barter ideology of traders and middlemen was becoming obsolete in the contemporary context of PNG development. It was being replaced by the cash-based ideology of market economics—that of *producers* and mass *accumulation* of wealth. In Siassi, as of this writing, this meant wage employment, "business," or cash cropping.[1] The Mandok's economic system was a *distributive* (as opposed to a redistributive or accumulative) economic system (after Sahlins 1963; Freedman 1967). This means that although goods, people, and foodstuffs were in constant motion along the trade routes and among Mandok villagers, either in formal distributions or in day-to-day exchanges, one man never amassed a significant amount of anything—whether goods, money, food, or pigs—on a long-term basis. The fact that the social system discouraged the formation of rigid land-based descent groups in favor of task-specific work assemblages of changing participants also inhibited the grouping of resources on a scale described for other Melanesian social and economic systems (notably, Goroka coffee growers; see Finney 1973).

The Mandok were not the only subsistence traders in Melanesia. Other Melanesian societies also depended on trade as a major element of their precolonial subsistence economy (Barlow and Lipset 1982; Carrier and Carrier 1989; Gewertz 1983; Munn 1982). In those societies in which *overseas* trade was a major element in the status mobility system, however, the primary mode of *subsistence* was fishing and/or horticulture, including pig husbandry (Malinowski 1922; Young 1971; Weiner 1976). Moreover, in some of these societies, yams were accumulated and allowed to rot, an occurrence that provided additional visible evidence of "strength" and the abundance of an individual's resources (Malinowski 1922; Young 1971). What distinguished the Mandok from other traders, perhaps, was the fact that trade was the pivotal element in *both* the status mobility systems and the local subsistence economy. It is here that my earlier contention that the Mandok were "middlemen who fished" rather than "fishermen who traded" becomes especially illuminating. Without local trade, the Mandok could not survive; they traded to eat. By combing the high seas they sustained their subsistence economy and prestige systems from a centralized and environmentally marginal location. Over the generations, the dependence on local trade for subsistence and the centrality of overseas trade to the *bigman* status system made "maritime middleman trade" both the key symbol around which the Mandok worldview revolved and the metaphor through which the Mandok interpreted their economic and social relationshps among themselves and with others.

Just as education and advanced technology seem always to go hand-in-hand in developing nations, so do development and cash cropping become synonymous in countries like PNG, where horticulture and animal husbandry remain the predominant means of subsistence. In societies in which fishing is a major feature of the local subsistence economy, fishing industries have developed (see for example, Smith 1977; Spoehr 1980). This is not surprising. Wherever these projects are successful, they seem logically to harness preexisting societal mechanisms and adapt them to a more sophisticated system of resource exploitation. But the Mandok's reef-fishing tradition was not suited to large-scale commercial fishing (Cragg 1981). Even if technological changes were made to change fishing techniques, preexisting social and cultural systems might undermine a successful transition. These systems were oriented toward *manipulation and distribution of others' products* for subsistence, rather than toward production for the group. As such, Mandok's subsistence economy was not pre-adaptive to such an intensification of environmental exploitation, and in fact it worked *against* such a transition.

The Mandok's plight in education and other development projects is not an isolated case peculiar to their tiny island in the Vitiaz Strait. Nor are these problems exclusive to PNG. The interface between any given community's cultural values and motivations for achievement on the one hand and those of its community school on the other becomes the interface of comparative investments in differentially perceived processes of development. On Mandok, these perceptions of investment and development were tied to perceptions of individual and cultural identity that are not so easily altered.

Throughout their contact history, Mandok participation and performance in "development" reflected both their perceived identities as mobile traders and middlemen and a rational evaluation of comparative investments and return on social and economic transactions consistent with this image. For a while, education offered the Mandok a workable alternative by enabling them to utilize their most valuable resource—the ever-growing population of children on the island. When education ceased to reap the expected returns on parents' rising investments in school fees, the Mandok stopped investing.

So often in technological societies the solution to a development problem is phrased in technological terms. Isolation of the various integrated elements of culture and society in this manner reflects a particularly Western viewpoint. Anthropologists have long recognized the fact that in nontechnological societies, various categories such as "religion," "economics," "politics," "society," and so on are not segregated but instead form part of a multifaceted, integrated whole. When development agencies plan "practical" changes, however, these insights are lumped under the vague label of "other constraints" (World Bank 1982:i). Consideration of these cultural factors is often cast aside in favor of "technological" answers. For small island societies like that of the Mandok, the most exploitable resource may just be the ever-rising population of children on the island (see, for example, Carrier and Carrier 1989). Perhaps more sensitivity to "cultural identity," to local interpretations of "development," and to permutations of "government" policy might serve as a guiding principle by which to plan curricula so that developing nations might indeed create appropriate education and development strategies in different geographic and cultural regions.

The Mandok case raises the following question regarding "development": When government development strategies stress land productivity and technological development, what can be done in those societies in which land is absent (or land development is at best supplementary) and in which cultural traditions militate against the development of a local "industry"? This question remains to be answered, both for the Mandok and for other similar communities. Although I have no ready answer, I would recommend that we heed the warning that the Mandok and others are sounding. As LeVine (1966) pointed out, everyone would agree that they want their children to "succeed," but villagers and government officials may have very different notions of what "success" means. To isolated rural villagers in developing nations, development may not imply advanced technology at all. The Mandok wanted access to European cash, knowledge, and "power" (whether medical, personal, or spiritual) to harness for the successful achievement of their own goals. Those goals were island-focused, not land- or urban-centered. Islanders wanted better health care and better markets for their products, themes that persisted since the islanders' first contact with Europeans (see Chapter 7). Development for them meant increased access to and control of an economic exchange system of which these goods were a part.

Throughout the various twists and turns of government policies, the Mandok maintained a fairly consistent set of cultural and social values. Every firstborn child had to "have a name" on Mandok, regardless of its parents' achievements elsewhere. Thus, although the means by which the foods and items of formal exchange were obtained changed somewhat (e.g., with cash instead of, or in addition to, local bartering), the essential goals remained consistent with both village standards of excellence and the traditional system for establishing renown. Personal achievement required the active support of extended kin and trade relations, but it was primarily an *individual* rather than a group-oriented endeavor. Personal strength was demonstrated in feasts and food distributions, which in turn reinforced the internal status mobility system. Remittances from town workers were sent to village parents: they were therefore sent to individuals, not to the community as a whole. Money and gifts remained in ego-based networks of circulation and exchange.

Like the profits of the traditional trade system, remittances rarely got reinvested in communal enterprises.

The Mandok liked to view themselves as "kings of the sea." As such, they continued to search for business projects that kept them on their island. As of this writing, they were still trying to talk themselves into changing this view, but alternatives still precluded such changes. Four short examples will illustrate both the process and its enduring relevance to development.

ALTERNATIVE DEVELOPMENT STRATEGIES, 1987–90

Relocation III: The Earthquake

On February 9, 1987, the Siassi region was rocked out of its predawn somnolence by an earthquake that measured 7.4 on the Richter scale (see Figure 10.1 and Pomponio 1990b). Some village elders and church councillors had been trying to revive interest in moving the community to Muru; the earthquake ended the debates and provided the needed catalyst. The threat of a tidal wave, the dilapidated buildings, and the dead fish floating belly up after the quake heightened people's sense of the precariousness of island life. They fled for higher and more solid ground. For the next three months the island remained underinhabited.

On February 26, the core elders, along with some key younger leaders and the school teachers, held a large and formal community meeting in Muru. I was invited to come and listen, which I did. Within minutes after the meeting began, however, it became evident that I would also be expected to give an "anthropological analysis" of the relocation proposal. Over the years I had had several lengthy conversations with these same individuals about my work and about the very issues under discussion. Feeling strongly that as an anthropologist I was ultimately accountable to the people about whom I write, and knowing that they were counting on me to say something comprehensible and intelligent on the subject, I complied.

I addressed three issues: population increase, decrease in education, and PNG's cash economy upon which, like it or not, they were now dependent. Before, I pointed out, there had been about 100 people living on the 4-hectare sand dune that was Mandok; now there were over 500. Women used to marry around age 20; now they were bearing their first children at ages 16 through 19. The first group to attend secondary schooling delayed marriage and childbirth; their expenses were few, so they could send a lot of money home to their parents and siblings. By now these people had two to five children each. With the inflation of the late 1970s (because I was there during that period they remembered it well), their expenses had risen, too—for rent, electricity, transportation

FIGURE 10.1 *Maramba carries valuable bowls and clay pots to safety as he helps Aibung and Atene assess the damage caused when an earthquake rocked their house (left) off its elevating stilts.*

to work, food, clothing, and school fees. Generally, town workers simply did not have the disposable cash their village relatives thought they had. This last point was the most difficult to convey, as their only view of town workers' cash resources came from remittances and from the lavish feasts they held in the village for their firstborn children.

In the meantime, villagers had become more dependent on cash. The Mandok trade stores had a much wider variety of things to buy in 1987 than there had been in 1980. More people seemed to be eating more rice and canned-fish or meat dinners. They also had a much wider variety of consumables from which to choose: peanut butter, bread (occasionally), instant noodle soup, cheese pops, different kinds of cookies, and so on. Even the local barter system used cash: Umboi trade partners sometimes preferred to eat canned fish over the freshly smoked fish the islanders traded. With increased dependence on cash and a decrease in remittances, villagers needed to pay attention to how they received money and how they spent it. Native canoes were giving way to the flashier *mon* industry, but could the islanders afford the gasoline and service required to run *mon*s? Would they be able to do so in the future?

Many speeches were given that day; this chapter began with excerpts from some of them. Finally the talk came around to the school. The headmaster reported that the bishop had offered money to build sorely needed new classrooms. The school, built in 1960, was by 1987 a dilapidated disaster; the earthquake had further weakened its already cracking structure. It would have to be completely rebuilt. But where? This question revived previous debates (see Chapter 9) and was approached very cautiously. The villagers were divided. Some wanted the new school built in Muru, to underscore this renewed commitment to "move to solid ground." Others wanted to wait one year and settle the community before moving the school. The first group felt this latter approach was a ploy to avoid the inevitable.

Someone then pointed out that people had not yet even built houses in Muru. After the earthquake, Muru refugees slept for four rainy days under worn and leaking tarpaulins rather than risk returning to Mandok (Pomponio 1990b). The thing to do, they reasoned, was to settle first and then move the school. In the meantime, word would be sent to ask the bishop what his timetable might be for supplying the funds needed for the new school.

A silent current of doubt ran beneath the surface in these debates. What would become of "sea people" who tried to change into "bush people"? Mandok was tiny, it was true, but it was also safe and comfortable. It was home. Eating fish was preferable to living on sweet potatoes. For generations the sea, giver of life, also protected them while they slept (e.g., from hostile invasion). There were fewer mosquitoes, fewer diseases, and fewer fears than those lurking in an unknown jungle night. People could walk around the village freely and visit each other at will. In Muru, in contrast, houses were built in scattered hamlet clusters because family groups built their homes close to their gardens. This arrangement produced entirely different patterns of social interaction from those to which the Mandok were accustomed. All of these factors were negatives weighed silently against the positive points discussed publicly.

For the next several months the villagers worked to overcome their shock and repair the damages caused by the earthquake. The northwest monsoon saw the return of Fr. Anton, a much-loved former priest, and by Christmas most of the Mandok were back on their island. The school was rebuilt on Por.

The Wokabaut So

After the earthquake the Catholic mission allotted funds to its affected parishes to aid in the construction process. On Mandok a handful of houses had collapsed completely; several more were tilted or damaged but were reparable. Other events surrounding the earthquake put the village, indeed the entire area, in a tense emotional state (discussed in Pomponio 1990b). The mission viewed the impetus to move to Muru, coming as it did from inside the village, as a good sign. The entire process involved in coping with the disaster helped spawn another new business venture.

After some discussion the village decided to invest "the bishop's money" in a portable sawmill (in TP, *wokabaut so*). With this, they reasoned, the relocation project and the Mandok village repairs could proceed more quickly. When these jobs had been accomplished, the Mandok could cut timber for cash, just as a new company was doing on Umboi.[2] Mandok youths could be employed at home, and the villagers could earn money from the timber on their land, just as the Umboi bush people had been doing for almost ten years. The government had purchased the rights to the timber and paid them, at regular intervals, for timber that as yet had not been touched. Only the few Mandok with close relatives at Gauru and Yangla received any of this money, and it had only been about K10, intermittently offered. With the *wokabaut so* the village could get a jump on land-based business projects and start earning money while their (planned) new coconut palms matured.

The sawmill was purchased and timber was felled. The younger men were so exuberant in their new project that the priest warned them about exhausting the resource (Mulderink 1988). Within one year, however, the project as a communal enterprise disintegrated. Finances had not been clearly separated from the trade store's accounts, and there was a power struggle over control of the sawmill.

By March 1990, two more *wokabaut so* businesses had been established, for a village total of three: one run by Panu Lupung, one by Ovesoso (both as part of their larger trade-store concerns), and one owned by an individual and his family. From the beginning of 1989 to March 1990, their combined sales netted over K11,500. Much of the early profits went to paying off the saws, which had been purchased on credit. Still, by March 1990 there were on Mandok eight permanent houses built with this timber and ten more under construction—each measuring nine by five meters (Mulderink 1990).

The Rebound of Education

In 1986 a committee headed by Sir Paulias Matane convened to examine PNG's education system. The resultant report noted that although the country had had some 14 different ministers of education over the years, it never really had a philosophy of education. Informed by the previous weaknesses and failures of the education system (see Chapter 8), this committee developed a philosophy of education based on a concept of integral human development, or IHD (Matane 1986). This philosophy is

> **integral**, in the sense that all aspects of the person are important; **human**, in the sense that social relations are basic; and [involves] **development**, in the sense that every individual has the potential to

grow in knowledge, wisdom, understanding, skill and goodness. (Matane 1986:6, emphasis in the original)

This approach provided a clear statement that recognized the need for a "Melanesian" blending of material and spiritual worlds (see Chapters 7 and 8). It had the express aim of developing an educational system that treated the child as a moral, spiritual, social, and potentially economic being. The report acknowledged that this being would most likely live in a rural village. It thus merged into one comprehensive philosophy selected aspects of previous policies administered since European contact, and it recognized explicitly rather than by default the role of the church in the educative process (regardless of religion, even though the report was written by members of the National Catholic Education Secretariate).

The Matane report was a timely one for Mandok children. By 1986 some of the students who would be ready for secondary school were children of parents who themselves had been denied secondary education. Many of them also had relatives in town who saw in the late 1970s and early 1980s what they felt to be destructive trends and who were determined to turn the villagers' attention back to education. They started with their own relatives.

The repeated failures and only occasional successes of businesses also encouraged skeptical parents. Some were just resigned to the need for more than elementary education for their children (cf. Pomponio and Lancy 1986). There were also local practical considerations. The new *mon* industry required mechanics. The 1987 earthquake reminded villagers that few youths were being trained as carpenters. Parents with large families were projecting future financial needs. For a variety of reasons, by 1988 parents had started to support secondary schooling again (Figure 8.1, p. 161). By March 1989 there were 12 students (both boys and girls) attending Siassi High School in Lablab and nine boys at St. Joseph's Technical School In Lae (Mulderink 1989).

The Siassi Development Corporation

In October 1986, FISIKA held a gala celebration for the opening of a new cooperative business called the Siassi Development Corporation (SDC). SDC was to have two functions. It was hoped that Siassi villagers would stock their village trade stores from a local bulk store, built at Lablab and staffed by a German expatriate, rather than go to Lae. The second function was to create and maintain the superstructure by which to market Siassi products in Lae. Once the bulk store became solvent, this latter goal included a fishing and shell-collecting business intended to be specifically for the islanders. In addition, the manager experimented with the collection of lobsters and the production of charcoal. The manager's wife started her own business of purchasing local crafts for subsequent sale to expatriates in Finschhafen and Lae.

At first, though excitement seemed high, business was poor for several reasons. First, the manager was new to PNG and new to Siassi. He had been a business-school teacher in Germany and had come to PNG for a new experience. It took a while for him to get used to local customs, peoples, and business practices. Second, the fish, shellfish, and crafts end of the business seemed to serve only the Aromot. Aromot was the closest island to Lablab, and therefore it cost the Aromot people less to get to the store; other islanders had to pay upwards of K21 for the trip by *mon* (see Chapter 9). Third, SDC's boat, the *M.V. Siassi*, arrived late, and then it kept breaking down. Fourth, freezers for the fishing business took much longer to procure and to distribute. This fact also gave the Aromot an edge on SDC in the market: because they were so close, they did not need the freezers. By this time the Mandok freezers were rusty and inoperative (see Chapter 9). Immediate transportation of the perishable fish necessitated the use of *mons*. Back to square one. The Mandok did not at first sell anything to SDC except for some sea-shells, but they were not entirely closed out of "development." It was around this same time that the trepang business started on Mandok (see Chapter 9).

SDC also had technological difficulties:

SDC started the Fish Marketing again after the coolroom was fixed in February 1988. But after two months of operation on a small scale the next generator break-down stopped this service again. For more than six months the generator was not working. Installation mistakes caused the break-down for the second time. After everything was checked the generator was working again [by the] end of December. The Ice-Block supply could not be improved before December 1988, when the DPI Fisheries in Lae got the second Ice-Making-Machine. As we have no funds to buy our own [ice maker] we are depending on Ice out of Lae. (SDC Annual Report 1988)

SDC recovered from its technological setbacks by January 1989 and seemed to be doing well after some administrative changes were made. First, shareholders in FISIKA were given priority over nonshareholders for selling their products. The Aromot, who had previously flourished, were shut out until they bought shares in the larger, umbrella cooperative organization. Second, the islanders no longer had to transport the fish themselves. When the boat finally got organized it made regular circuits of the Siassi region, and occasionally went across the Dampier Strait to Kilenge, to collect all cash-earning products from copra to grass skirts. The Mandok, largest of the Siassi shareholders in FISIKA, now had a clear path to a market for their goods. Finally, freezers were placed on each island and put in the care of one designated manager. The manager

T A B L E 1 0. 1 *Money earned by Siassi communities from Siassi Development Corporation.*

	1986	1987	1988
Copra	K5,301.84	K16,790.75	K52,022.58
Fish	—	4,148.90	1,828.55
Artifacts	—	1,748.25	2,898.77
TOTALS	K5,301.84	K22,687.90	K56,749.90

NOTE: The low total for fish sold in 1988 reflects technological difficulties with the boat and the coldroom (see text). Projections for 1989 were for K12,000.

SOURCE: Siassi Development Corporation Annual Report 1988.

was also given K500 with which to buy fresh fish on the spot, at a rate of K1/kg, after inspecting them for proper handling and cleaning.

March and April 1989 was a banner fishing season in Siassi. SDC sent to Lae about 16,000 kg of fish bought from fisherfolk on Mandok, Malai, and Aromot. These islanders were paid a total of K21,000 within four months (Jakob 1989). Total annual receipts from 1986 through 1988 for fish, artifacts, and copra (mostly from Umboi and Kilenge) are shown in Table 10.1. Shells were also collected and sold for the prices listed in Table 10.2. SDC seemed finally to be functioning according to plan.

There were several problems, though, that plagued this and all other development projects in Siassi (and elsewhere); foremost among them were market trends and personnel transience. The fish was sold in Lae, first in a supermarket that catered largely to expatriates and later in SDC's newly opened fish store. One of the vagaries of a world (or even regional) market system is that commodities produced at farther distances are often less expensive than those produced locally. Compared to fish and shellfish imported from New Zealand, Siassi fish was very expensive— good, but costly. The fish became more of a specialty item than a staple (Mulderink 1989). The second problem, personnel transience, surfaced at the end of 1989, which marked the end of the manager's contract. He and his family returned to Germany. A new manager was hired, but by March 1990 the fishing project had run aground again from the third and fourth perennial problems; ice supplies and bad weather during the northwest monsoon (Mulderink 1990).

SDC offered quick cash returns for fish, shellfish, shells, and crafts, but it was an externally initiated business run by transient outsiders. Siassi peoples were the producers, not the managers. Nevertheless, the cooperative provided a workable means by which islanders could remain on

TABLE 10.2 *Shell prices paid by Siassi Development Corporation, 1987.*

SHELL	SIZE	PRICE EACH
Triton	L	K3.00
	M	2.00
	S	1.00
Nautilus		1.00
Helmit	L	3.00
	M	2.00
	S	1.00
Strombids	XL	2.00
Volutes	M (20 cm.)	1.00–1.50
Murex	L	1.00
	S	.50
White cowry		.20
Turbins and other small shells	S	.10

their tiny islands and continue their maritime subsistence activities. It, along with the trepang business on Mandok, was therefore very popular.[3]

THE NEXT GENERATION

While villagers continued to resist relocation and sedentary life on Umboi, their town-dwelling relatives looked on with fear and apprehension about the islanders' future. Lewis Kusso-Alless expressed these fears most eloquently:

▼ *Anau eta irov ila su,* "some seagulls [do] fly into the bush." The population is increasing so rapidly. Hygiene is so poor and neglected. Erosion is distinctive. Bartering is becoming non-exist[ent] given a push aside by marketing services and values. *Mailaŋ* ["feasting"] is becoming [a] burden for the sponsors and less distinctive [than] it was at one time. Food shortage is evident. Yet the Mandoks choose to live on and on at the island. . . .

I saw them at Muru with [the tools for sago processing] every day of the weeks I was there. [Sago is a kind of starch processed from the pulp of the sago palm, which grows along the rivers of Umboi. Its use as a staple was usually reserved for lean times when there was

▼ no other vegetable staple available.] I even took pictures of them. They were not middle-aged men, but young, newly married men with just a kid or two each. I saw them carrying tons and tons of coconuts to Mandok, as if there were *mailaŋ* or copra-making activities on. I saw them carrying very green banana on their canoes. I saw empty beds of canoes with loads of betel nuts. I witnessed them buying tapioca from my own [adoptive] parents. I heard them complaining about the Gauru's not bartering with them. I felt a gutty twist every time I saw this played in my face. (Kusso-Alless 1989)

FINALE

Development in third-world communities is not a one-time effort, nor does it follow a unidirectional sequence. It involves a long, uneven struggle against local environments and economic, social, political, and cultural factors that sometimes cause setbacks or necessitate adjustments. Throughout their development history up to this writing, the Mandok were above all resourceful. Their decisions over time showed a commitment to their cultural heritage and a pragmatic adaptability that will serve them well, whatever their future decisions. It is one of my greatest hopes that this account is not only comprehensible to them, but also to administrators, developers, volunteers, and other kinds of outsiders who work with them or other third-world peoples.

As we have noted, however, some things are not easily changed. Self-perception is one of them. The dancing feast depicted in Figure 4.2 (p. 85) shows some of the complex blend of old and new on Mandok. The "purist" might bristle at the blend of traditional and modern building constructions side by side, the men in shorts and T-shirts, and the occasional wristwatch. The women, dressed in a combination of *laplap*, bra, and grass skirt, bob reverently with averted eyes as they escort the *nakamutmut* from the lane leading to the *pulat*. In the focal center of the photograph, in profile, a young man carrying a large black cassette recorder is recording the ceremony for people who could not be present and for his own future enjoyment.

At six o'clock the church bell calls everyone to evening prayer. The *nakamutmut*s retreat to the *pulat* and the dancers stop in place. The missionary priest, who has come to watch this final ceremony for this year's cycles, indicates that adjournment to the church is not necessary. All heads bow in place as the catechist leads the community in prayer. After the prayers, a line of women from the sponsor's *baliŋwaro* files into the village plaza carrying oblong wooden bowls with manioc or taro pudding, pots of rice, tea, branches of betel nut, and packets of betel pepper for the performers. The community takes a short break.

When the meal is finished, the men return to the center of the village plaza. One of the drummers calls out a new song phrase. He beats his

FIGURE 10.2 *The* baliŋwaro *men entwine themselves in the sago fronds as they escort the departing* nakamutmut.

drum in the BA-BOOM, BOOM rhythm of this dance, and soon the other men join in. On the third or fourth refrain the *nakamutmut*s return to the plaza, and the dancing resumes.

Men carry bamboo poles festooned with tobacco leaves and strips of newspaper for the dancers and singers to roll into long cigarettes. Baskets filled with strands of shell money, dogs' teeth, pigs' tusks, cash, *laplap*s, manioc bread, and other items that the sponsor has accumulated are presented to the *baliŋwaro* for working so hard on the feast cycle and maintaining the sponsor's masked figure throughout. Larger baskets hung on poles in the *nakamutmut*'s path are filled with manioc bread baked in an oven of hot stones. The *nakamutmut* will take the baskets when it leaves the island. The excitement mounts as the entire village gears up for the grand finale.

The ceremony climaxes when the departing *nakamutmut*, surrounded by other figures and all the different *baliŋwaro*s, enters the plaza for the last time. Male members of the *baliŋwaro lain* entwine themselves in the figure's sago fronds as it makes its last round of the plaza (see Figure 10.2). The sponsors cry as their *nakamutmut* returns to its home place. As the figure makes its final turn toward the sea, all the women and children are herded in the opposite direction, so as not to see anything. There they wait until the all-clear signal is given.

The villagers can finally relax. The dance is over, the exchanges are completed, the figure has left, and the immediate danger is gone. Women and children do not leave their compounds this night unless there is a good reason, for "the *mariam*s are walking around." Grandfathers tell stories to their grandchildren as they weave bracelets and necklaces for them from the fallen fronds the children collected after the ceremony. These will bring them blessings and good luck. The sponsors collapse from exhaustion. They will not have bathed or eaten yet, for they were collecting the wealth objects and food for the baskets and supervising their distribution. Almost too tired to chew, they squat in the gloaming around the fire, speaking little. For them, the pressure is finally off. The *baliŋwaro*s are also exhausted. They, too, have delayed their evening bath and meal until they finished distributing all of the sponsor's food and completed the ceremony. They, too, collapse by their fires in subdued exhaustion. As they total up all the sponsors' distributions they contemplate how, when their firstborns come of age, they will return this feast.

Notes

PREFACE

1. "Smallholder" is a term generally used to mean "all indigenous farmers, regardless of the actual size of their holding, and to distinguish them from plantations or large-scale operations which were deemed to be foreign owned" (Good 1986:50*n*.). See Good (1986:50–51) for a discussion of the problems with this definition in the context of economic realities in PNG.

INTRODUCTION

1. I use "traditional" and "modern" after Shils's (1960) discussion of the formulation of "New States." New States are characterized by (1) recent acquisition of sovereignty after a substantial period of foreign (i.e., Western) rule, (2) the "massively traditional character" of the social structure and culture, and (3) an elite concerned with modernization of the social structure, culture, and political life and outlook of the people (1960:267–268). In contrast, "traditional societies" are those that "are attached to beliefs and rules which guided past practices, and which are regarded as guides to right practice in the present" (1960:282).

CHAPTER ONE

1. Lewis Kusso-Alless, who used to spell his name "Lew Allace," is an avid student of his own culture. In 1976 he wrote an article entitled "Siassi Trade" (Allace 1976), upon which I draw extensively in the next two chapters.

2. Other anthropologists have worked on Mandok as well, mostly for short periods of time. In the 1970s and 1980s a Japanese museum collector named Kobayashi visited intermittently to collect artifacts. As far as I know he writes only in Japanese. The linguist Geoff Smith studied Mandok's counting system in 1978 (reported in Lancy 1978, 1983). Anton Ploeg worked in Barang village on Umboi Island and visited Mandok briefly in 1979 (Ploeg 1984, 1985). Ian Lilley dug test pits for archaeological research on Mandok in 1983 (Lilley 1986:111; 1988), and Pieter ter Keurs studied the woodcarving and canoe industries in 1983–84 (ter Keurs 1985, 1989).

3. The severe drop in both Tuam's and Malai's populations from 1963 to 1980 is probably the result of migrations to Umboi and to town. I suspect that these figures reflect only *residential* populations, not including absentee workers in towns. For example, my own census of Mandok in 1980 gives a residential population of 437. Subsequent figures and percentages used in this study are based on my figures.

4. Though the Mandok have their own names for these distinctions, for the sake of clarity I have chosen to follow the usage already established in the bulk of the literature.

5. "Kowai" and "Kaimanga" are Yabim terms introduced by German Lutheran missionaries during the German Era (late 19th/early 20th centuries). Most of the literature describes two dialects of Mutu, which is also called Tuam-Mutu in some sources, because most of the data analyzed were collected on Tuam (Hooley 1971, 1976; Hooley and McElhanon 1970). See Chowning (1986) and Lincoln (1977) for more comparative analyses. My own linguistic data, gathered in 1987, indicate that there are three dialects: one on Tuam, one on Malai, and one shared among Aromot, Mandok, and Aronaimutu islands.

6. The literature does not always use consistent spellings. "Siassi," for example, contains the medial *ss*, most likely to indicate a voiceless sibilant in English or German. This is not necessary in local, unwritten languages or in Tok Pisin, and some linguists use the latter phonetic spelling with only one *s*. My informants changed their spellings to match writing conventions in different languages, and that is the usage I follow.

7. For a comprehensive listing and discussion of the objects of trade in the Vitiaz trade system, see Allace (1976) and Harding (1967, 1989).

8. For a critique of Lilley's conclusions, see Harding and Clark (1990:12–18).

9. When Chinnery visited Mandok in about 1926, he made no mention of the Mandok carving anything but canoes. The only island on which carving bowls was then documented was Tami (Chinnery n.d.:33–41).

CHAPTER TWO

1. For a detailed review and analysis of these versions and their role in local theology, see Pech (1979). For other versions of the legend, see Allace (1976); for the Rai Coast version, see Lawrence (1964). David Counts and Martin Zelenietz made different Kilenge versions available to me, and Eldon Ball gave me a tape recording of an Arop version. My thanks to Michael Mote and Gabriel Aipake from Mandok, who told me the version presented here, and to Pius Metke from Aupwel for telling me an Aupwel version in December 1980. Responsibility for the interpretation of these accounts is of course my own.

2. There is a cover term in Mutu that describes the entire groin area and includes the upper part of the thigh and the genitals. In other versions it is stated clearly that he tattooed her *pudenda* (Lawrence 1964:22).

3. This is an English translation of a direct translation into Mutu from Tok Pisin. The Mandok have no word for "number"; numbers were not conceived as abstract concepts but were attached to specific items. The Tok Pisin expression *kisim namba* "to get/take [one's] number" was very popular in PNG during both my field stays. It got translated literally into Mutu as "*nagam namba toni wa*"—the Tok Pisin word *namba* was inserted directly into the Mutu phrase.

4. Betel nut is the mainstay of social life in many areas of PNG. The nut of the areca palm is chewed with a mixture of slaked lime, made from coral, and betel pepper (sometimes including the leaves). The combination produces a chemical reaction that results in increased salivation and a wad that is blood-red. Chewing betel, which can have both stimulating and narcotic effects

on the chewer, occurs all over PNG and other parts of Melanesia in ritual life and magical incantations, as we shall see as the legend unfolds.

5. This trend of local legends presupposing the creation of humanity is also present in other Austronesian island cultures. See, for example, Hogbin (1970:38). But compare Lawrence (1964:13) for the Rai Coast, where local cosmogony does explain the creation of humans. The study of comparative Austronesian cosmogony raises interesting questions that unfortunately lie beyond the scope of the present study. My thanks to Richard Scaglion and Thomas Harding for raising the question of human origins in this comparative sense.

6. I am indebted to Fr. Anton Mulderink for this observation regarding real and apparent conflicts in Siassi social life.

7. According to Allace (1976, [Kusso-Alless] 1984), Gainor, the woman Kilibob married at Arop, was one of the last people made, and she was made for Kilibob to marry. She was from Tarawe (Kusso-Alless 1984). Allace also notes that, in traveling inland, Kilibob makes a special point of avoiding Barang, Omom, and Gom, which are all *Kowai* communities on Umboi. This sequence thus gives the islanders a few examples of where they can and cannot travel safely on Umboi.

8. Ficus and callophyllum trees figure prominently in Mandok mythology and belief as homes for different kinds of spirits. Some are ancestral and protective spirits, others are malevolent (see Chapter 3).

9. Decorative and fragrant shrubs were inserted into these armlets, enhancing the dancer's attractiveness as they swished and swayed rhythmically with the dancer's movements. Love magic was also performed on the shrubs to enhance further a dancer's attractiveness to the opposite sex. Such shrubs were considered so vital a part of the costume that a person would not dance without them. Certain feasts favored different types; the feast mentioned at this point in the legend was the *Bukumu singsing*, and therefore the desired arm bracelet was *ngas*. Ngas could also be woven into anklets.

10. I am indebted to Fr. Anton Mulderink for his exegesis of this part of the episode and for his analysis of the meaning for the Mandok of tree symbolism more generally. Responsibility for interpretation of his comments is of course mine.

11. The phrase "we do not know" has several connotations. As a rhetorical device, it may mean that this section of the legend is obscure. On the other hand, it might also imply that because Kilenge is out of Siassi, the narrators "do not know" because they *have no rights* to use this particular capsule of knowledge.

12. My tellers were not sure why he was angry with the Kilenge but conjectured that they must have done something to offend him. One Aromot version claims that the spectacle caused when Namor subsequently sold the canoe preempted other trade, and the Kilenge traders were angry (Mulderink 1989). Allace (1976:12) mentions that the Kilenge had sexual intercourse on the fallen *malaz* tree, which caused the bridge to crack and fall into the sea. This event presumably prompted Namor to take the two-masted canoe from them. In any case, this is the Siassi explanation for why the Kilenge do not manufacture canoes.

13. See Errington (1974), McDowell (1985), and selections in Gewertz and Schieffelin (1985) for comparative examples of Melanesian concepts of both time and the recording of history.

CHAPTER THREE

1. During World War II there was a "black market" trade in gelignite, which was used for blowing up reefs as a means of catching fish (see Chapter 7). Crocodile hunters were also credited with the demise of certain *puʀun* with crocodile forms.

2. In August 1980 the Mandok purchased an additional parcel of land from Gauru village that extended the garden boundaries to the Izon River. This land is not yet, to my knowledge, officially registered.

CHAPTER FOUR

1. Unmarried women and all men were barred from seeing childbirth. The Mandok said that if unmarried women saw childbirth, "they would be afraid to marry."

2. *Nakamutmut* are similar to the *nausang* masked figures in Kilenge (Grant and Zelenietz 1981) and the *kamutmut* figures from the Möwehafen area of southwest New Britain (Todd 1934).

3. Firstborns could also be introduced to the dance with the *Sia* feasting complex; see Chapter 6 and Figure 6.1, page 117.

4. See Counts and Counts (1983) for similar themes for Kaliai, west New Britain. My thanks to Dorothy and David Counts for reminding me of this article. See also Goodale (1985) and Scaletta (1985) for additional examples from neighboring New Britain groups.

5. Freedman (1967:190) translates the Mandok term *maron* as "leader." Harding (1967:67) translates the Sio term *maro* as "great" or "great one" and also mentions adoption of the term by Lutheran missionaries for translating "God." In a later work (1985), Harding distinguishes between *maro*, "the leaders of men's clubhouses," and *koipu*, "a feast maker." He further notes that "*maro* and *koipu* were normally one and the same" (1985:39). The Sio system offers interesting comparisons with the Mandok; interested readers should consult Harding (1985:39–45).

6. In emphasizing the hereditary basis of the Mandok's political system, my interpretation here departs from statements in Pomponio (1983). Compare also Harding (1967) and Freedman (1967).

CHAPTER FIVE

1. When I returned to Mandok in 1986, *runai* membership had been reorganized to accommodate the rising population and several new houses built since 1981. Three of the larger groups divided to make three more groups, for a total of ten. People explained the splits as a practical means by which ceremonial food distributions could be accomplished more efficiently.

2. My account and interpretation of Mandok *runa* is contrast with those offered by Freedman (1967:210–212). For a detailed discussion of particular points of difference, see Pomponio (1983:170–175).

3. Freedman (1967, 1970) has characterized Siassi social organization as having a lattice structure. I prefer the concept of a "social fishnet" not to argue metaphors but to provide an image of the nature of various categories of relatedness on Mandok and the flexibility of the system. This kind of social organization pulls in a wider array of people in much the way Mandok men cast their fishnets to catch many fish.

4. The recent increase in off-island marriages was partly the result of over-inbreeding, as noted in the text. Several young women were sent to visit relatives in towns in the hope that each would find a suitable marriage partner. A concentrated increase in intermarriage with Kilenge occurred in the mid-1980s, due, it seems, to the introduction and proliferation of *mons* (motorized dugout canoes, discussed in Chapter 9). This new canoe gave the Mandok a direct route to west New Britain, whereas between the mid-1960s and 1980 they were entirely dependent on commercial shipping lines; in order to get to Kilenge, they had to take a circuitous route through Finschhafen and Lae.

5. I know of only one case of a legitimate firstborn being adopted.

CHAPTER SIX

1. There is also a long tradition of documentation of this relationship in anthropology. See, for example, Barry et al. (1959), Whiting and Child (1953), Whiting (1963), Sahlins (1963), LeVine (1966), and Edgerton (1971).

2. See also Atkinson (1958) and McClelland (1961). Ruth Finney applied these concepts in a pioneering study of achievement motivation in high-school students in PNG (Finney 1971).

3. Bamler (cited in Chinnery n.d.:44) describes the *atam* relationship as a "recompenser," noting the difficulty of adequately translating the concept into English.

4. In fact, children will see this need less and less as time goes on. During Christmas of 1988, the elders decided to make all firstborn ceremonies optional, with three exceptions: the *nakamutmut* "beating," boys' superincision, and the first dancing feast (Mulderink 1990).

CHAPTER SEVEN

1. For an excellent, comprehensive review of early exploration in this area (focusing on Long Island), see Ball (1982) and Ball and Hughes (1982).

2. For more information on the role of trade as an agent of peace in northeast New Guinea, see Harding (1970).

3. Money also recruited labor for his plantation while he owned it, so he was well known to Siassi peoples by this time (Ploeg 1989).

4. For additional information on education and development in PNG, see Pomponio and Lancy (1986), Swatridge (1985), and Weeks and Guthrie (1984).

5. *Runai* refers to the group; *rumai* refers to the group's ceremonial house. Compare Freedman (1967), who records one term, *rumai*, for both. Modern Mandok also used *rumai* to mean a church. Speakers were not consistent, however, and sometimes used the terms interchangeably.

6. The "T" stands for "Territory." The colonial administration maintained for many years a dual education system that recognized the profound background differences of native and expatriate children. Primary "T" schools served native Papua New Guinean children. Primary "A" schools catered to (primarily) Australian and other expatriate children.

7. This was not the case throughout the Territory. In Kaliai, western New Britain, true leaders often recommended "nothing men" because they could be counted on not to cause problems (Counts and Counts 1990).

CHAPTER EIGHT

1. Ownership of some of this land was still under dispute throughout the 1980s. In 1988 a court case regarding land rights in the Mantagen/Masele area of north Umboi was pending (Mulderink 1989).

2. This was a common, stereotypical insult the bush communities liked to hurl at the sea people. The islanders retorted by questioning the intelligence and cleanliness of the bush people. Islanders also liked to laugh at the obvious fear the "landlubbers" had of the sea and their consequent inability to swim or paddle canoes.

3. Local lore maintained that the bodies of the dead Gomlonggons were never buried, and many floated out to sea; subsequently the Mandok and other islanders ate nothing from the sea for many months afterward. There is no written documentation for this, but clearly the episode was not a happy one in Mandok history.

4. Although 1971–72 marks the beginning of the decline of Mandok high-school enrollments, Gelem was better situated, from the Mandok point of view, than Lablab. Many Mandok had matrilateral kin, trade, and affinal relatives at Barim and on Aronaimutu Island. They were therefore still within reach of a support group.

5. Other problems that had to do with the social relationships between particular teachers and the community contributed to the extraordinarily high dropout rate in 1979 (see Pomponio 1985).

6. Signs of the deterioration of the carving tradition were also visible in the previous generation of workers returning from plantations. They were absent from the village during some of the years in which they would have been under the tutelage of their elder male kinsmen in learning the carving tradition, patterns, and so on. These returning men would sneak over to the mission at night to look at the priest's copies of their *runai* designs (Mulderink 1980).

7. These figures applied to government and mission high schools; international high schools were much more expensive.

CHAPTER NINE

1. In the early 1960s the Catholic mission collected trochus and green-snail shells from the islanders at a rate of about three tons per year (Patrol Report Finschhafen 9, 1961–62:7). Ted Foad collected three tons in 1964 (Harding 1989). Trochus and green-snail shells remained on the list of produce items sold to the Gizarum plantation through 1970 (Patrol Report Finschhafen 1, 1970–71:2).

2. Whenever a *luluai* or a *tultul* was appointed during the early 1960s, great care was taken to provide one man from each moiety (Patrol Report Finschhafen 17, 1961–62, App. C:3).

3. Keke's father, a World War II veteran, used his compensation money to buy an outboard motor and had a *mon* built in the village. She still had to buy fuel for it and pay for a "captain" to run it, as this would have been inappropriate for a woman to do.

4. Gregory's formulation is much more complex and on the whole is less applicable than my interpretation and application of it here. I am using only the parts of his definitions that apply to the Mandok case.

5. As of 1989, one group, "Parang Petrol," run by one family *lain*, was still doing well (Mulderink 1989).

CHAPTER TEN

1. The Umboi Timber Project might constitute an exception to this pattern (see *Post Courier* 1981; *Niugini Nius* 1982). However, this project was not perceived by the Mandok to be anything that concerned them particularly because the land in question was not theirs—it belonged to several Umboi communities. The only plans in which islanders figured at all were a small number of stevedoring jobs to pole felled logs out to ships anchored in Bunsil harbor (FISIKA 1986). The entire project was disbanded by late 1989 when the company was found to be in violation of its contract with the provincial government.

2. The Umboi Timber Project got under way just as I was leaving Mandok in 1987. Over the years, the project was the subject of much controversy, which space precludes elucidating here.

3. SDC sold the *M.V. Siassi* after the Siassi member of Parliament, the Hon. Peter Garong, donated speedboats to eight villages (Jakob 1989). The donation decreased SDC's costs, but villagers now had to supply gasoline and upkeep for their new boats (see Chapter 9).

Glossary

aidaba Firstborn person, regardless of sex.

aisor Song of mourning, sung during the all-night vigil held for a firstborn or other important member of the community who has died.

anunu Inner self, likeness, reflection; also translated to express the Christian concept of "soul."

baliŋ Generic term for any kind of wealth object, including brideprice, land purchase, or trade object; sometimes pronounced *mbaliŋ*.

bêche de mer See *trepang*.

bigman TP, "big man"; a traditional leader, elder, or otherwise high-status man.

bikhet TP, "big head"; used to describe spoiled children and people who are stubborn, contradictory, or in any way contrary or difficult.

bisnis TP, "business"; any cash-rendering project.

borou A polysemous term applied to deaf or mentally impaired people, uneducated people, stupid people, and animals; defined by the lack of ability to hear (and speak) and thus to learn.

classificatory kin Any person(s) classified as belonging to a kinship position not held biologically. For example, classificatory siblings are classed as siblings but do not share the same biological parents.

consanguineal Related by blood.

copra The dried meat of coconuts, used in the food and cosmetics industries worldwide. Copra was a major cash crop in Siassi, as in other areas of PNG and the Pacific.

Ego Anthropological term used to designate the individual from whose perspective a genealogical chart is to be interpreted; can be applied to real and hypothetical cases.

FISIKA Acronym for Finschhafen-Siassi-Kabwuum Development Authority.

gohet TP, "go ahead," "approval," "go forward"; used to mean "development." See also *kirapim ples*.

gol Generic term for mollusc.

gorgor A man of many talents, a "Renaissance man"; sometimes pronounced *ngorngor*.

guruba Trade partner (*gurubadi*, pl.).

ig Moving creatures of the sea, especially fish.

iza "His/her/its name"; also a form of adoption in which the adopting parent "calls the name" for the child but does not take the child into a new home. Compare *paroŋ* and *utuŋ*.

Kai The daytime part of the Sia dancing feast. See also *Sia*.

Kaimanga   Yabim word introduced by Lutheran missionaries to describe the language group, peoples, and southeast region of Umboi Island. Compare *Kowai*.

Kakam   Special mourning name given to a woman whose firstborn child has died. Compare *mandaat*.

kamos   Sacred legend or history.

kirapim ples   TP, "to get up/bring up the place/village"; used to describe development. See also *gohet*.

Kowai   Yabim word introduced by Lutheran missionaries to describe the language, peoples and northwest region of Umboi Island. Compare *Kaimanga*.

kwila   TP for *Intsia bijuga*, a valuable hardwood with worldwide commercial value.

lain   TP for any categorical grouping of people based on blood, age, household membership, or other social or political criteria.

laplap   TP for a length of cloth (usually about two meters long and one meter wide) wrapped around the waist and worn by both men and women.

las   Leatherskin or queenfish (*Scomberoides commersonianus*).

levirate   Marriage custom in which a widow marries her dead husband's real or classificatory brother.

liva   Woman, female.

mailaŋ   Dancing feast entailing village-wide distributions of pigs, wealth objects, and vegetable foods.

maluum   Smaller of two types of fishnets used in Siassi. Compare *palpal*.

Mandaat   Special mourning name for a man whose firstborn child has died.

maran   The ceremonial plaza in the center of the village.

mariam   Spirit of a dead person, a ghost.

maron   Traditional leader, involving hereditary advantage and superior peace-making abilities.

Maron tiina   "Big/great *maron*"; Used to translate "God."

Mata   Moiety and east side of Mandok Island. Compare *Sangup*.

matrilateral   Relatives on the mother's side, not necessarily in the mother's lineage.

matrilineal   Descent traced through the mother.

meri blaus   TP, "woman's blouse"; a loose-fitting "Mother Hubbard" type of blouse introduced by missionaries.

misis   TP for European woman.

moiety   One of two approximately equal divisions of a society.

mon   Motorized dugout canoe. Compare *waŋ*.

mos   A complex creation, a piece of artwork, or a design.

motak   (*?Polymesoda palustris*), a mangrove bivalve similar to steamer clams but rounder.

mutu Island. When capitalized, refers to the language of the Siassi small islanders.

nakamutmut Masked figures who link Mandok people with their sacred ancestral past and who have a prominent role in ceremonial life. *Nakamutmut* are the repositories of Mandok law and order and the ultimate traditional sanctions within Mandok village.

naŋur Trevally (*Gnathanodon speciosus* and *Caranx* spp.).

ndaab Items appropriated or people taken in or sponsored by a *bigman*, either as a result of a death or other catastrophe.

ngar Knowledge, intelligence, breeding; also used to mean personality and temperament.

ngarawat tidi Firstborn daughter of a *maron*.

ngas Black vine from Umboi that is woven into armlets and leglets for dancing feasts.

ngeu ariaŋa A "strong man," used to describe a *bigman* or an otherwise powerful or successful man. See also *ngeu tiina*. Note too that all constructions of the form *ngeu to_____* , a "man of_____," can also be used for women. In that case the structure would be *liva to _____ , a "woman of _____ ."*

ngeu ee moɤon A man who is "one of a kind." The phrase is sometimes used to describe a particularly successful *bigman*, but it can also be applied to a woman (*liva ee moɤon*).

ngeu tiina A *bigman*; used to describe strong, successful, and powerful men. See also *ngeu ariaŋa*.

ngeu to mos Artisan, particularly a master carver or canoe builder.

ngeu to ngar Man of knowledge. The term implies a man of good judgment, one who knows how to do many things (e.g., build canoes, carve, perform rituals and feasts correctly) and who knows different forms of important and sacred knowledge. Can also be applied to a woman (*liva to ngar*).

olman Elder. Used both as an adjective and a noun. Its plural form, *dolman*, describes village leaders as a group.

olya Social replacement. Firstborn boys especially are considered to be their fathers' *olya,* but the term can also be applied to any child named specifically for an important or deceased relative.

on Oblong wooden bowl carved by Mandok men and used in several types of ceremonial exchange. It is a major trade and wealth item in the Vitiaz Strait trade network.

palpal Large fishnet used for fishing and hunting dugong. Compare *maluum*.

paroŋ Polysemous term meaning succor, nurture, or fosterage of a child. Compare *utuŋ*.

patrilateral Relatives on the father's side, not necessarily in the father's lineage.

patrilineal Descent traced through the father's line.

polysemous Having many meanings.

pulat Men's sacred area.

puɤun A malevolent spirit, usually in the form of a snake, crocodile, or other reptile.

Rag Southeast monsoon. Compare *Yavar.*

rumai Ceremonial men's house associated with a *runai*; also used for "church."

runai Nominally patrilineal descent group. Compare *rumai.*

Sangup Moiety and west side of Mandok Island. Compare *Mata.*

SDC Siassi Development Corporation.

Sia Traditional dancing feast imported from Arop Island in which male dancers imitate cockatoos and other birds, as well as a variety of scenes from nature. The name is applied both to the nighttime part of a feast that lasts several days and to the entire feasting and dancing complex that can last for years. Compare *Kai.*

singsing TP for dancing feast.

small-holder General term applied by development specialists to mean any native landholder; used to distinguish native landholdings from larger, foreign-owned plantations.

sup Kingfish (*Seriola* spp.).

superincision Surgical procedure performed on all boys in which the top of the foreskin is slit vertically to the back of the glans penis.

tan Land, ground. *Tan tiina*, "big ground," refers to a "mainland" (as opposed to a coral island) such as New Guinea or Umboi Island.

tiwai (*Polymesoda cyrenoididae*), a mangrove bivalve similar to cherrystone clams.

totoɤoŋ The noun that describes the action of punting a canoe across a reef or shallows.

trepang Sea cucumber.

trochus *Trochus niloticus*, or top shell. Mandok women incise armlets from the base ring of this shell. These armlets are a major trade item in the Vitiaz trade system.

tutaŋ Sacred or important knowledge; for example, knowledge imparted to initiates during their seclusion and to betrothed individuals before marriage.

utuŋ Formal adoption. Compare *paroŋ.*

vuvuaŋ A story. From the verb root *-vuvub,* "to tell a story."

waŋ Canoe. *Waŋ modiŋ ru* was a two-masted sailing canoe used in overseas trade.

waro Line or vein. For example, *baliŋwaro* means "line of wealth," whereas *siŋwaro* means "blood vein."

wasoŋ Net fishing.

ɤoliŋ Purchase, price; also used to describe the second of two stages of brideprice.

Yabim A language and ethnic group located in the Huon Peninsula area of northeast New Guinea. Early German Lutheran missionaries used the Yabim language as a lingua franca throughout their areas of influence. Also spelled *Jabêm* after a German pronunciation.

Yavar Northwest monsoon. Compare *Rag.*

References

ALLACE, L.
1976   Siassi Trade. Oral History 4(10):2–22.

AMARSHI, A., K. GOOD, AND R. MORTIMER
1979   Development and Dependency: The Political Economy of Papua New Guinea. Melbourne: Oxford University Press.

ATKINSON, J. W. ED.
1958   Motives in Fantasy, Action, and Society: A Method of Assessment and Study. Princeton: Van Nostrand.

BALL, E.
1982   Long Island, Papua New Guinea: European Exploration and Recorded Contacts to the End of the Pacific War. Records of the Australian Museum 34(10):447–461.

BALL, E., AND I. M. HUGHES
1982   Long Island, Papua New Guinea—People, Resources and Culture. Records of the Australian Museum 34(10):463–525.

BAMLER, G.
1892   Report of First Trip to Siasi-Rook-Maligep. Unpublished typescript dated 15 January 1892. Ampo; Papua New Guinea: Lutheran Mission Archives. Translated by R. Pech, May 1987.

BARLOW, K., AND D. LIPSET
1982   Personal communication.

BARRY, H. H., CHILD, I. L., AND M. K. BACON
1959   Relation of Child-Rearing to Subsistence Economy. American Anthropologist 61:51–63.

BARTH, F.
1969   Ethnic Groups and Boundaries. Boston: Little, Brown.

BRADY, I., ED.
1976   Transactions in Kinship: Adoption and Fosterage In Oceania. Honolulu: University of Hawaii Press.

CARRIER, J., AND A. H. CARRIER
1989   Wage, Trade, and Exchange in Melanesia. Berkeley: University of California Press.

CARROLL, V., ED.
1970   Adoption in Eastern Oceania. Honolulu: University of Hawaii Press.

CHINNERY, E. W. P.

n.d.   Certain Natives in South New Britain and Dampier Straits. Anthropological Report No. 3, Territory of New Guinea. Melbourne: Government Printer.

CHOWNING, A.

1979   Leadership in Melanesia. Journal of Pacific History 14(2):66–84.

1986   Refugees, Traders, and Other Wanderers: The Linguistic Effects of Population Mixing in Melanesia. *In* P. Geraghty, L. Carrington, and S. A. Wurm, eds., Focal II: Papers From the Fourth International Conference on Austronesian Linguistics. Pacific Linguistics C-94:407–434.

COUNTS, D., AND D. COUNTS

1983   Father's Water Equals Mother's Milk: The Conception of Parentage in Kaliai, West New Guinea. Mankind 14(1):46–56.

1990   Personal communication.

CRAGG, S. M.

1981   The Subsistence Economy of Umboi Island With Special Reference to the Role of Mangrove Swamps: A Preliminary Report. Waigani, Papua New Guinea: Office of Environment and Conservation.

1982   Coastal Resources and the Umboi Logging Project: An Environmental Impact Study. Waigani, Papua New Guinea: Office of Environment and Conservation.

DE LEPERVANCHE, M.

1973   Social Structure. *In* I. Hogbin, ed., Anthropology in Papua New Guinea: Readings from the Encyclopaedia of Papua and New Guinea (1973). Melbourne: Melbourne University Press.

EDGERTON, R.

1971   The Individual in Cultural Adaptation. Los Angeles: University of California Press.

EPSTEIN, T. S.

1968   Capitalism, Primitive and Modern: Some Aspects of Tolai Economic Growth. Canberra: Australian National University.

ERRINGTON, F. K.

1974   Karavar: Masks and Power in a Melanesian Ritual. Ithaca: Cornell University Press.

EVANS-PRITCHARD, E. E.

1940   The Nuer: A Description of the Modes of Livelihood and Political Institutions of Nilotic People. Oxford: Clarendon.

FELDT, E.

1946   The Coastwatchers. Melbourne: Geoffrey Cumberlege and Oxford University Press.

FINNEY, B. R.

1973   Bigmen and Business: Entrepreneurship and Economic Growth in the New Guinea Highlands. Honolulu: University of Hawaii Press.

FINNEY, R.

1971   Would-Be Entrepreneurs?: A Study of Motivation in New Guinea. New Guinea Research Bulletin No. 41. Canberra: New Guinea Research Unit, Australian National University.

FIRTH, S.

1986 [1983]   New Guinea Under the Germans. Port Moresby: Web Books.

FISIKA

1986   Umboi Timber Project: Report of Meeting Between FISIKA Delegation and Departmental Committee on Umboi Timber. Mimeo dated 5 December 1986.

FORTES, M.

1974   The First Born. Journal of Child Psychology 15:81–104.

FORTUNE, R.

1932   Sorcerers of Dobu. New York: Dutton [1963 ed.].

FOSTER, B.

1974   Ethnicity and Commerce. American Ethnologist 1(3):437–448.

1977   Mon Commerce and the Dynamics of Ethnic Relations. Southeast Asian Journal of Social Science 5(1–2):111–122.

FOSTER, G.

1965   Peasant Society and the Image of Limited Good. American Anthropologist 67:293–315.

FREEDMAN, M. P.

1967   The Social and Political Organization of the Siassi Islands. Doctoral dissertation, University of Michigan. Ann Arbor: University Microfilms.

1970   Social Organization of a Siassi Island Community. *In* T. G. Harding and B. J. Wallace, eds., Cultures of the Pacific. New York: Free Press.

GEERTZ, C.

1957   Ethos, Worldview, and the Analysis of Sacred Symbols. Antioch Review 17(4):421–437.

1966   Religion as a Cultural System. *In* M. Banton, ed., Anthropological Approaches to the Study of Religion. London: Tavistock.

1973   Interpretation of Cultures: Toward an Interpretive Theory of Culture. New York: Basic Books.

GELL, A.

1975   Metamorphosis of the Cassowaries: Umeda Society, Language, and Ritual. London: The Athlone Press.

GEWERTZ, D.

1983   Sepik River Societies: A Historical Ethnography of the Chambri and Their Neighbors. New Haven: Yale University Press.

GEWERTZ, D., AND E. SCHIEFFELIN, EDS.

1985   History and Ethnohistory in Papua New Guinea. Oceania Monograph No. 28. Sydney: University of Sydney.

GOOD, K.

1986   Papua New Guinea: A False Economy. Anti-Slavery Society, Indigenous Peoples and Development Series No. 3.

GOODALE, J. C.

1985   Pig's Teeth and Skull Cycles: Both Sides of the Face of Humanity. American Ethnologist 12(2):228–244.

GRANT, E. M.

1973   Guide to Fishes (4th ed.). Brisbane: Queensland Government, Department of Harbours and Marine.

GREGORY, C. A.

1980   Gifts to Men and Gifts to God: Gift Exchange and Capital Accumulation in Contemporary Papua. Man 15:626–652.

HALLOWELL, A. I.

1955   Culture and Experience. New York: Schocken Books [1967 ed.].

HARDING, T. G.

1967   Voyagers of the Vitiaz Strait: A Study of a New Guinea Trade System. Seattle: University of Washington Press.

1970   Trade in Northeast New Guinea. *In* T. G. Harding and B. J. Wallace (eds.), Cultures of the Pacific. New York: Free Press.

1985   Kunai Men: Horticultural Systems of a Papua New Guinea Society. University of California Publications in Anthropology, Vol. 16. Berkeley: University of California Press.

1989   Objects and the Scale of Melanesian Trade: Trading and Agricultural Societies. Paper presented to "Object Informs, Objects in Form: The Ethnography of Oceanic Art," conference sponsored by the Baltimore Museum of Art and the Program in Art History and Anthropology at Johns Hopkins University. Baltimore, April 14–15.

HARDING, T. G., AND S. CLARK

1990   Sio's Story of Male. Paper presented to the Association for Social Anthropology in Oceania Working Session, "Children of Kilibob: Creation, Cosmos and Culture." Kaua'i, Hawaii, March 21–24.

HERDT, G.

1981   Guardians of the Flutes: Idioms of Masculinity. New York: McGraw-Hill.

HOGBIN, I.

1970   The Island of Menstruating Men. Toronto: Chandler.

HOLZKNECHT, H.

1980   Personal communication.

HOOLEY, B.

1971   Austronesian Languages of the Morobe District, Papua New Guinea. Oceanic Linguistics 10(2):79–151.

1976   Austronesian Languages: Morobe Province. *In* S. A. Wurm, ed., New Guinea Area Languages and Language Study. Pacific Linguistics Series C, No. 39, Vol. 2:355–357.

HOOLEY, B., AND K. McELHANON
1970   Languages of the Morobe District, New Guinea. *In* S. A. Wurm and D. C. Laycock, eds., Pacific Linguistic Studies in Honour of Arthur Capell. Canberra: Australian National University, Series C, No. 13.

HOWARD, A., R. HEIGHTON, JR., C. JORDAN, AND R. GALLIMORE
1970   Traditional and Modern Adoption Patterns in Hawaii. *In* V. Carroll, ed., Adoption in Eastern Oceania. Honolulu: University of Hawaii Press.

ISOAIMO, A.
1980   Circular to All Headmasters and Teachers: Grade 6 Class Achievements, 1979. Unpublished mimeo, Morobe Province Department of Education.

JAKOB, V.
1987, 1989   Personal communication.

JORGENSEN, D., ED.
1983   Concepts of Conception: Procreation Ideologies in Papua New Guinea. Special Issue, Mankind 14(1).

KAHN, M.
1986   Always Hungry, Never Greedy: Food and the Expression of Gender in a Melanesian Society. New York: Cambridge University Press.
1990   Stone-Faced Ancestors: Physical and Spatial Anchoring of Myth in Wamira, Papua New Guinea. Ethnology 29(1):51–66.

KEKE, A. H.
1990   Personal communication.

KENEHE, S. N.
1981   In Search of Standards: Report of the Committee of Enquiry into Educational Standards Established by The Honourable Mr. Sam Tulo, M.P., Minister for Education. Gordon, Papua New Guinea: Hebamo Press.

KEURS, P. J. TER
1985   An Island of Woodcarvers: Mandok, Papua New Guinea. Unpublished fieldwork report. University of Leiden, the Netherlands.
1989   Some Remarks on Seafaring, Trade, and Canoe-Construction of the Siassi of Mandok Island (Papua New Guinea). Baessler-Archiv 37:373–400.

KIGASUNG, W.
1976   Mission Pioneering in Siassi Island, 1847–1947. Unpublished master's thesis, 1976, University of Papua New Guinea.

KUSSO-ALLESS, L.
1984–1989   Personal communication.

LANCY, D. F.
1978   Cognitive Testing in the Indigenous Mathematics Project. *In* D. F. Lancy, ed., The Indigenous Mathematics Project. Papua New Guinea Journal of Education, Special Issue 14:114–142.
1979a   Education Research 1976–1979: Reports and Essays. Port Moresby, Papua New Guinea: UNESCO/Education.

1979b Introduction. *In* D. F. Lancy, ed., The Community School, Papua New Guinea Journal of Education, Special Issue 15:1–26.

1983   Cross-Cultural Studies in Cognition and Mathematics. New York: Academic Press.

LAWRENCE, P.

1964   Road Bilong Cargo: A Study of the Cargo Movement in the Southern Madang District, New Guinea. Melbourne: Melbourne University Press.

1967   Land Tenure Among the Garia. *In* I. Hogbin and P. Lawrence, eds., Studies in New Guinea Land Tenure. Sydney: Sydney University Press.

LEACH, E. R.

1961   Rethinking Anthropology. New York: Humanities Press.

LENSSEN, FR. F., C.M.M.

1979–1983   Personal communication.

LeVINE, R.

1966   Dreams and Deeds: Achievement Motivation in Nigeria. Chicago: University of Chicago Press.

LILLEY, I.

1986   Prehistoric Exchange in the Vitiaz Strait, Papua New Guinea. Doctoral dissertation, Australian National University.

1988   Prehistoric Exchange Across the Vitiaz Strait, Papua New Guinea. Current Anthropology 29(3):513–516.

LINCOLN, P.

1977   Subgrouping Across a Syntactic Isogloss. Paper presented to the Austronesian Symposium, Hawaii, August.

MAIR, L.

1948   Australia in New Guinea. London: Christophers.

MALINOWSKI, B.

1922   Argonauts of the Western Pacific. London: Routledge and Kegan Paul.

1948   Magic, Science, and Religion. New York: Doubleday [1954 ed.].

MATANE, P.

1986   A Philosophy of Education for Papua New Guinea. Ministerial Committee Report, November 1986. Boroko: National Catholic Education Secretariate.

McCLELLAND, D.

1961   The Achieving Society. Princeton: Van Nostrand.

McDOWELL, N.

1985   Past and Future: The Nature of Episodic Time in Bun. *In* D. Gewertz and E. Schieffelin, eds., History and Ethnohistory in Papua New Guinea. Oceania Monograph No. 28. Sydney: University of Sydney, pp. 26–39.

McKINNON, B.
1968   Education in Papua and New Guinea: Current Directions and Future Challenges. Australian Journal of Education 12(1):102–105.

MICHAEL
1957   75 Glorious Years 1882–1957. Vunapope: Catholic Mission.

MIEGS, A. S.
1984   Food, Sex, and Pollution: A New Guinea Religion. New Brunswick: Rutgers University Press.

MOROBE PROVINCE
1980   National Census: Morobe Province Preliminary Field Counts. Port Moresby, Papua New Guinea.

MULDERINK, FR. A., C.M.M.
1979–1990   Personal communication.
1980   Aibale Timotheus: One of Papua New Guinea's Remarkable Men. Northeast New Guinea 1(2):13–19.

MUNN, N.
1982   Personal communication.
1986   The Fame of Gawa: A Symbolic Study of Value Transformation in a Massim (Papua New Guinea) Society. New York: Cambridge University Press.

NEUHAUSS, R.
1911   Deutsch Neu-Guinea, Vol. 1. Berlin: Reimer.

NIUGINI NIUS
1982   August 5:14–15.

O'NEILL, T.
1961   And We, the People: Ten Years with the Primitive Tribes of New Guinea. New York: P. J. Kenedy and Sons.

ORTNER, S.
1973   On Key Symbols. American Anthropologist 75:1338–1346.

PANOFF, M.
1968   The Notion of Double Self Among the Maenge. Journal of the Polynesian Society 46:275–295.

PAPUA NEW GUINEA
1969–1970   Annual Reports.

PATROL REPORTS, VARIOUS
        National Archives, Port Moresby, Papua New Guinea.

PECH, R.
1979   Myth, Dream, and Drama: Shapers of a People's Quest for Salvation. Unpublished M.S.T. thesis, Trinity Lutheran Seminary, Columbus, OH.

PLOEG, A.

1984   Development Administration in an Isolated Sub-District. Administration for Development 22:1–17.

1985   Dependency Among the Kovai, Siassi, Morobe Province, Papua New Guinea. Oceania 55:252–271.

1989   Personal communication.

POMPONIO, A.

1983   Namor's Odyssey: Education and Development on Mandok Island, Papua New Guinea. Doctoral dissertation, Bryn Mawr College. Ann Arbor: University Microfilms.

1985   The Teacher as a Key Symbol. Papua New Guinea Journal of Education 21(2):237–252.

1990a   Seagulls Don't Fly Into the Bush: Cultural Identity and the Negotiation of Development on Mandok Island, Papua New Guinea. *In* J. Linnekin and L. Poyer, eds., Cultural Identity and Ethnicity in the Pacific. Honolulu: University of Hawaii Press, pp. 43–69.

1990b   What Did the Earthquake Mean? *In* P. R. DeVita, ed., The Humbled Anthropologist: Tales From the Pacific. Belmont: Wadsworth, pp. 35–45.

1991   Namor's Odyssey: Mythical Metaphors and History in Siassi. Paper given at the Working Session, "Children of Kilibob: Creation, Cosmos, and Culture." Association for Social Anthropology in Oceania annual meetings. Victoria, B.C.: March 27–30, 1991.

n.d.   Education IS Development on a Ten-Acre Island. *In* T. Harding, B. Wallace, and V. Lockwood, eds., Contemporary Pacific Societies. Englewood Cliffs: Prentice-Hall.

POMPONIO, A., AND D. LANCY

1986   A Pen or a Bushknife? School, Work, and "Personal Investment" in Papua New Guinea. Anthropology and Education Quarterly 17(1):40–61.

POST COURIER (PORT MORESBY, PNG)

1981   February 27:21; June 18:19.

ROSS, M.

1986   Proto Oceanic and the Austronesian Languages of Western Melanesia. Pacific Linguistics Series C, No. 98. Canberra: Australian National University.

SACK, P.

1972   Dukduk and Law Enforcement. Oceania 43:96–103.

SACK, P., AND D. CLARK EDS.

1979   German New Guinea: The Annual Reports. Canberra: Australian National University.

SAHLINS, M.

1963   Poor Man, Rich Man, Big-man, Chief: Comparative Types of Melanesia and Polynesia. Comparative Studies in Society and History 5(3):285–303.

1965   On the Sociology of Primitive Exchange. *In* M. Banton, ed., The Relevance of Models for Social Anthropology. A.S.A. Monographs. London: Tavistock.

1972   Stone Age Economics. Chicago: Aldine.

SALISBURY, R.

1962   From Stone to Steel. Cambridge: Cambridge University Press.

1970   Vunamami: Economic Transformation in a Traditional Society. Berkeley: University of California Press.

SCAGLION, R.

1976   Seasonal Patterns in Western Abelam Conflict Management Practices: The Ethnography of Law in the Maprik Subdistrict. Doctoral dissertation, University of Pittsburgh. Ann Arbor: University Microfilms.

SCALETTA, N.

1985   Primogeniture and Primogenitor: Firstborn Child and Mortuary Ceremonies Among the Kabana (Bariai) of West New Britain, Papua New Guinea. Doctoral dissertation, MacMaster University, Hamilton, Ontario, Canada.

SCHIEFFELIN, E. L.

1976   The Sorrow of the Lonely and the Burning of the Dancers. New York: St. Martin's Press.

SHILS, E.

1960   Political Development in the New States. Comparative Studies in Society and History 2:265–292.

SIASSI DEVELOPMENT CORPORATION

1988   1988 Annual Report. Lablab, Papua New Guinea: Siassi Development Corporation Pty. Ltd. Unpublished mimeo.

SMITH, E. M., ED.

1977   Those Who Live From the Sea. New York: West.

SPOEHR, A.

1980   Protein From the Sea: Technological Change in Philippine Capture Fisheries. Ethnology Monographs No. 3. University of Pittsburgh Department of Anthropology.

STANDARD DICTIONARY OF FOLKLORE, MYTHOLOGY, & LEGEND.

1972   New York: Funk & Wagnalls.

STRATHERN, A.

1971   The Rope of Moka: Big Men and Ceremonial Exchange in Mount Hagen, New Guinea. Cambridge: Cambridge University Press.

STRATHERN, A., AND M. STRATHERN

1971   Self Decoration in Mount Hagen. Toronto: University of Toronto Press.

SWATRIDGE, C.

1985   Delivering the Goods: Education as Cargo in Papua New Guinea. Melbourne: Melbourne University Press.

TODD, J. A.

1934   Report on Research Work in Southwest New Britain. Oceania 5(1 and 2):80–101, 193–213.

TURNER, V.

1967   The Forest of Symbols: Aspects of Ndembu Ritual. Ithaca: Cornell University Press.

TUZIN, D.

1972   Yam Symbolism in the Sepik: An Interpretive Account. Southwestern Journal of Anthropology 28:230–254.

UNITED NATIONS

1962   U.N. Visiting Mission to the Trust/Territories of Nauru and New Guinea. New York: United Nations.

WATSON, J. B.

1970   Society as Organized Flow: The Tairora Case. Southwest Journal of Anthropology 26(2):107–124.

1990   Other People Do Other Things: Lamarckian Identities in Kainantu Subdistrict, Papua New Guinea. *In* J. Linnekin and L. Poyer, eds., Cultural Identity and Ethnicity in the Pacific. Honolulu: University of Hawaii Press, pp. 17–42.

WEEDEN, W. J., C. BEEBY, AND G. GRIS

1969   Report of the Advisory Committee on Education in Papua New Guinea. Canberra: Department of External Territories.

WEEKS, S., AND G. GUTHRIE

1984   Papua New Guinea. *In* R. M. Thomas and T. N. Postlethwaite, eds., Schooling in the Pacific Islands: Colonies in Transition. Oxford: Pergamon.

WEINER, A.

1976   Women of Value, Men of Renown: New Perspectives in Trobriand Exchange. Austin: University of Texas Press.

WHITING, B.

1963   Children of Six Cultures: Studies of Child Rearing. New York: Wiley.

WHITING, J. W. M., AND I. L. CHILD

1953   Child Training and Personality: A Cross-Cultural Study. New Haven: Yale University Press.

WILTGEN, R. M.

1979   The Founding of the Roman Catholic Church in Oceania, 1825–1850. Canberra: Australian National University.

WORLD BANK

1982   Papua New Guinea: Selected Development Issues. Washington, D. C.: East Asia and Pacific Regional Office.

WORSLEY, P.

1984   The Three Worlds: Culture and World Development. Chicago: University of Chicago Press.

YOUNG, M.

1971   Fighting With Food: Leadership, Values, and Social Control in a Massim Society. Cambridge: Cambridge University Press.

ZELENIETZ, M., AND J. GRANT

1980   The Ambiguities of Education in Kilenge, Papua New Guinea. Paper presented at the International Conference on Education in Oceania, March 1980, Victoria, Canada.

1981   Kilenge *Narogo*: Ceremonies, Resources and Prestige in a West New Britain Society. Oceania 51(2):98–117.

1986   Personal communication.

Index

References to figures, tables, or photographs are indicated in **bold** type.